FOUR FAMILIES

FOUR FAMILIES: A TETRALOGY

Reader's Guide to *Western Pilgrims, Quakers and Puritans, Fundy to Chesapeake,* and *American Dreams*

Synopsis of 481 Immigrants and First Known
Ancestors in America from Northern Europe
in the
Families of :
George J. Hill and Jessie F. Stockwell
William T. Shoemaker and Mabel Warren
William H. Thompson and Sarah D. Rundall
John Zimmermann and Eva K. Kellenbenz

with
Outlines of Their Descent
from the Immigrants

By

George J. Hill, M.D., M.A., D.Litt.

HERITAGE BOOKS
2017

HERITAGE BOOKS

AN IMPRINT OF HERITAGE BOOKS, INC.

Books, CDs, and more—Worldwide

For our listing of thousands of titles see our website
at
www.HeritageBooks.com

Published 2017 by
HERITAGE BOOKS, INC.
Publishing Division
5810 Ruatan Street
Berwyn Heights, Md. 20740

Heritage Books by the author:

*American Dreams: Ancestors and Descendants of John Zimmermann and
Eva Katherine Kellenbenz Who Were Married in Philadelphia in 1885*

Edison's Environment: The Great Inventor Was Also a Great Polluter

Four Families: A Tetralogy Reader's Guide to Western Pilgrims, Quakers and Puritans, Fundy to Chesapeake, *and* American Dreams*;
Synopsis of 481 Immigrants and First Known Ancestors in America from Northern Europe in the Families of George J. Hill
and Jessie F. Stockwell, William T. Shoemaker and Mabel Warren, William H. Thompson and Sarah D. Rundall,
John Zimmermann and Eva K. Kellenbenz, with Outlines of Their Descent from the Immigrants.*

*Fundy to Chesapeake; The Thompson, Rundall and Allied Families: Ancestors and Descendants of
William Henry Thompson and Sarah D. Rundall, Who Were Married in Linn County, Iowa, in 1889*

*Hill: The Ferry Keeper's Family, Luke Hill and Mary Hout,
Who were Married in Windsor, Connecticut, in 1651 and Fourteen Generations of Their Known and Possible Descendants*

John Saxe, Loyalist (1732–1808) and His Descendants for Five Generations

*Quakers and Puritans: The Shoemaker, Warren and Allied Families; Ancestors
and Descendants of William Toy Shoemaker and Mabel Warren, Who Were Married in Philadelphia in 1895*

*Western Pilgrims: The Hill, Stockwell and Allied Families;
Ancestors and Descendants of George J. Hill and Jessie Fidelia Stockwell, Who Were Married in Wright County, Iowa, in 1882*

*Cover image is from an old map of British Colonies in North America 1763–1775, from Ayrshire Roots.com;
frontispiece is a collage of the Four Families covers; statue of Samuel Chapin (viii) and Roger Conant's statue
(xviii) are from Google Images; gravestone of Maj. Gen. Humphrey Atherton (p.151) is from Find A Grave*

Cover designed by Debbie Riley

International Standard Book Numbers
Paperbound: 978-0-7884-5789-0

FOUR FAMILIES

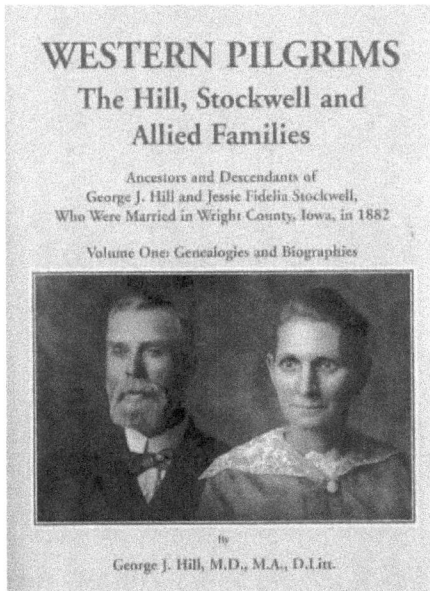

GEORGE J. HILL AND JESSIE STOCKWELL

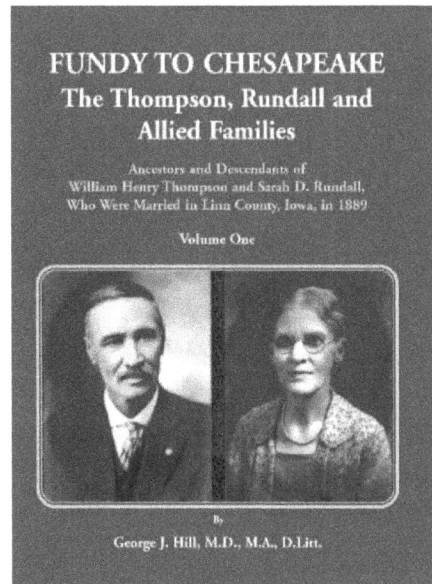

WILL THOMPSON AND SARAH RUNDALL

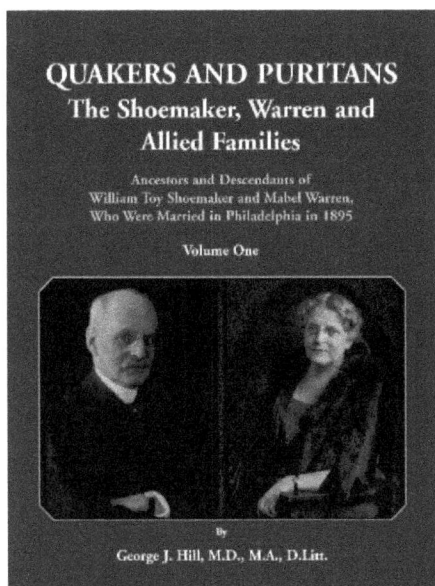

WILLIAM SHOEMAKER AND MABEL WARREN

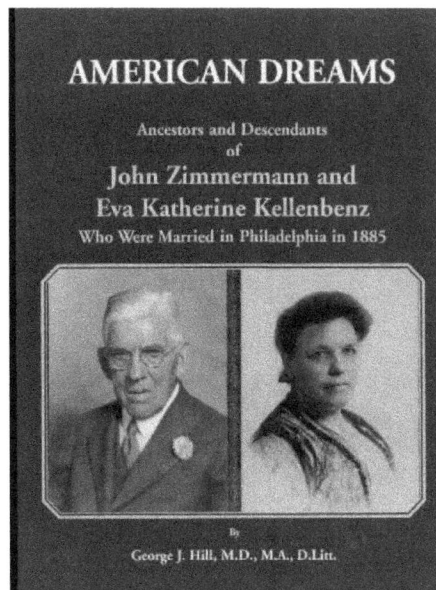

JOHN ZIMMERMANN AND EVA KELLENBENZ

For Lanie

The American Dream

The American Dream is that dream of a land in which life should be better and richer and fuller for everyone, with opportunity for each according to ability or achievement.

—James Truslow Adams
The Epic of America (1931)

FOREWORD

Dr. George J. Hill has provided us with a great collection of life stories of successful businessmen. You'll enjoy these biographies.

The need for achievement is distinct from the need for wealth, the need for power, or the need for fame, etc., although it may be hard to distinguish which is the driving force behind the result. The need for power may be the source of a person's drive for wealth if he believes money brings power. Or the need for power may drive a person's need for fame if he believes fame will result in power. But the need for achievement doesn't need money or fame.

It might be an interesting effort to do an analysis of the folklore of our current American culture. The result may show that there is a special need for and value in Dr. Hill's collection of success stories of a previous generation beyond what even he expected. I would make it required reading for history teachers and school superintendents.

—George J. Downing
Sewell, New Jersey
Professor Emeritus of Social Science
Rowan College of Gloucester County

FROM THE FOREWORD TO *AMERICAN DREAMS: ANCESTORS AND DESCENDANTS OF JOHN ZIMMERMANN AND KATHERINE KELLENBENZ*

At a time when issues surrounding immigration are prominent in the public dialogue, *American Dreams* usefully reminds us of the contributions that immigrants have made to American society.

An immigrant is like a seed that falls on soil far from the place of its origin. What will grow from it depends upon the nature of the seed, but also on the fertility of the soil, and the salubriousness of the climate. They and their many descendants exemplify the American Dream. As we contemplate today's immigrants, let us hope that the American Dream remains comparably vivid and inspiring.

—Michael Scott Swisher
Stillwater, Minnesota
Governor General
National Society, Sons of Colonial New England

From Google Images

SAMUEL CHAPIN

Detail of Statue of "The Puritan" by Augustus Saint-Gaudens
Said to represent Rev. Samuel Chapin
Springfield, Massachusetts

Ancestor of Jessie Fidelia Stockwell

Contents

Preface

I wrote this book to enable readers to navigate through four books – a tetralogy – of family history and genealogy. *Four Families* tells the history and genealogy of my family and the family of my wife, Helene Zimmermann. Each book in the *Four Families* tetralogy was based on the model used for a book that was written more than a century ago about one branch of Helene's family: *The Warren, Jackson and Allied Families*. There is some overlap in these four books, because long ago, I discovered that my wife and I were distant cousins. As I pursued my research, I found that we have other additional ancestors-in-common.

My initial goal was to write the genealogical history of each pair of our eight grandparents. The task would be to do the research and write four books: two books would be about each of my four grandparents, and two would be about my wife's. My next goal was to bring the four books together with this Synopsis, which is intended serve as a guide to all the books.

Genealogy is never completed, and it is always a work-in-progress – even when published. In the Synopsis, I have added some new information that I have discovered, and I mention a few corrections.

This Synopsis shows, in alphabetical order, brief summaries of the lives of more than 500 men and women: 481 men and women who emigrated and a few others who are the first known in America in the Four Families – and of 31 others, selected to exemplify the many ancestors who died before them in Europe.

These Four Families are formed from the four men and four women who are our eight grandparents. This Synopsis also shows in outline form, the genealogical line that proceeds from the European immigrant to one or more of our eight grandparents.

—George J. Hill

Introduction

This book draws together and concludes the work that I first began as a school boy, when I became interested in my family's history, and which I am now able to close. I hope that in the future, others may enjoy adding to what I have found, and correcting my errors.

My curiosity about family history developed as we drove home after attending my father's family's summer picnic in the town park in Clarion, Iowa. I asked my mother about my many cousins, who they all were, and who were there parents? She answered my question by writing down a list of my nineteen Hill family cousins, and then she added the names of my father's brothers and sisters to show how they were related to each other, and to me and my brother.[1] Her list in clear, beautiful, handwriting was my first guide to the Hill Family. Soon after this, she gave me a mimeographed typescript that was printed many years earlier, entitled "Genealogy of the Hill Family in America." Much later, I learned that this 12-page mimeographed document was compiled in 1921. It began as follows:

1 Isaac Hill was born about 1740
He married
He was a soldier in the Revolutionary War   d. about 1830
    2-1 Ephraim b. May 1778 d. July 14, 1832 m. Charlotte Prince
    3-2 Luke b. d. (April 7 1803)
    4-3 VanAger b. d.
    5-4 Isaac b.
    6-5 Seth b.
2   Ephraim Hill, son of Isaac Hill, was born May 1778 and died July 24, 1832.

This mimeographed document was the starting point for my research. It eventually led to the publication in 2011 of my 600-page book on the Hill Family in America.[2] The book carried this branch of the Hill family back for three more generations to the immigrant, Luke Hill, and his wife, Mary Hout, who were married in Windsor, Conn., in 1651. Along the way, I had a lot of help from members of the Hill family, and others who were interested in genealogy. After I learned that professional help was available, I began to work with several professional genealogists, in different parts of America and in England. I thus learned that Charlotte Prince, shown above as the wife of my ancestor Ephraim Hill, was a descendant of a *Mayflower* passenger. I also learned that one of my great-aunts had joined the D.A.R., and with the help of the record copy of her application, I applied for membership in the Sons of the American Revolution. These two societies' registrars were very helpful to me, as I continued my pursuit of family history and genealogy. With guidance from professionals and knowledgeable family historians, I finally completed my work on the Hill family. I suspected that there might be more to do, but I believed then that it was time to publish it, and let others add to it – as I had already added to the original "Hill Family in America."

As I was working of the Hill family genealogy, I began to think of a larger project. Who were all my ancestors? For instance, who were the ancestors of Charlotte Prince, and for that matter, who was the wife of that soldier of the Revolutionary War, Isaac Hill? I found the model for this project in the study of my wife's parents' home, in Haverford, Pennsylvania, in 1961. It was a book by Betsey Warren Davis, my wife's great-aunt, entitled *The Warren, Jackson, and Allied Families*. The book was about my wife's maternal grandparents and their ancestors. It was divided into two parts – the Warren family and the Jackson family – and into chapters for each of the ancestral branches of the married couple who were my

---

[1] George J. Hill, *Hill: The Ferry Keeper's Family: Luke Hill and Mary Hout, Who Were Married in Windsor, Connecticut, in 1651, and Fourteen Generations of Their Known and Possible Descendants* (Westminster, Md.: Heritage Books, 2011). The nine children and twenty-one grandchildren of George J. Hill and Jessie F. Stockwell are shown on pp. 278-83.

[2] Hill, *The Ferry Keeper's Family*.

wife's great-grandparents, Jeduthan Warren and Betsy Jackson. I decided that I would do something like this for the ancestors of each of my grandparents and the same for each of my wife's grandparents. My research would be divided into four parts, each of which would be named for a set of grandparents: The Hill, Stockwell, and Allied Families; Thompson, Rundall, and Allied Families; Shoemaker, Warren, and Allied Families; and Zimmermann, Kellenbenz, and Allied Families. The four file titles would be abbreviated: HSAF, TRAF, SWAF, and ZKAF. There would be eight major sections, one for each grandparent. I had no idea how large and difficult the project would become, especially after I discovered that there were several marital connections between my family and the family of my wife, and that we were, in fact, distant cousins. How to handle all this information?

Fortunately, I discovered in 1994 that I could use a computer to store, sort, and print the information. Sad to say, I chose software (Family Tree/Sierra®) that looked very good, but in the end, wasn't well supported. In retrospect, I should have used Family Tree Maker®. The manufacturer of Family Tree/Sierra went out of business sometime after 2000. Fast forward to the present: My four books were finally completed and published in seven volumes, between 2014 and 2016. I knew that the work was still unfinished – genealogy never is – and that additions and corrections would be needed. However, it was time to put an end to the work, because my old computer was dying and the software program that I was using was extinct. The Sierra software could not be installed into a new computer. Although my basic genealogical files (i.e., names, dates, and places) were transferrable by Gedcom into new software and into a new computer, all the narrative text, citations, and references would be lost. And as I expected, about two months after I completed the fourth book in the series, my old computer took its last gasp and crashed.

This Synopsis summarizes, with brief biographies, about 500 men and women. Each biography includes the dates and locations of birth, death, and marriage, and for the 481 immigrants and first known American ancestors, what is known about their arrival in America, and in many cases, something significant that they accomplished, or that happened to them. Many of the immigrant wives do not have a surname that been identified. Brief biographies of 203 of these women appear immediately after their husbands' names. The immigrants' names are shown in normal font. The names of about 31 others are shown in italics, referring to those who did not emigrate from Europe. The names of 16 are shown in brackets for those whose lines were once proposed, but have now been discredited, or who are related by marriage to one or more of our families.

The descendants of the immigrants show the development in America of a relatively classless system, in contrast to Europe. Some of those who emigrated came with wealth and power, and were city dwellers. A few of them continued to live well in the cities on the northeast coast of America. On the other hand, some who came as indentured servants or prisoners rose from poverty within a few years, and had descendants with comfortable means. However, in most cases, within a generation or two, most of the descendants of the immigrants became farmers. There was a "tendency to the mean," to use the term from statistics. The Synopsis does not show the details of the lives of the descendants, but a few generalizations can be made. One is that in the small towns in colonial America, marriages usually were between families that were acquainted with each other in the same town, and who went to the same church. Another is that in the colonial era, most of the men served in the militia, and many were involved in the series of wars with the French and the Indians. The four books, in which nearly four hundred families are profiled, are a potentially rich source for future studies of social history and demography.

There are many family connections in three of these four books, as can be seen in the Indexes for *Western Pilgrims*, *Quakers and Puritans*, and *Fundy to Chesapeake*. In three instances, closer relationships exist: The Hill-Stockwell and Shoemaker-Warren Families are shown to have ancestors-in-common from four immigrants: Thomas Trowbridge, William Ward, and Sarah (_____) (Pellet) Underwood are ancestors of both George J. Hill, the Iowa Pioneer, and Betsey Warren; and William Underwood, Sarah's second husband, married again and he is an ancestor of both Betsey Warren and Jessie Stockwell. Additionally, one of William Fletcher's children is an ancestor of Betsy Warren, and another of his children is probably an ancestor of George J. Hill. David and Sarah Phippen are ancestors of both George J. Hill and Jessie

Stockwell. Connections between these two families also occur in Europe, through at least five and possibly six Gateway ancestors to Charlemagne: Thomas Trowbridge (an ancestor of both George J. Hill and Betsey Warren); John Thorndike (ancestor of Betsey Warren); Matthew Allyn (ancestor of George J. Hill); and Jane Lawrence, wife of George Giddings (ancestor of George Hill); Griffith Bowen (ancestor of Jessie Stockwell), and perhaps also Obadiah Bruen (possibly an ancestor of Jessie Stockwell). And there is James Prescott, an ancestor of Sarah D. Rundall, whose English ancestry is unproven, but he may have Royal ancestors; and perhaps George Morton, whose English Royal ancestry has been suggested, but is unproven.

Two of the lines mentioned in these books are considered "probable but unproved," but they pass the "White Queen Test" of Robert Charles Anderson.[3]

One line poses the question: "Is Jerusha ___, wife of Rufus Herrick (III) and mother of Sarah Herrick, a third wife, or was she his second wife, Jerusha Pierce?" The answer I give is: Yes, she is Jerusha Pierce. The rationale for this answer is shown in the Herrick chapter of *Western Pilgrims* (p. 45, *et seq.*)

The other line poses the question: "Is Hannah ___, wife of James Thompson, Sr., and mother of Joseph Scott Thompson, Hannah Scott, daughter of Joseph Scott of Colchester County, Nova Scotia"? The answer I propose is: Yes, Hannah ____ is Hannah Scott, daughter of Joseph Scott. The discussion of this question is given in the Introduction to the Thompson family (pp.3-4) in *Fundy to Chesapeake*. Research by AncestryProGenealogists has subsequently affirmed this conclusion, based on the preponderance of evidence and with nothing to contradict it. However, no direct proof has yet been found (See Appendix to this book).

I have tried to do my best to accept what I found, even though it wasn't always what I hoped for. Perhaps I have hoped for too much. It's easy to fall into the trap of false hopes. I have seen false hopes in other genealogies over the past two decades. One of the first was in the Lyon family volumes, in which Royal ancestors were said to be found – but this was false. And in the Prescott family, in the Prescott Memorial volumes, two lines of Prescotts were shown to be related, and that they had Royal ancestors – but this has also been discredited. And I now know that the connection of the Herrick family in colonial America with the wealthy Herrick family of London, that was posited in the Herrick genealogy, is also incorrect.

The papers, notes, and books that were used in the research for these four books were transferred to the Gloucester Co. Library in Woodbury, N.J. I am grateful to Barbara Price, librarian, and the staff and volunteers of the library and the adjacent Gloucester County Museum for accepting these items. At the time of writing, they are being prepared for inventory, filing, and internet access.

---

[3] The White Queen Test was named by Robert Charles Anderson, quoted as follows by Denwood Nathan Stacy Holmes in "'The Black Sheep of Some Good Family': The Essex Ancestry of John Holmes, Gentleman, Messenger of the Plymouth Court," *New England Historic Genealogical Register* 171 (Spring 2017):85-92, as follows:

> Once you have reached a genealogical conclusion, with whatever degree or confidence, you should apply one final test, the White Queen Test, named for the White Queen in Lewis Carroll's *Alice Through the Looking Glass*. The White Queen assured Alice that she was quite capable of believing six impossible things before breakfast. In this test, you emulate the White Queen by turning your conclusion on its head and asking what you would have to believe if the conclusion were *untrue*. As the proposition you must believe in order to *disprove* your hypothesis becomes more and more unbelievable (to anyone but the White Queen), so your proposed conclusion gains in strength.

Four Groups of Interesting Persons,
Shown with their Immigrant Ancestors printed in CAPITAL LETTERS

A Partial List of Notable Immigrants, including Some Who Arrived in the Great Migration, the Winthrop Fleet, on the *Mayflower*, in the Welcome Fleet, or with Royal Ancestors

Major-General HUMPHREY ATHERTON was chosen major-general on 22 May 1661 to command the military forces of the colony of Massachusetts.

PHILIP ATWOOD arrived in 1635, in the Great Migration to Massachusetts.

ALEXANDER BAKER came in the *Elizabeth and Ann* in April 1635, in the Great Migration.

JOHN BAKER came to Massachusetts in 1637, or possibly as early as 1634.

GEORGE BARBOUR sailed from Gravesend, 4 July 1635 on *Transport*.

ABRAHAM BELKNAP, father-in-law of Nathaniel Singletary, was a proprietor of Lynn in 1638.

ROBERT BLOTT came to Boston in about 1634. He became the official swineherd of the town.

RICHARD BORDEN was the father of the first white child to be born in Rhode Island.

NATHANIEL BOULTER was the husband and father of two women who were accused of witchcraft in Hampton, N.H., in 1680.

Governor WILLIAM BRADFORD, who arrived on the *Mayflower*, was leader of the Plymouth Colony.

JOHN BUDD built what is now the oldest frame house in New York State, in Southold, Long Island.

ALICE CARPENTER married Governor William Bradford. Her sister, JULIANA CARPENTER married GEORGE MORTON, who was a major sponsor of the voyage of the *Mayflower*.

ROGER CONANT was Governor of the Beverly Colony in Massachusetts in 1626.

ALICE DICKINSON arrived in Pennsylvania in 1682 on the *Submission*, part of the Welcome Fleet. She married EDMOND McVAUGH.

ELIZABETH (FONES) (WINTHROP) (FEAKE) HALLETT, known as "That Winthrop Woman," was the first mother-in-law of Thomas Lyon, Sr., an ancestor of Sarah D. Rundall by his second wife.

EDWARD FULLER and his wife "Mrs. Fuller" came on the *Mayflower* in 1620.

THOMAS HOLBROOK, who came in the Great Migration in March 1634/5, is an ancestor of President James A. Garfield

Rev. OBADIAH HOLMES was famously whipped in Boston for preaching, as a Baptist, without a license. He was an early landowner in New Jersey.

Mr. EDWARD HOWELL, gent., was a Lord of the Manor in England when he came to America. He is the founder of the town of Easthampton. He is of Royal Descent.

ALICE (____) LAKE, wife of the immigrant Henry Lake, a laborer, was hanged as a witch in Boston in 1650-1 after the death of her fifth child, who she claimed she could still see, even though he was dead.

JANE LAWRENCE, daughter of Thomas Lawrence and Joan Antrobus, was of proven Royal Descent.

TOBY LEECH came to Pennsylvania with the Welcome Fleet in 1682. His estate was known as "Fox Chase," still remembered in the northern part of Philadelphia.

JAN LUKENS, who married MARY (Maria) TYSON (TEISSEN) (DOORS), was one of the founders of Germantown, Philadelphia, Pennsylvania.

JOHN MANLEY, who appeared in Cecil Co., Md., in the late 17th century, was probably one of the famous "Pirates of the Chesapeake."

PATIENCE (____) MILLER was "a skilled physician and surgeon," an unusual occupation. She died at Northampton, Mass., 16 March 1716. She was the wife of John Miller, a planter.

JOHN OGDEN was Deputy Governor of the Connecticut Colony.

GEORGE MORTON, whose wealth was a major sponsor of the *Mayflower*, published *Mourt's Relations,* the first book about the Plymouth Colony.

JACOB PARKER is an ancestor of President Franklin Pierce.

BARTHOLOMEW PENROSE was a well-known ship builder in Philadelphia. He built *Diligence*.

HENRY PENNNINGTON, an original settler of Cecil County, Maryland, founded one branch of the Pennington Family in America.

WILLIAM PHELPS was Governor of the Windsor Colony in Connecticut in 1641.

Rev. ABRAHAM PIERSON, Sr., is the father of Rev. Abraham Pierson, Jr., who was the first President of Yale University (by its present name and title).

JOHN PUTNAM, immigrant to Salem, founded the Putnam family in America.

EZEKIEL RICHARDSON, Esq., came in the Great Migration with the Winthrop Fleet in 1630.

WILLIAM RUNDLE was one of the twenty-seven proprietors of Greenwich, Conn., in 1667.

JOHN SAXE, a Tory and spy, was expelled to Canada with his family after the Revolutionary War.

JOHN SHARPLES came to America with his family on the *Friendship* in 1682 with the Welcome Fleet.

SARAH SHOEMAKER, widow of George Shoemaker, came to Philadelphia in 1685. Her husband was buried at sea. Her son, George Shoemaker, Jr., founded Shoemakertown (now known as Elkins Park).

RICHARD SINGLETARY, whose descendants changed the family name to Dunham, is an ancestor of President Barack Obama.

MARGARET STEPHENSON was hanged on the last day that witches were hanged in Salem.

WILLIAM STOCKWELL, Sr., was an original settler of Sutton, Mass. His house, built in 1717, is the oldest house still standing in that town in central Massachusetts.

ARCHIBALD THOMPSON is said to have brought the first spinning foot-wheel to New England.

Mr. JOHN THORNDIKE was buried at Westminster Abbey.

Rev. PARDON TILLINGHAST was said to be the "father of the commerce of Rhode Island."

REBECCA TOWNE, known from her married name as "Goody Nurse," was hanged in Salem during the witchcraft delusion of 1692. She was one of three sisters who were accused; two were hanged.

JOHN TOWNSEND and his brother RICHARD TOWNSEND were founders of Oyster Bay, Long Island. They signed the Flushing Remonstrance.

THOMAS TROWBRIDGE, of Taunton, was the founder of the Trowbridge family in America.

RICHARD WALL and his wife JOANE WHEEL came to Pennsylvania in the Welcome Fleet. Their home in Cheltenham Township has been preserved as a museum.

JOHN WHITNEY, tailor of London, and his wife ELINOR came in 1635 in the Great Migration.

Major SIMON WILLARD was appointed to lead the military forces of the United Colonies of New England in their expedition against the Indians in the fall of 1654.

Immigrants and their Ancestors with Notable Descendants

HENRY ADAMS is an ancestor of Presidents John Adams and John Quincy Adams.

BENJAMIN ALBEE built one of the first water powered mills for grinding grain in New England.

JOHN ALCOCK appeared as early as 1639 in Gorgeana (now York), Mass., which is now in Maine. He is a qualifying ancestor for the Order of the First Families of Maine.

SAMUEL ALLEN is an ancestor of Ethan Allen, the legendary Revolutionary War commander.

SARAH ALLERTON was the sister of Isaac Allerton, who came to New England on the *Mayflower*.

ROBERT ARCHIBALD is an ancestor of Sir Mathew George Adams Archibald, Governor of Manitoba.

CHRISTOPHER AVERY is an ancestor of Lucy Avery, grandmother of John D. Rockefeller, Sr.

ANN BAGLEY, WILLIAM BRINTON, HENRY DIXON and ROBERT PENNELL, Jr., are ancestors of President Richard M. Nixon.

JOANNA "JOAN" BLESSING was the mother of three women who were convicted of witchcraft in Salem in 1692, including Rebecca (Towne) Nurse, known as "Goody Nurse" in *The Crucible.*

GRIFFITH BOWEN, gent., of Boston in 1638/9, was an ancestor of President Franklin Pierce.

EDWARD HOWELL is an ancestor of Fleet Admiral William F. Halsey, hero of World War II.

JONATHAN HYDE is the ancestor of the man who built the oldest log cabin in Vermont.

EDWARD JACKSON, Esq., was the founder and principal first citizen of Cambridge, Mass.

JOHN JOHNSON is an ancestor of President Franklin D. Roosevelt.

THOMAS OVIATT is the ancestor of Captain Miles Mason Oviatt, USMC, who won the Medal of Honor for his actions at the Battle of Mobile Bay, 5 August 1864.

GRACE RAVENS is an ancestor of Roger Sherman, Signer of the Declaration of Independence.

JOHN CADWALADER and SARAH ROBERTS are the parents-in-law of Griffith John, a prominent freeholder in the Welsh tract of Chester Co., Pennsylvania.

Deacon SAMUEL CHAPIN is memorialized in the statue, "The Puritan." His descendants include Presidents Grover Cleveland and William Howard Taft, and the abolitionist, John Brown.

ALICE DICKINSON, wife of EDMOND McVAUGH, is an ancestor of President Theodore Roosevelt.

JOHN FOLGER and his wife Meribah GIBBS were great-grandparents of Benjamin Franklin.

_____GOODSPEED, perhaps *WILLIAM*, was an ancestor of John Putnam of Salem. The Goodspeeds are ancestors of three U.S. Presidents: Gerald R. Ford, Calvin Coolidge, and Herbert Hoover.

Deacon ROBERT HALE is an ancestor of the Patriot spy Nathan Hale.

JOHN SHARPLES is an ancestor of the First Lady of the Confederacy, Virginian (Howell) Davis

ELIZABETH STRATTON, wife of Mr. John Thorndike, was the mother-in-law of John Proctor, who was hanged at Salem in 1692. He was the flawed star of Arthur Miller's play *The Crucible*.

RICHARD SWAINE's daughter, Grace Swaine, and her daughter, Mary Boulter, were accused of witchcraft in Hampton, N.H.

JOHN TOMPKINS was the ancestor of 1st Sgt. Aaron Burr Tomkins, 1st N.J. Cavalry, who was awarded the Medal of Honor in the Civil War; and Daniel D. Tompkins, 6th Vice President of the United States.

WILLIAM WARD is the ancestor of General Artemas Ward, who was second in command to George Washington at the beginning of the Revolutionary War.

JOHN WHITNEY was the ancestor of Eli Whitney, inventor of the cotton gin.

Notable Collateral Relatives of Descendants of Immigrants

Walter ANTROBUS was the father-in-law of Thomas Lawrence, whose father was of European Royal Ancestry. Thomas Lawrence's son was an early Mayor of New York City.

Rev. COTTON MATHER married and had children by a granddaughter of MARY MILLER.

David Lake, son of the immigrant THOMAS LAKE, married Sarah (Earle) Cornell, widow of Thomas Cornell, Jr., who was falsely accused and executed for killing his mother.

Mr. WILLIAM DENISON and his wife MARGARET CHANDLER had a son, Maj. Gen. Daniel Denison, who married Patience Dudley, daughter of Governor Thomas Dudley of Massachusetts.

Notable Ancestors of Immigrants

MATTHEW ALLYN was the son of Margaret Wyatt. He was also the husband of a woman known as Margaret Wyatt. The Wyatts and their Chichester ancestors are descendants of European royalty.

RALPH de ARUNDEL was the son of Sir Richard de Arundel, 10th Earl of Arundel and Surrey. The family has been traced to William the Conqueror and Charlemagne.

JOSIAH BALDWIN is the father of Mary Baldwin, who may be the Mary ___ who married Samuel Oviatt. Josiah Baldwin's mother, Mary (Bruen) Baldwin, is a descendant King Henry II of England.

OBADIAH BRUEN is the presumed great-grandfather of Mary ___ ("maybe" Mary Baldwin), who married Samuel Oviatt. Obadiah Bruen has many Royal ancestors, and signers of the Magna Charta.

GRIFFITH BOWEN, gent., who appeared in Boston in 1638/9, was a descendant of King Henry I of England and Charlemagne.

JAMES FEAKE, goldsmith of London, invested in the Jamestowne Company.

_____ *GOODSPEED* is the ancestor of John Putnam, who emigrated to Salem, and Presidents Gerald R. Ford, Calvin Coolidge, and Herbert Hoover.

Mr. EDWARD HOWELL, gent. is a descendant of European Royalty, including Charlemagne, William the Conqueror, and other notables in English history, such as William of Warrenne.

WILLIAM MUNROE was captured and sent to America as a prisoner. He was the son of Robert of Aldie, Commissary of Caithness, in the 17th generation in the line of the Head of Clan Munro.

HERMANN ISAAC Op den GRAEFF is probably the son of Johann Wilhelm de la Marck, Graff of Julich-Cleves-Berg. He is the grandnephew of Anne of Cleves, fourth wife of Henry VIII.

Acknowledgements

I give special thanks to fellow members of lineage societies who have recently been involved and have supported me in this project, including: Mike Bates, Glen Beebe, John Bourne, Linda Boyd, William B. Brown III, Dr. Frank Clarke Jr., Lt. Col. Larry Casey, Char Edson, Jane Engleman, Barry Christopher Howard, Lea Filson, Tim Finton, Harry Folger III, John Harman, John Mauk Hilliard, Linda Hoffman, Wick Hollingshead, Ed Horton, Andrew Huston, Jack Idenden, Tom Jacks, Brantley Knowles, David Kollock, Col. Charles Lucas, Tim Mather Maybee, Clark McCullough, Karen McLendon, Karen Avery Miller, Carla and Bob Odom, Dr. John M. Pogue, Bill Reutelhueber, Davine Roberts, Diane Robinson, John Shannon, Tom Showler, Brenton Simons, Heather Speas, David Stringfellow, Alice Teal, Robert Pond Vivian, Jim Ward, Andrew Webster, Denis Woodfield, Shari Worrell, and Debbie Yingst.

I thank the Gloucester County Library, Museum, and Historical Society, which accepted the books, papers, and reference materials that were used for these four books. I thank especially Barbara Price, who has archived this material as the George J. Hill Collection.

Thanks to members of our families, without whose help it would have been impossible to compile these books. Some are now deceased: My mother, Essie Mae (née Thompson) Hill, author and family historian; and our daughters, Sarah and Helena Rundall Hill. Also, in alphabetical order: Ralph Bassett; Michael Bowman; Sue (née Kelley) Carnwath; Kevin Corwin; Avis (née Boyington) Hill; Alton Herrick; William Edwin Hill, Secretary of the Hill Family in the 1920s; Barbara (née Zimmermann) Johnson, and her son-in-law, Thomas Riley; Jeanine (née Humbert) Johnson, my first cousin, once removed; Dolly Jean (née Goldsberry) Koon; Anne Mitchell; Jean (née Hoxie) Naples; Arthur Putnam; Mrs. Kenneth (Natalie) Rose; George Ardell Rundall; Andrew Saxe; Foster Stockwell; Dr. Margaret "Peg" Thompson; Ruby (née Hill) Woodin; and John Zimmermann, a great-grandson of John Zimmermann, the Emigrant.

In this project, I was guided by the following books: Betsey Warren Davis, *The Warren, Jackson, and Allied Families*; Bart Anderson, *The Sharples-Sharpless Family*; Robert Charles Anderson, *The Great Migration Begins*; David Hackett Fisher, *Albion's Seed: Four British Folkways in America*; David Lines Jacobus, *Families of Old Fairfield*; and Frank J. Doherty, *Settlers of the Beekman Patent*.

The present work would have been difficult if not impossible, had it not been for the internet searches that were facilitated by the New England Historic Genealogical Society (NEHGS); Ancestry.com, especially with its soundex name searches, although entries in family trees were often conflicting and obviously erroneous; FamilySearch.org; Google books, with immediate, free access to pdf copies of books in the public domain; Wikipedia, for clues to searches; and other internet search engines

I am indebted to several professional genealogy researchers who worked on this project, including: Pauline Lucille Austin, Johanne Gervais, Diane Snyder Ptak, Michael Wickes, and Jane Wile.

Many family associations and leaders of these associations have been helpful, including Liane Townsend Fenimore of the Townsend Society of America; Gene Pennington and the Pennington Research Association; the Towne Family Association; and the Fuller Society.

Many lineage society genealogists who approved the qualifying lines and offered invaluable suggestions, including: Alex Bannerman, Timothy Field Beard, Richard Burr, Paul Cook, Tracy Ashley Crocker, Phyllis Hansen, John Harman, Lyndon H. Hart III, Phil Livingston, Maureen McGowan-Singer, Dr. Evelyn Ogden, Henry Peden, Michel Racicot, David Carline Smith, and Kelly Lloyd Stewart.

I thank my teachers, including: Mrs. Ralston, who taught me about American history in eighth grade; Professors of History Robert "Bob" Woolsey and Frederick Kilgour at Yale, who encouraged me; Professor Clement Alexander Price, who taught me how to look at history from the Other side; Mervin Rummels, who introduced me to Shakespeare and the beauties of English grammar; Professor Jan Ellen Lewis, who taught me how history should be written; and Professor J. Perry Leavell, who taught me that the best dissertation is a finished dissertation.

And finally, I am glad to thank my publisher, Leslie Wolfinger, and my editor, Debbie Riley, of Heritage Books, who have always supported me.

From Google Images

ROGER CONANT
Governor of the Beverly Colony
Statue in Salem, Massachusetts

Ancestor of
Betsey Warren

IMMIGRANTS TO AMERICA

IN

FOUR FAMILIES

FEATURED NAMES

SIXTY-EIGHT IMMIGRANTS

HENRY ADAMS	GEORGE MORTON
SAMUEL ALLEN	JOHN OGDEN
SARAH ALLERTON	MARY OP den GRAEFF
MATTHEW ALLYN	WILLIAM PALMER
ROBERT ARCHIBALD	JOHN PEIRCE
HUMPHREY ATHERTON	ABRAHAM PIERSON
CHRISTOPHER AVERY	DAVID POTTS
RICHARD BORDEN	PHINEAS PRATT
WILLIAM BRADFORD	JAMES PRESCOTT
JOHN BUDD	DEGORY PRIEST
JOHN CADWALADER	JOHN PRINCE
JULIANA CARPENTER	JOHN PUTNAM
SAMUEL CHAPIN	GRACE RAVENS
ROGER CLAPP	WILLIAM RUNDLE
HENRY COMLY	JOHN SAXE
ROGER CONANT	JOHN SHARPLES
JUDITH FEAKE	GEORGE SHOEMAKER
ROBERT FLETCHER	RICHARD SINGLETARY
JOHN FOLGER	WILLIAM STOCKWELL
EDWARD FULLER	ARCHIBALD THOMPSON
JONATHAN GILLETT	PARDON TILLINGHAST
ROBERT HALE	JOHN TOWNSEND
HENRY HERRICK	RICHARD TOWNSEND
LUKE HILL	JOHN THORNDIKE
JOHN HOBBY	WILLIAM TOWNE
THOMAS HOLBROOK	THOMAS TROWBRIDGE
OBADIAH HOLMES	MARY TYSON
EDWARD HOWELL	WILLIAM UNDERWOOD
EDWARD JACKSON	RICHARD WALL
JOHN JOHNSON	WILLIAM WARD
JANE LAWRENCE	ARTHUR WARREN
TOBY LEECH	JOHN WHITNEY
JAN LUKENS	SIMON WILLARD
JOHN MANLEY	JOHN ZIMMERMANN

HENRY ADAMS

HENRY ADAMS,[4] youngest son and fourth child of John and Agnes (Stone?) Adams, called "Henry the Patriarch" by his descendant John Quincy Adams, was born at Barton St. David, co. Somerset, England, in about 1583; died at Braintree, Mass., 8 October 1646. He was the ancestor of **Presidents John Adams and John Quincy Adams**, and of the patriot **Samuel Adams**. Henry Adams was a yeoman in England, and a farmer and brewer in Massachusetts. He married, at Charlton Mackrell, co. Somerset, 19 October 1609, **EDITH SQUIRE,** eldest child of Henry Squire of co. Somerset. Their great-granddaughter, Edith Adams, is probably an ancestor of George J. Hill, the Iowa Pioneer.

Henry ADAMS = Edith SQUIRE
Thomas ADAMS = Mary BLACKMORE
Pelataih ADAMS = Ruth PARKER
James BRADFORD = Edith ADAMS
Jonathan PELLET = Jerusha BRADFORD
Willard PIERCE = Jerusha PELLET
Rufus HERRICK [III] = Jerusha P. _____ (prob.) PIERCE
William Prince HILL = Sarah P. "Sally" HERRICK
Charles W. HILL = Adelia Catherine RILEY
George J. HILL = Jessie Fidelia STOCKWELL

BENJAMIN ALBEE

BENJAMIN ALBEE[5] came to America from England before 1641 with his brother, John. He first settled at Braintree, Mass., and from there he moved in 1649 to Medfield, Mass. He built one of the first water powered mills for grinding grain in New England. He married **HANNAH ____**. They had four children, of whom the eldest, James, born 1640, is a candidate to be the father or grandfather of William Alleby, who married Sarah (Davis) Sheffield in 1716. Their other sons, John and Benjamin, are also considered as candidates to be the father or grandfather of William Alleby, who is an ancestor of Jessie Stockwell.

Benjamin ALBEE = Hannah _____
(possibly) James ALBEE = Hannah COOK
William ALLEBY = Sarah DAVIS, widow of _____ SHEFFIELD
Jesse IRISH = Mary ALLBEE
William IRISH = Dolly _____
Freeborn POTTER = Dolly IRISH
Harvey HYDE = Fidelia Gadcourt POTTER
Benajah Flavel STOCKWELL = Emily Lodiweska HYDE
George J. HILL = Jessie Fidelia STOCKWELL

HANNAH (_____) ALBEE

HANNAH _____ was the wife of **BENJAMIN ALBEE**, immigrant from England. They were married in Massachusetts and had four children. Her origin is unknown (see preceding).

JOHN ALCOCK

JOHN ALCOCK[6] is said to have been born in Mersham, England; died between 1671 and 6 July 1675, probably in York, Maine. He appeared as early as 1639 in Gorgeana (now York), Mass., which is now in Maine. He was sergeant of the train band of York in 1659. He married, probably in England, **ELIZABETH _____**, who died, probably in York, Maine, after 29 October 1675. They had seven children; their daughter Sarah married Lieut. John Giddings and is an ancestor of Jessie Stockwell.

---

[4] Hill, *Western Pilgrims*, 112-7. The descent to George J. Hill depends on the assumption that Jerusha P., wife of Rufus Herrick (III), was Jerusha Pierce. (See discussion of this question in *Western Pilgrims*, 45, Herrick Family.)
[5] Hill, *Western Pilgrims*, 357-8.
[6] Hill, *Western Pilgrims*, 295-6.

John ALCOCK = Elizabeth _____
Lieut. John GIDDINGS = Sarah ALCOCK
Thomas GIDDINGS = Sarah ANDREWS
Capt. Joseph GIDDINGS = Eunice ANDREWS
Benjamin GIDDINGS = Martha SEELEY
Luther HYDE = Phoebe GIDDINGS
Harvey HYDE = Fidelia Gadcourt POTTER
Benajah Flavel STOCKWELL = Emily Lodiweska HYDE
George J. HILL = Jessie Fidelia STOCKWELL

ELIZABETH (_____) ALCOCK

ELIZABETH _____ was the wife of **JOHN ALCOCK**, immigrant to Massachusetts. They were probably married in England. Her ancestry is unknown (see preceding).

SAMUEL ALLEN

SAMUEL ALLEN[7] was born in co. Essex, England, about 1588; died at Windsor, Conn., 28 April 1648. He came with the Dorchester Company in 1630 – possibly with his brother, Thomas, and Matthew Allyn. He married in 1633 **ANN** ____; died 13 November 1687. Samuel Allen had seven children. His eldest, Samuel, is an ancestor of Jessie Stockwell. His second child, Nehemiah, is an ancestor of **Ethan Allen**.

Samuel ALLEN = Ann _____
Samuel ALLEN = Hannah WOODFORD
Deacon Samuel ALLEN = Sarah RUST
Samuel ALLEN = Hannah MILLER
Jabez WARD = Jemima ALLEN
Henry HYDE = Thyrina WARD
Luther HYDE = Phoebe GIDDINGS
Harvey HYDE = Fidelia Gadcourt POTTER
Benajah Flavel STOCKWELL = Emily Lodiweska HYDE
George J. HILL = Jessie Fidelia STOCKWELL

ANN (_____) ALLEN

ANN _____ was the wife of **SAMUEL ALLEN**, immigrant, probably to Massachusetts, who died at Windsor, Conn., in 1648. They married in 1633. She married (2) **William HURLBUT** (see preceding).

SARAH ALLERTON

SARAH ALLERTON[8] was born say 1582; died at Plymouth Colony in 1633. She was the daughter of _____ Alllerton. He had two children: **Sarah** and **Isaac,** a merchant, born in perhaps London, in 1586; died at New Haven, Conn., in Feb 1658/9. He came to New England on the *Mayflower*. Sarah Allerton married (1) **John VINCENT**, who died before November 1611, without issue. She married (2), at Leiden, 4 November 1611, **DEGORY PRIEST**, hatter, of London; born about 1579; died at Plymouth Colony, 1 January 1620/1; they had two children. Their daughter Mary married PHINEAS PRATT and is believed to be an ancestor of William Henry Thompson. Sarah married (3), at Leiden, as his second wife, **Godbert GODBERTSON**; born about 1592; died between July and October 1633.

Degory PRIEST = Sarah ALLERTON
Phineas PRATT = Mary PRIEST
Joseph PRATT = Dorcas FOLGER
Joseph EDMANDS = Mary PRATT

---

[7] Hill, *Western Pilgrims*, 328-9.

[8] Hill, *Fundy to Chesapeake*, 39-40. This genealogy depends on the presumption that Hannah _____, wife of James Thompson, Sr., is Hannah Scott, daughter of Sheriff Joseph Scott. For discussion, see *Fundy to Chesapeake*, 3-4.

Lieut. Joseph SCOTT = Mary EDMANDS
Sheriff Joseph SCOTT = Sarah CUTTING
James THOMPSON Sr. = Hannah _____, prob. Hannah SCOTT
Joseph Scott THOMPSON = Ruth E. ARCHIBALD
James Everett THOMPSON = Jane GRANT
William Henry "Will" THOMPSON = Sarah D. "Sadie" RUNDALL

MORGAN ALLOTT

MORGAN ALLOTT,[9] of Ware, England, had a son, *Robert ALLOTT*, who had a daughter, *Elizabeth ALLOTT*, baptized at Ware, 17 March 1582/3; buried 28 March 1671. *Elizabeth ALLOTT* married, 28 April 1606, *Adrian PORTER*. Adrian and Elizabeth (Allott) Porter are ancestors of Jessie Stockwell.

Morgan ALLOTT = _____
Robert ALLOTT = Joan _____
Adrian PORTER = *Elizabeth ALLOTT*
Capt. Isaac JOHNSON = Elizabeth PORTER
(see JOHN JOHNSON and ELIZABETH PORTER)

MATTHEW ALLYN

Hon. MATTHEW ALLYN,[10] a wealthy merchant, son of Richard and Margaret (Wyatt) Allen of Braunton, co. Devon, baptized 17 April 1605; died at Windsor, Conn., 1 February 1670/1. He married, at Braunton, 2 February 1626/7, **MARGARET WYATT**, daughter of John Wyatt and *FRANCES CHICHESTER*; baptized 8 March 1594/5; died at Windsor, 12 September 1675. They came in 1633.

Matthew ALLYN = Margaret WYATT
Capt. Benjamin NEWBERRY = Mary ALLYN
Preserved CLAPP = Sarah NEWBERRY
Abraham MILLER = Hannah CLAPP
Samuel ALLEN = Hannah MILLER
Corporal Jabez WARD = Jemima ALLEN
Private Henry HYDE = Thyrina (Therina) WARD
Luther HYDE = Phoebe GIDDINGS
Harvey HYDE = Fidelia Gadcourt POTTER
Benajah Flavel STOCKWELL = Emily Lodiweska (Emma F.) HYDE
George J. HILL = Jessie Fidelia STOCKWELL

ABIGAIL AMBROSE

ABIGAIL AMBROSE[11] died in New Hampshire after 1756, but probably soon before 1763; married, as his first wife, in about 1739, **Joshua PRESCOTT [II]**, grandson of the immigrant, **JAMES PRESCOTT**.

Joshua PRESCOTT [II] = Abigail AMBROSE
William PUTNAM = Dorothy "Dolly" PRESCOTT
William ARCHIBALD = Susannah "Susan" PUTNAM
Joseph Scott THOMPSON = Ruth E. ARCHIBALD
James Everett THOMPSON = Jane GRANT
William Henry "Will" THOMPSON = Sarah D. "Sadie" RUNDALL

JOHN ANDREWS

Lieutenant JOHN ANDREWS[12] was born, probably in England, about 1618 to 1621; died at Chebacco Parish, Ipswich, Mass., 20 April 1708. He first appeared in the records of Ipswich in 1637. He married

---

[9] Hill, *Western Pilgrims*, 245-6.
[10] Hill, *Western Pilgrims*, 345-7. Margaret Wyatt has **Royal ancestors**. Richardson, *Royal Ancestry*, 1:114-5.
[11] Hill, *Fundy to Chesapeake*, 93-4.
[12] Hill, *Western Pilgrims*, 301-4.

Jane JORDAN, born in England, say 1626, daughter of STEPHEN JORDAN of Ipswich, and later of Newbury; died after John Andrews made his will in 1705. Their son Joseph Andrews is an ancestor of Jessie F. Stockwell, by the marriage of two of his grandchildren, who were first cousins.

Lieut. John ANDREWS = Jane JORDAN
Joseph ANDREWS = Sarah RINDGE
John ANDREWS = Elizabeth WALLIS   Thomas GIDDINGS = Sarah ANDREWS
Capt. Joseph GIDDINGS = Eunice ANDREWS
Benjamin GIDDINDGS = Martha SEELEY
Luther HYDE = Phoebe GIDDINGS
Harvey HYDE = Fidelia Gadcourt POTTER
Benajah Flavel STOCKWELL = Emily Lodiweska (Emma F.) HYDE
George J. HILL = Jessie Fidelia STOCKWELL

JOHN ANTHONY

John ANTHONY,[13] a freeman of Portsmouth R.I., in 1665, may have come in the *Hercules* in 1634 from Hempstead, near London, and may have removed to Providence, R.I. Accounts of his life vary in different sources. It is said that by his wife **Frances ___**, he had several children, including a son, John Anthony [II]. Isabel Anthony, said by some to be a daughter of John [I] and Frances Anthony, or John [II] and Susannah Anthony, married Robert Potter.

John [I] ANTHONY = Frances _____   or   John [II] ANTHONY = Susannah _____
Robert POTTER = Isabel ANTHONY
John POTTER = Ruth FISHER
John POTTER = Jane BURLINGAME
William POTTER = Martha TILLINGHAST
Capt. Oliver POTTER = Mary COLVIN
Capt. Freeborn POTTER = Dolly IRISH
Harvey HYDE = Fidelia Gadcourt POTTER
Benajah Flavel STOCKWELL = Emily Lodiweska HYDE
George J. HILL = Jessie Fidelia STOCKWELL

WALTER ANTROBUS

WALTER ANTROBUS,[14] who died in April 1614, married in St. Albans, England, 8 February 1586/7, **JOAN ARNOLD**, who died perhaps in New England in 1635, or later. Her daughter, Joan (Antrobus) (Lawrence) Tuttle, and her granddaughter, Jane (Lawrence) Giddings, came to America on the *Planter* in 1635, with Jane's husband George Giddings and several members of their families. Her grandmother, Joan (Arnold) Antrobus, was admitted as a passenger, and it is assumed that she made the trip, although there is no record of her arrival in America. The descendants of Thomas Lawrence and his wife Joan Antrobus include JANE LAWRENCE, who married GEORGE GIDDINGS.

Walter ANTROBUS = Joan ARNOLD (widowed; was admitted as passenger on *Planter*)
Thomas LAWRENCE = Joan ANTROBUS (married [2] John Tuttle; came with him on *Planter*)
George GIDDINGS = Jane LAWRENCE (they came on *Planter*)
John GIDDINGS = Sarah ALCOCK
Thomas GIDDINGS = Sarah ANDREWS
Joseph GIDDINGS = Eunice ANDREWS
Benjamin GIDDINGS = Martha SEELEY
Luther HYDE = Phoebe GIDDINGS
Harvey HYDE = Fidelia Gadcourt POTTER

---

[13] Hill, *Western Pilgrims*, 254. Also see Hill, *Fundy to Chesapeake*, 778-84, which tells how this John Anthony was also believed to be an ancestor of the Townsends of Long Island, and thus of Sarah D. Rundall. (See Appendix for discussion of disproved lines of HARCOURT, WESTON, POTTER, and ANTHONY.)

[14] Hill, *Western Pilgrims*, 299-300. Richardson, *Royal Ancestry* 3:551-2, for Jane Lawrence = George Giddings, and the **Royal Line** of Jane Lawrence; and *Western Pilgrims*, 293-4.

Benajah Flavel STOCKWELL = Emily Lodiweska (Emma F.) HYDE
George J. HILL = Jessie Fidelia STOCKWELL

ROBERT ARCHIBALD

Robert ARCHIBALD.[15] born about 1668; died in Londonderry, N.H., in 1765. He married **ANN BOYD,** born in Northern Ireland in 1668; died at Londonderry, N.H., 5 April 1765. Their son John Archibald, Sr., is an ancestor of William H. Thompson through the marriage of two of his grandchildren.

Robert ARCHIBALD = Ann BOYD
John ARCHIBALD, Sr. = Margaret WILSON
Samuel ARCHIBALD = Eleanor TAYLOR   William James FISHER = Eleanor ARCHIBALD
Lt. Col. John ARCHIBALD 2nd = Margaret FISHER
William ARCHIBALD = Susannah "Susan" PUTNAM
Joseph Scott THOMPSON = Ruth E. ARCHIBALD
James Everett THOMPSON = Jane GRANT
William Henry "Will" THOMPSON = Sarah D. "Sadie" RUNDALL

JOAN ARNOLD

JOAN ARNOLD,[16] born about 1578 in England, probably co. Hertford, married, at St. Albans, co. Hertford, ***WALTER ANTROBUS***, who died there, 5 April 1614. Joan (Arnold) Antrobus survived her husband, and in 1635 she registered to come to America with her daughter, Joan (Antrobus) (Lawrence) Tuttle, and her granddaughter, Jane (Lawrence) Giddings. She is an ancestor of Jessie Stockwell.

RALPH de ARUNDEL

RALPH de ARUNDEL,[17] son of Sir Richard de Arundel, 10th Earl of Arundel and Surrey, married ***Juliane ?GRENVILLE***, The Arundel (Fitz Alan) family descends from **Charlemagne**.

Ralph de ARUNDEL = Juliane ?GRENVILLE
Bartholomew COLLINGRIDGE = Alice ARUNDEL
William COLLINGRIDGE = Sarah ___
Geoffrey DORMER = Alice COLLINRIDGE
Thomas CROKER = Alice DORMER
John CROKER = Isabell SKINNER
Edward HAWTEN = Margery CROKER
Henry HOWELL = Margaret HAWTEN
Mr. Edward HOWELL, Lord of the Manor of Westbury = *Frances PAXTON*
(See EDWARD HOWELL)

ESTHER ASHMEAD

ESTHER (Hester) ASHMEAD,[18] was born at Cheltenham, Gloucestershire; died at Cheltenham Twp., Pa., 11 August 1726. She married **TOBY LEECH,** 26 Oct 1679 in Gloucestershire. She is an ancestor of Dr. William T. Shoemaker.

HUMPHREY ATHERTON

Major-General HUMPHREY ATHERTON,[19] probably the son of Edmund Atherton, of Winstanley, co. Lancaster, was born before 1615; died at Boston, Mass., 17 September 1661. He was first mentioned in the records of New England on 18 March 1637/[?8]. On 22 May 1661, he was chosen major-general.

---

[15] Hill, *Fundy to Chesapeake*, 49-53.
[16] Hill, *Western Pilgrims*, 299-300.
[17] Hill, *Western Pilgrims*, 153-6.
[18] Hill, *Quakers and Puritans*, 110.
[19] Hill, *Quakers and Puritans*, 263-5, for the descent to Mabel Warren. And Hill, *Fundy to Chesapeake*, 3-4; 46-7. This genealogy depends on the presumption that Hannah _____, wife of James Thompson, Sr., is Hannah Scott.

He married, in England, **MARY WALES,** daughter of John and Margaret Wales, and sister of NATHANIEL WALES, of West Riding, Yorkshire; died at Dorchester, Mass., in 1672. Humphrey Atherton is an ancestor of Mabel Warren and probably also of William H. Thompson.

Humphrey ATHERTON = Mary WALES
Lieut. James TROWBRIDGE = Margaret ATHERTON
John GREENWOOD, Esq. = Hannah TROWBRIDGE
Isaac JACKSON = Ruth GREENWOOD
Sgt. Josiah JACKSON = Mary DARBY
Oliver JACKSON = Mary PEIRCE
Jesse WARREN = Betsy JACKSON
Herbert Marshall WARREN = Eliza Caroline COPP
William Toy SHOEMAKER = Mabel WARREN

\-\-\-\-\-\-\-\-\-\-\-\-\-\-

Humphrey ATHERTON = Mary WALES
Nathaniel WALES, Jr. = Isabel ATHERTON
Jonathan WALES = Sarah BAKER
David CUTTING = Elizabeth WALES
David CUTTING = Sarah EDMUNDS
Sheriff Joseph SCOTT = Sarah CUTTING
James THOMPSON Sr. = Hannah ____, prob. Hannah SCOTT
Joseph Scott THOMPSON = Ruth E. ARCHIBALD
James Everett THOMPSON = Jane GRANT
William Henry "Will" THOMPSON = Sarah D. "Sadie" RUNDALL

PHILIP ATWOOD

PHILIP ATWOOD[20] arrived in New England in 1635, probably on the *Susan & Ellen*, and first resided at Charlestown. He had wide-ranging interests in exploration and land development in Massachusetts. He married (1) in Massachusetts, by 1653, **Rachel BACHELOR,** daughter of WILLIAM BACHELOR; born in England, say 1633; died at Malden, 5 February 1673/4.

Phillip ATWOOD = Rachel BACHELOR
Andrew MITCHELL = Abigail ATWOOD
Ebenezer NURSE = Elizabeth MITCHELL, prob. dau. of Andrew Mitchell
Caleb PUTNAM = Elizabeth NURSE
William PUTNAM = Dorothy "Dolly" PRESCOTT
William ARCHIBALD = Susannah "Susan" PUTNAM
Joseph Scott THOMPSON = Ruth E. ARCHIBALD
James Everett THOMPSON = Jane GRANT
William Henry "Will" THOMPSON = Sarah D. "Sadie" RUNDALL

CHRISTOPHER AVERY

CHRISTOPHER AVERY,[21] son of Christopher and Johann Avery, was born in co. Devon, England, about 1590; died at New London, Conn., and was buried there, 12 March 1679. His first appearance in the record of New England was in April 1642, when he purchased two acres of marsh by the sea at Cape Ann, Massachusetts Bay Colony. He married, at Ipplepen, co. Devon, about 26 August 1616, *Margery STEPHENS*. It appears that his wife never came to the New World. One of his descendants is Lucy Avery, grandmother of **John D. Rockefeller, Sr.,** founder of Standard Oil Co.

Christopher AVERY = *Margery STEPHENS*
Capt. James AVERY = Joanna GREENSLADE
John AVERY = Abigail CHESEBROUGH
Capt. William DENISON = Mary AVERY

---

[20] Hill, *Fundy to Chesapeake*, 88-9.
[21] Hill, *Western Pilgrims*, 72-6.

Edward HERRICK = Mary DENISON
Col. Rufus HERRICK = Miss GIBBS, prob. Myra "Mary" GIBBS
Capt. Rufus HERRICK Jr. = Lydia NEWMAN
Rufus HERRICK [III] = Jerusha P. _____ (prob.) PIERCE
William Prince HILL = Sarah P. "Sally" HERRICK
Charles W. HILL = Adelia Catharine "Delia" RILEY
George J. HILL = Jessie Fidelia STOCKWELL

WILLIAM BACHELOR

WILLIAM BACHELOR,[22] victualler of Charlestown, Mass., was born about 1596; died at Charlestown, February 1669/[70]. He probably came to Massachusetts in December 1634. He married (1), probably in England, by 1632, **JANE** _____; died after 1 July 1637.

William BACHELOR = Jane _____
Phillip ATWOOD = Rachel BACHELOR
Andrew MITCHELL = Abigail ATWOOD
Ebenezer NURSE = Elizabeth MITCHELL, prob. dau. of Andrew Mitchell
Caleb PUTNAM = Elizabeth NURSE
William PUTNAM = Dorothy "Dolly" PRESCOTT
William ARCHIBALD = Susannah "Susan" PUTNAM
Joseph Scott THOMPSON = Ruth E. ARCHIBALD
James Everett THOMPSON = Jane GRANT
William Henry "Will" THOMPSON = Sarah D. "Sadie" RUNDALL

JANE (_____) BACHELOR

JANE _____ married, as his first wife, probably in England, **WILLIAM BACHELOR** (see preceding).

GEORGE BACON

GEORGE BACON,[23] a mason, was born about 1592, co. Suffolk, England; died at Hingham, Plymouth Colony, Mass., and was buried there, 3 May 1642. He came in 1635 on the ship *Increase* with three children, his wife having died by 1623. He married (2), at Hingham, Mass., between 1635 and 1640, **MARGARET** _____; she died at Hingham, in February 1682/3, having married (2) **Edward GOLD**.

George BACON = Margaret _____
Thomas BACON = Mary GAMLIN
Joseph BACON = Margaret BOWEN
Henry BACON = Hannah WOODWARD
Jabez HYDE = Hannah BACON
Private Henry HYDE = Thyrina (Therina) WARD
Luther HYDE = Phoebe GIDDINGS
Harvey HYDE = Fidelia Gadcourt POTTER
Benajah Flavel STOCKWELL = Emily Lodiweska (Emma F.) HYDE
George J. HILL = Jessie Fidelia STOCKWELL

MARGARET (_____) BACON

MARGARET _____ married, as his second wife, **GEORGE BACON** (see preceding).

ANN BAGLEY

ANN BAGLEY[24] died at Birmingham, Chester Co., Pa., in 1699. She married, in England, in 1659, **WILLIAM BRINTON**, in about 1633. She is an ancestor of Sarah D. Rundall.

---

[22] Hill, *Fundy to Chesapeake*, 88.
[23] Hill, *Western Pilgrims*, 239-40.
[24] Hill, *Fundy to Chesapeake*, 329.

ALEXANDER BAKER

ALEXANDER BAKER,[25] collarmaker and ropemaker, was born in England in about 1607; died at Boston, Mass., between 18 February 1684/5 (will) and 11 May 1685 (probate). He came with his wife and three daughters in the *Elizabeth and Ann* in April 1635. He married by 1632, **ELIZABETH ____**; born about 1612; died after 18 February 1684/5.

Alexander BAKER = Elizabeth ____
Jonathan WALES = Sarah BAKER
David CUTTING = Elizabeth WALES
Sarah EDMUNDS = David CUTTING (Jr.)
Sheriff Joseph SCOTT = Sarah CUTTING
James THOMPSON Sr. = Hannah ____, prob. Hannah SCOTT
Joseph Scott THOMPSON = Ruth E. ARCHIBALD
James Everett THOMPSON = Jane GRANT
William Henry "Will" THOMPSON = Sarah D. "Sadie" RUNDALL

ELIZABETH (_____) BAKER

ELIZABETH _____ married, in England, by 1632, **ALEXANDER BAKER**. They came to America in 1635 with their three daughters. She died after 1684/5 (see preceding).

JOHN BAKER

Mr. JOHN BAKER[26] was born in England in 1598; was of co. Norwich when he came to America in 1637 at age 39; died, probably at Ipswich, Mass., between 1661 and 1666. He was first recorded as a freeman of Ipswich on 14 May 1634, with a "prefix of respect." He married, in England, **ELIZABETH _____**; she died sometime after giving testimony in 1666.

Mr. John BAKER = Elizabeth _____
Thomas BAKER = Elizabeth _____
Sebas "Seaborn" JACKSON = Sarah BAKER
Edward JACKSON = Mary _____
Isaac JACKSON = Ruth GREENWOOD
Sgt. Josiah JACKSON = Mary DARBY
Oliver JACKSON = Mary PEIRCE
Jesse WARREN= Betsy JACKSON
Herbert Marshall WARREN = Eliza Caroline COPP
William Toy SHOEMAKER = Mabel WARREN

ELIZABETH (_____) BAKER

ELIZABETH _____ married, in England, **JOHN BAKER**. They came to Massachusetts in 1637, and she died after giving testimony in 1666 (see preceding).

JOHN BALDWIN

JOHN BALDWIN,[27] an early resident of Milford, Conn., married **Mary BRUEN**, daughter of OBADIAH BRUEN and SARAH SEELEY. John and Mary (Bruen) Baldwin are the parents of Josiah Baldwin, who was the father of Mary Baldwin. She may be the Mary ___, who married Samuel Oviatt son of THOMAS OVIATT.

---

[25] Hill, *Fundy to Chesapeake*, 46. For the question of Hannah ___ (?SCOTT), see *Fundy to Chesapeake*, 3-4.
[26] Hill, *Quakers and Puritans*, 208-10.
[27] Hill, *Western Pilgrims*, 139, 689; Mary Baldwin is a great granddaughter of Obadiah[1] Bruen (*Mary*[4], *Josiah Baldwin*[3], *Mary*[2], *Obadiah*[1] *Bruen*), who is of **Royal descent**.

John BALDWIN = Mary BRUEN
Josiah BALDWIN = Mary CAMP
Samuel OVIATT = Mary _____ ("maybe BALDWIN")
John OVIATT = Susanna HINE
John OVIATT (Jr.) = Abigail SMITH
Edward Howell PRINCE = Huldah OVIATT
Ephraim HILL = Charlotte PRINCE
William Prince HILL = Sarah P. "Sally" HERRICK
Charles W. HILL = Adelia Catharine "Delia" RILEY
George J. HILL = Jessie Fidelia STOCKWELL

GEORGE BARBOUR

Capt. **GEORGE BARBOUR**[28] was born in England in 1615; died before his estate was inventoried, 23 April 1685. He sailed from Gravesend, 4 July 1635 on *Transport*, was a townsman of Dedham in 1640 and became freeman there in 1647. He married (1), in 1642, **ELIZABETH CLARK**, who died in 1683.

Capt. George BARBOUR = Elizabeth CLARK
Jonathan MORSE = Mary Marie BARBOUR
Jonathan MORSE (Jr.) = Jane WHITNEY
Joseph PARTRIDGE = Eunice MORSE
Lt. Aaron HOLBROOK = Hannah PARTRIDGE
Ebenezer STOCKWELL = Abi HOLBROOK
Joseph H. STOCKWELL = Anna Maria SAXE
Benajah Flavel STOCKWELL = Emily Lodiweska (Emma F.) HYDE
George J. HILL = Jessie Fidelia STOCKWELL

ABRAHAM BELKNAP

ABRAHAM BELKNAP[29] was probably the son of Bennet or Benedict Belknap of co. Herts. He died in Massachusetts on 1(7)1643. He was said to be "of Boston" and was a proprietor of Lynn in 1638. His inventory was presented by his widow **MARY**.

Abraham BELKNAP = Mary _____
Nathaniel SINGLETARY = Sarah BELKNAP, prob. dau. of Abraham Belknap
John SINGLETARY = Mary GREELEY
Ebenezer STOCKWELL = Mary SINGLETARY
Benajah STOCKWELL = Hannah GALE
Ebenezer STOCKWELL = Abi HOLBROOK
Joseph H. STOCKWELL = Anna Maria SAXE
Benajah Flavel STOCKWELL = Emily Lodiweska (Emma F.) HYDE
George J. HILL = Jessie Fidelia STOCKWELL

MARY (_____) BELKNAP

MARY _____ married **ABRAHAM BELKNAP**, immigrant to Massachusetts, who died in 1643. She survived him and is probably an ancestor of Jessie Stockwell (see preceding).

FRANCIS BELL

Lieut., the Hon. **FRANCIS BELL**[30] was in Wethersfield, Conn., by about 1640 or 1641, "still quite young"; died in Stamford, Conn., 8 January 1689/90. In 1653, he represented Stamford in the General Court. He married in about 1640, **REBECCA** _____, who died at Stamford, 7 May 1684.

---

[28] Hill, *Western Pilgrims*, 210.
[29] Hill, *Western Pilgrims*, 184.
[30] Hill, *Fundy to Chesapeake*, 189-90.

Hon. Lieut. Francis BELL = Rebecca _____
Capt. Jonathan BELL = Susannah PIERSON
Ebenezer WEED = Mary BELL
David BROWN = Sarah WEED, prob. dau of Ebenezer Weed
David BROWN (II) = Deborah JESSUP
Shadrack RUNDALL Sr. = Phebe BROWN
Reuben John RUNDALL = Martha TOMPKINS
Silas William RUNDALL = Rachel MANLY
William Henry "Will" THOMPSON = Sarah D. "Sadie" RUNDALL

REBECCA (_____) BELL

REBECCA _____ married **FRANCIS BELL,** immigrant to America. They were probably married before he arrived at Wethersfield, Conn., in about 1640; she died in 1684 (see preceding).

ANN BIDDLE

ANN BIDDLE[31] was born in England in 1609; died in 1684. She married *Thomas BRINTON Jr.,* born in 1607; died in 1687 at co. Stafford, England. They were ancestors of Quaker immigrants to Pennsylvania. Their descendants include **President Richard M. Nixon** and Sarah D. Rundall.

Thomas BRINTON Jr. = Ann BIDDLE
William BRINTON the Elder = Ann BAGLEY
(see WILLIAM BRINTON)

WILLIAM BIGWOOD

WILLIAM BIGGWOOD,[32] of Frome, St. John, co. Somerset, married there, *Jane BAYLIE*; she was buried there, 4 June 1629. William and Jane (Baylie) Biggwood are 6th great-grandparents of Eliza Caroline Copp, who came to America to marry Herbert Marshall Warren.

William BIGGWOOD = Jane BAYLIE
John BEGWOOD = Mary _____
William BIGWOOD = Mary _____
William BIGWOOD = Mary BAKER
William BIGWOOD = Mary MILLARD
William BIGWOOD = Mary _____
John BIGWOOD = Sarah _____
James BIGWOOD = Anne WALBURTON
James John COPP = Caroline BIGWOOD
Herbert Marshall WARREN = Eliza Caroline COPP
William Toy SHOEMAKER = Mabel WARREN

HANNAH BIRTHS

HANNAH BIRTHS,[33] who died on 15 September 1662, was the second of the four wives of **HENRY JEFTS,** who emigrated from England. She is an ancestor of Mabel Warren.

HUMPHREY BLAKE

HUMPRHREY BLAKE,[34] gent., was born in say 1494; died at Over Stowey, co. Somerset, 19 November 1558; buried there 28 December 1558. He married *Anne/Agnes* ___; buried 24 June 1585. One line of Humphrey Blake's descendants is that of THOMAS RICHARDS of Weymouth, Mass.

---

[31] Hill, *Fundy to Chesapeake*, 325-8.
[32] Hill, *Quakers and Puritans*, 197-200.
[33] Hill, *Quakers and Puritans*, 154.
[34] Hill, *Western Pilgrims*, 103-6. The supposition that Maj. William Bradford is an ancestor of George J. Hill depends on the assumption that Rufus Herrick's wife Jerusha P. was Jerusha Pierce. See *Western Pilgrims*, 45.

Humphrey BLAKE = Anne/Agnes ____
John BLAKE, the Elder = Joan ____
Thomas RICHARDS = Alice BLAKE
Thomas RICHARDS (Jr.) = Welthean ?LORING
Major William BRADFORD, Jr. = Alice RICHARDS
(also see WILLIAM BRADFORD)

JOANNA BLESSING

JOANNA BLESSING,[35] aka Joan, was the daughter of John and Joane (Priest) Blessing. She married WILLIAM TOWNE, and died at Topsfield, Mass., in 1682. Ten years after she died, three of her daughters were convicted of witchcraft at Salem, Mass. She is an ancestor of William H. Thompson.

ROBERT BLOTT

ROBERT BLOTT,[36] perhaps son of Robert Blott of Harrold, co. Bedford, was born in Puddington, co. Bedford, England, in say 1584; died in Boston, Mass., in 1665. He appears to have come to Massachusetts in about 1634. He married, in Harrold, co. Bedford, England, 31 August 1609, **SUSANNAH SELBEE**; probably born there; died in Boston, Mass., 20 January 1659/60.

Robert BLOTT = Susannah SELBEE
Thomas WOODFORD = Mary BLOTT
Samuel ALLEN = Hannah WOODFORD
Deacon Samuel ALLEN = Sarah RUST
Samuel ALLEN = Hannah MILLER
Jabez WARD = Jemima ALLEN
Henry HYDE = Thyrina WARD
Luther HYDE = Phoebe GIDDINGS
Harvey HYDE = Fidelia Gadcourt POTTER
Benajah Flavel STOCKWELL = Emily Lodiweska HYDE
George J. HILL = Jessie Fidelia STOCKWELL

RICHARD BORDEN

RICHARD BORDEN,[37] son of Matthew and Joan Borden of Headcorn, co. Kent, England, was baptized at Headcorn 22 February 1595/6; died at Portsmouth, R.I., 25 May 1671. He was Deputy to the Rhode Island General Assembly. He acquired land in New Jersey by 1667. He married **JOANE FOWLE**; born in say 1604 in co. Kent, England; died in Portsmouth, R.I., 15 July 1688.

Richard BORDEN = Joane FOWLE
Captain Jonathan HOLMES = Sarah BORDEN
Phillip TILLINGHAST J.P. = Martha HOLMES
William POTTER = Martha TILLINGHAST
Capt. Oliver POTTER = Mary COLVIN
Capt. Freeborn POTTER = Dolly IRISH
Harvey HYDE = Fidelia Gadcourt POTTER
Benajah Flavel STOCKWELL = Emily Lodiweska HYDE
George J. HILL = Jessie Fidelia STOCKWELL

NATHANIEL BOULTER

NATHANIEL BOULTER,[38] a pipestave maker, was born in about 1625; died at Hampton, N.H., 14 March 1693. He married, at Hampton, N.H., 5 April 1647, **Grace SWAINE**, daughter of RICHARD

---

[35] Hill, *Fundy to Chesapeake*, 84.
[36] Hill, *Western Pilgrims*, 332-3. Anderson, *Great Migration* 1:334-8 (ROBERT BLOTT).
[37] Hill, *Western Pilgrims*, 284-9.
[38] Hill, *Fundy to Chesapeake*, 100-1.

SWAINE and his wife BASILL; baptized at Easthamstead, Berks, 25 February 1627/8. Grace (Swaine) Boulter and her daughter, Mary (Boulter) Prescott, were accused of witchcraft in 1680.

Nathaniel BOULTER = Grace SWAINE
James PRESCOTT Sr. = Mary BOULTER
Joshua PRESCOTT = Sarah CLIFFORD, prob. dau. of Israel Clifford
Joshua PRESCOTT (Jr.) = Abigail AMBROSE
William PUTNAM = Dorothy "Dolly" PRESCOTT
William ARCHIBALD = Susannah "Susan" PUTNAM
Joseph Scott THOMPSON = Ruth E. ARCHIBALD
James Everett THOMPSON = Jane GRANT
William Henry "Will" THOMPSON = Sarah D. "Sadie" RUNDALL

THOMAS BOURNE

Mr. THOMAS BOURNE,[39] born about 1581, said to be from co. Kent; died at Marshfield, Mass., and was buried there, 11 May 1664, age 83. Bourne received a land grant in Plymouth Colony on 2 January 1636 and was a freeman at Plymouth on 7 February 1636/7. He married **ELIZABETH _____** in England, probably by say 1610; born about 1589; died at Marshfield, Mass., in 1660, age 71.

Mr. Thomas BOURNE = Elizabeth _____
Mr. Nehemiah SMITH = Anne BOURNE
Deacon Joshua RAYMOND = Elizabeth SMITH
Lieut. Thomas BRADFORD = Ann RAYMOND
James BRADFORD = Edith ADAMS
Jonathan PELLET = Jerusha BRADFORD
Willard PIERCE = Jerusha PELLET
Rufus HERRICK [III] = Jerusha P. _____ (prob.) PIERCE
William Prince HILL = Sarah P. "Sally" HERRICK
Charles W. HILL = Adelia Catherine RILEY
George J. HILL = Jessie Fidelia STOCKWELL

ELIZABETH (_____) BOURNE

ELIZABETH _____ was the wife of **Mr. THOMAS BOURNE,** immigrant to Plymouth Colony, was a freeman in 1636/7. They married in England and she died in Marshfield, Mass., in 1660 (see above).

GRIFFITH BOWEN

GRIFFITH BOWEN, gent.,[40] son of Francis and Ellen (Franklyn) Bowen, was born about 1600, probably at Langwith, Wales; died after 11 March 1660, probably in London. He married, in 1627, **MARGARET FLEMING,** who came with him to America, and returned with him to Swanzey, Wales. He was a descendant of **King Henry I**, and an ancestor of **President Franklin Pierce**.

Griffith BOWEN, gent. = Margaret FLEMING
Lieut. Henry BOWEN = Elizabeth JOHNSON
Joseph BACON = Margaret BOWEN
Henry BACON = Hannah WOODWARD
Jabez HYDE = Hannah BACON
Private Henry HYDE = Thyrina (Therina) WARD
Luther HYDE = Phoebe GIDDINGS
Harvey HYDE = Fidelia Gadcourt POTTER
Benajah Flavel STOCKWELL = Emily Lodiweska (Emma F.) HYDE
George J. HILL = Jessie Fidelia STOCKWELL

---

[39] Hill, *Western Pilgrims*, 107-8. The descent to George J. Hill depends on the assumption that Jerusha P., wife of Rufus Herrick (III), was Jerusha Pierce. (See discussion in *Western Pilgrims,* 45, Herrick Family.)
[40] Hill, *Western Pilgrims*, 242-3. The line from Alice ferch John to Griffith Bowen is shown in Roberts, *600 Immigrants*, 485-6; and Weis, *Ancestral Roots*, 8th ed., 170-1.

ERROLL BOYD

ERROLL BOYD[41] was born in about 1752, perhaps in Scotland; died at Halifax, Nova Scotia, 24 February 1828, "aet 76." He was probably in one of the septs (families) of Clan Boyd who were loyal to the Crown. He married **JEAN WILSON**, whose ancestry is unknown.

Erroll BOYD = Jean WILSON
William GRANT = Margaret BOYD
James Everett THOMPSON = Jane GRANT
William Henry "Will" THOMPSON = Sarah D. "Sadie" RUNDALL

WILLIAM BRADFORD

Governor **WILLIAM BRADFORD**,[42] son of William and Alice (Hanson) Bradford, was born at his father's house in Austerfield, co. York, England, in about March 1589/90; died at Plymouth Colony, New England, 9 May 1657. He was Governor of the Plymouth Colony in 1621-33, 1635, 1637, 1639-43, and 1645-56. He married (2), at Plymouth, Mass., 14 August 1623, **ALICE (CARPENTER) SOUTHWORTH**, daughter of Alexander and Priscilla (Dillen) Carpenter and widow of Edward Southworth; she was born probably at Wrington, co. Somerset, England, say 1595 (or perhaps 3 August 1590); died at Plymouth, 26 or 27 March 1670.

Governor William BRADFORD = Alice CARPENTER
Major William BRADFORD, Jr. = Alice RICHARDS
Lieut. Thomas BRADFORD = Ann RAYMOND
James BRADFORD = Edith ADAMS
Jonathan PELLET = Jerusha BRADFORD
Willard PIERCE = Jerusha PELLET
Rufus HERRICK [III] = Jerusha P. _____ (prob.) PIERCE
William Prince HILL = Sarah P. "Sally" HERRICK
Charles W. HILL = Adelia Catherine RILEY
George J. HILL = Jessie Fidelia STOCKWELL

JOHN BRAY

JOHN BRAY,[43] tailor of London, was born in say 1520; died before 6 December 1615. He was a witness in the case against William Flower, who assaulted a priest at St. Margaret's and was martyred by being burned alive after his hand was cut off. He married, at St. Margaret's Westminster, London, on 13 August 1553, *Margaret HASLONDE*, who died on 28 March 1588. They are ancestors of Jessie F. Stockwell.

John BRAY = Margaret HASLONDE
Thomas WHITNEY = Mary BRAY
John WHITNEY = Elinor (Ellen, Ellin) _____
(see JOHN WHITNEY)

FRANCIS BREWSTER

Mr. FRANCIS BREWSTER,[44] a merchant, was born in England; died in New England before 1647. He came to New Haven by 1641. He was not related to William Brewster of the *Mayflower*. He married,

---

[41] Hill, *Fundy to Chesapeake*, 109.

[42] Hill, *Western Pilgrims*, 96-102. See Corrections for note on p. 96, in which Jerusha Pierce, wife of Rufus Herrick III, is erroneously called Sarah Pierce. The supposition that Gov. Bradford is an ancestor of George J. Hill depends on the assumption that Rufus Herrick's wife Jerusha P. was Jerusha Pierce. See *Western Pilgrims,* 45 (Herrick).

[43] Hill, *Western Pilgrims*, 211.

[44] Hill, *Fundy to Chesapeake*, 222.

in England, as her first husband, **LUCY ____**. She and her daughter Elizabeth gave testimony against a neighbor lady who was accused of witchcraft. The "absurd trial" ended with a verdict of "not guilty."

Mr. Francis BREWSTER = Lucy ____ (perhaps JONES, later known as "Mrs. Pell")
Nathaniel WHITE = Elizabeth BREWSTER
Nathaniel TOMPKINS = Elizabeth WHITE
Nathaniel TOMPKINS [II] = Elizabeth CORNELL
Nathaniel TOMPKINS [III] = Mary FORSHAY
Nathaniel TOMPKINS [IV] = Elizabeth "Polly" OAKLEY
Bartholomew TOMPKINS = [unmarried] Martha LAKE
Reuben John RUNDALL = Martha TOMPKINS
Silas William RUNDALL = Rachel MANLY
William Henry "Will" THOMPSON = Sarah D. "Sadie" RUNDALL

LUCY (_____) BREWSTER

LUCY _____ (perhaps JONES) married (1), in England, **Mr. Francis BREWSTER**, immigrant to New England by 1641. She married (2), **Dr. Francis PELL**, without further issue (see preceding).

WILLIAM BRINTON

WILLIAM BRINTON, the Elder,[45] son of Thomas and Ann (Biddle) Brinton, was born about 1633 in Nether Gornal, Sedgeley, Straffordshire; died 1699 or 1700, Birmingham, Chester Co., Pa. He is an ancestor of **President Richard M. Nixon**. He married, in 1659, probably at Sedgeley, **ANN BAGLEY**, born about 1635 in England; died in 1699, Birmingham, Chester Co., Pa.

William BRINTON = Ann BAGLEY
William BRINTON the Younger = Jane (or Jean) THATCHER
William BRINTON = Hannah BULLER
Joseph WALTER Sr. = Jane BRINTON
James WALTER = Sarah DIXON
William WALTER = Phebe MERCER
William H. MANLY = Sarah D. WALTER
Silas William RUNDALL = Rachel MANLY
William Henry "Will" THOMPSON = Sarah D. "Sadie" RUNDALL

JAMES BRISCOE

JAMES BRISCOE[46] married **SARAH WHEELER.** They were of Milford, Conn. Their origin is obscure.

James BRISCOE = Sarah WHEELER
John SMITH = Ruth BRISCOE
Caleb SMITH = Abigail CLARK
John OVIATT = Abigail SMITH
Edward Howell PRINCE = Huldah OVIATT
Ephraim HILL = Charlotte PRINCE
William Prince HILL = Sarah P. "Sally" HERRICK
Charles W. HILL = Adelia Catherine RILEY
George J. HILL = Jessie Fidelia STOCKWELL

FRANCIS BROWN

FRANCIS BROWN[47] was probably born in England in 1625 to 1628, perhaps in Somersetshire; died at Rye, N.Y., in 1707. He came to Windsor, Conn., in about 1641. He married, as his second wife, **Martha**

---

[45] Hill, *Fundy to Chesapeake*, 325-8.
[46] Hill, *Western Pilgrims*, 142.
[47] Hill, *Fundy to Chesapeake*, 177-82.

___ **(LAWRENCE) CHAPMAN**, and is an ancestor of Sadie Rundall by this marriage. He later married (3) **Judith (BUDD) OGDEN**, who is also an ancestor of Sadie Rundall (see JOHN BUDD).

Francis BROWN = Martha _____
Joseph BROWN = Mary _____
Francis BROWN = Mercy WEBB
David BROWN = Sarah WEED
David BROWN [II] = Deborah JESSUP
Shadrack RUNDALL Sr. = Phebe BROWN
Reuben John RUNDALL = Martha TOMPKINS
Silas William RUNDALL = Rachel MANLY
William Henry "Will" THOMPSON = Sarah D. "Sadie" RUNDALL

MARTHA (_____) (LAWRENCE) (CHAPMAN) BROWN

MARTHA _____, immigrant to America, married (3), as his second wife, **FRANCIS BROWN**. She previously married (1) **Thomas LAWRENCE** and (2) **John CHAPMAN** (see preceding).

HENRY BROWN

HENRY BROWN,[48] shoemaker; born 1615; died 6 August 1701. He was a proprietor of Salisbury, Mass., in 1643. He married **ABIGAIL ___**, who died 23 August 1702. They had seven children.

Henry BROWN = Abigail _____
Andrew GREELEY, Jr. = Sarah BROWN
John SINGLETARY = Mary GREELEY
Ebenezer STOCKWELL = Mary SINGLETARY
Benajah STOCKWELL = Hannah GALE
Ebenezer STOCKWELL = Abi HOLBROOK
Joseph H. STOCKWELL = Anna Maria SAXE
Benajah Flavel STOCKWELL = Emily Lodiweska (Emma F.) HYDE
George J. HILL = Jessie Fidelia STOCKWELL

ABIGAIL (_____) BROWN

ABIGAIL ___ married **HENRY BROWN**, shoemaker of Salisbury, Mass. (see preceding).

JOHN BROWN

JOHN BROWN[49] was born about 1600; buried at Watertown, Mass., 20 June 1636. He arrived in New England in 1632 on *Lyon*, and resided at Watertown. He married, by 1634, **DOROTHY _____**.

John BROWN = Dorothy _____
John MEAD = Hannah POTTER (originally prob. BROWN)
Ebenezer MEAD, J.P. = Sarah KNAPP
Jonathan HOBBY Sr. = Sarah MEAD
Jonathan HOBBY Jr. = Deborah LYON
Reuben RUNDLE Sr. = Amy HOBBY
Shadrack RUNDALL Sr. = Phebe BROWN
Reuben John RUNDALL = Martha TOMPKINS
Silas William RUNDALL = Rachel MANLY
William Henry "Will" THOMPSON = Sarah D. "Sadie" RUNDALL

---

[48] Hill, *Western Pilgrims*, 190.
[49] Hill, *Fundy to Chesapeake*, 149. John Brown's widow married William Potter, and his daughter Dorothy was called Hannah Potter.

DOROTHY (_____) BROWN

DOROTHY _____[50] married (1) by 1634, **JOHN BROWN**. After he died in 1636, she married (2) **William POTTER.** Her daughter, called Hannah Potter, married John Mead (see preceding).

MARY BROWNE

MARY BROWNE,[51] perhaps the wife of **MILES OAKLEY**, who was married at Saffron Walden, co. Essex, England; born at Saffron Walden, 10 August 1612. She is an ancestor of Sarah D. Rundall.

OBADIAH BRUEN

Mr. OBADIAH BRUEN,[52] a draper, son of John Bruen, Esq., and Anne Fox, was baptized at Tarvin, Cheshire, 25 December 1606; died, probably in Newark, N.J., after 1680. He married, at Warwickshire, 7 May 1633, **SARAH SEELEY.** They immigrated to America in 1640 and lived in Marshfield, Mass. His daughter Mary Bruen married John Baldwin. Their sons, Richard and Josiah Baldwin, may be connected with the descendants of THOMAS OVIATT and his wife FRANCES, probably BRYAN. If this is true, Samuel Oviatt's descendants would also be descendants of Obadiah Bruen, who had **Royal ancestors** and Barons who signed the Magna Charta. The unproved line of descent to George J. Hill is shown below.

Obadiah BRUEN = Sarah SEELEY
John BALDWIN = Mary BRUEN
Josiah BALDWIN = Mary CAMP
Samuel OVIATT = Mary _____ ("maybe BALDWIN")
John OVIATT = Susanna HINE
John OVIATT = Abigail SMITH
Edward Howell PRINCE = Huldah OVIATT
Ephraim HILL = Charlotte PRINCE
William Prince HILL = Sarah P. "Sally" HERRICK
Charles W. HILL = Adelia Catherine RILEY
George J. HILL = Jessie Fidelia STOCKWELL

ALICE BRYAN

ALICE BRYAN,[53] daughter of Thomas and Frances (Bowlinge) Bryan, was born 1 November 1609; died at Tring, co. Herts., England. She married *Thomas OVIATT*, son of John and Esther Oviatt, born in England in 1602. Their son THOMAS OVIATT appeared in Milford, Conn., in 1664/5 with his wife FRANCES, whose maiden name may have been Bryan. They are ancestors of George J. Hill.

Thomas OVIATT = Alice BRYAN
Thomas OVIATT = Frances, prob. BRYAN [possibly a relative of his mother]
(see THOMAS OVIATT)

JOHN BUDD

Lieut. JOHN BUDD,[54] whose origin is unknown, is believed to have come to New England on the ship *Hector*, arriving in Boston, Mass., 26 June 1637; died, probably at Rye, N.Y., in about 1700. His house, built in Southold, is the oldest frame house in New York State. He married, perhaps in England, **KATEREN** _____; she died, probably in Rye, N.Y., in 1669.

Lieut. John BUDD = Kateren (aka Katherine) _____
John OGDEN = Judith BUDD
Thomas LYON, Jr. = Abigail OGDEN

---

[50] Hill, *Fundy to Chesapeake*, 149.
[51] Hill, *Fundy to Chesapeake*, 227.
[52] Hill, *Western Pilgrims*, 139. Richardson, *Royal Ancestry*, 1:587-8.
[53] Hill, *Western Pilgrims*, 138.
[54] Hill, *Fundy to Chesapeake*, 165-76.

Jonathan HOBBY Jr. = Deborah LYON
Reuben RUNDLE Sr. = Amy HOBBY
Shadrack RUNDALL Sr. = Phebe BROWN
Reuben John RUNDALL = Martha TOMPKINS
Silas William RUNDALL = Rachel MANLY
William Henry "Will" THOMPSON = Sarah D. "Sadie" RUNDALL

KATEREN (_____) BUDD

KATEREN (aka KATHERINE) _____ married, perhaps in England, **Lieut. JOHN BUDD**. Her origin is unknown, but the original spelling of her name suggests that she may have been Dutch (see preceding).

[THOMAS BULL]

[**THOMAS BULL**[55] died between 1709 and 1716 in Cecil Co., Md. He is presumed to have emigrated from England. As a prosperous planter, he owned a property known as *Bull's Mountain*. JOHN MANLEY called him "cousin and he is included in the book *Fundy to Chesapeake* for that reason.]

JOHN BULLARD

JOHN BULLARD,[56] son of William and Grace (Bignett) Bullard, was born in about 1596, probably at Barnham, co. Suffolk; died at Medfield, Mass., 27 October 1678. He became a proprietor of Dedham on 6 July 1638. He married (1) **MAGDALEN ____ (maybe MARTIN)**, who died at Medfield, 29 November 1661. Their daughter Magdalen married JOHN PARTRIDGE.

John BULLARD = Magdalen _____ (possibly MARTIN)
John PARTRIDGE = Magdalen BULLARD
Eleazer PARTRIDGE = Elizabeth ALLEN
Joseph PARTRIDGE = Eunice MORSE
Lt. Aaron HOLBROOK = Hannah PARTRIDGE
Ebenezer STOCKWELL = Abi HOLBROOK
Joseph H. STOCKWELL = Anna Maria SAXE
Benajah Flavel STOCKWELL = Emily Lodiweska (Emma F.) HYDE
George J. HILL = Jessie Fidelia STOCKWELL

MAGDALEN (_____) BULLARD

MAGDALEN _____,[57] **perhaps MARTIN**, married, as his first wife and mother of his five children, **JOHN BULLARD.** She died at Medfield, Mass., 29 November 1661 (see preceding).

WILLIAM BULLER

WILLIAM BULLER,[58] probably born in Warwickshire, England; died at Concord, Chester Co., Pa., in 1719. He emigrated from Warwickshire with his wife and family with a certificate granted in 1715. He became a member of the Concord Monthly Meeting. He had five children.

William BULLER = _____ _____
William BRINTON = Hannah BULLER
Joseph WALTER Sr. = Jane BRINTON
James WALTER = Sarah DIXON
William WALTER = Phebe MERCER
William H. MANLY = Sarah D. WALTER
Silas William RUNDALL = Rachel MANLY
William Henry "Will" THOMPSON = Sarah D. "Sadie" RUNDALL

---

[55] Hill, *Fundy to Chesapeake*, 256.
[56] Hill, *Western Pilgrims*, 200.
[57] Hill, *Western Pilgrims*, 200.
[58] Hill, *Fundy to Chesapeake*, 333.

_____ (_____) BULLER

_____,[59] whose name is unknown, emigrated to Pennsylvania with her husband, **WILLIAM BULLER**. She is truly a *femme covert*. Her daughter Hannah is an ancestor of Sarah D. Rundall (see preceding).

ROGER BURLINGAME

ROGER BURLINGAME[60] appeared in Stonington, Conn., sometime before 1654, when he appeared as a witness in court. He died at Mashantatack Purchase (now Cranston, R.I.), 1 September 1718. He became a large land owner in Rhode Island, and was an original settler of the Mashantatack Purchase. He married, by 1663 (perhaps 3 October 1663), in Warwick, RI., **Mary ___**, possibly **Mrs. Mary BARLINGSTONE**. She may have been the childless widow of a man named William Barlingstone. She died at about the same time as her husband. Roger and Mary Burlingame are ancestors of Jessie Stockwell through two different lines of descent.

Roger BURLINGAME = Mary _____, possibly Mrs. Mary BARLINGSTONE
Sgt. Thomas BURLINGAME = Martha LIPPIT   John POTTER, Jr. = Jane BURLINGAME
Thomas BURLINGAME, Jr. = Eleanor RALPH   William POTTER = Martha TILLINGHAST
Benjamin COLVIN = Eleanor BURLINGAME
Capt. Oliver POTTER = Mary COLVIN
Capt. Freeborn POTTER = Dolly IRISH
Harvey HYDE = Fidelia Gadcourt POTTER
Benajah Flavel STOCKWELL = Emily Lodiweska (Emma F.) HYDE
George J. HILL = Jessie Fidelia STOCKWELL

MARY _____ (? BARLINGSTONE) BURLINGAME

MARY _____ (? BARLINGSTONE) married **ROGER BURLINGAME**, who emigrated in about 1654. She died in about 1718. Two of her twelve children are ancestors of Jessie Stockwell.

JOHN BURROUGH

JOHN BURROUGH,[61] of East Bergholt, co. Suffolk, died after making his will on 10 April 1577. He married *Margaret _____* and had two children. His daughter Alice Burrough married Nicholas Hedge. Their daughter, Elizabeth Hedge, married, in about 1588, the Rev. Richard Ravens; their daughter GRACE RAVENS, emigrated to Massachusetts. She married (1) John Sherman and was an ancestor of **Roger Sherman, Signer of the Declaration of Independence**; (2) THOMAS ROGERS, who emigrated to Watertown, Mass., sometime before 1636, and had a daughter, Elizabeth Rogers, an ancestor of Mabel Warren. Grace (Ravens) (Sherman) (Rogers) married (3) Roger Porter, and died without further issue.

John BURROUGH = Margaret _____
Nicholas HEDGE = Alice BURROUGH
Rev. Richard RAVENS = Elizabeth HEDGE
Thomas ROGERS = Grace RAVENS (m. [1] John SHERMAN)
(see THOMAS ROGERS and GRACE RAVENS)

HENRY BURT

HENRY BURT,[62] born about 1595 in England; died at Springfield, Mass., 30 April 1662. He arrived in Roxbury, Mass., in 1639. He married, on 28 December 1619, in England, **EULALIA MARCHE**, who

---

[59] Hill, *Fundy to Chesapeake*, 333.
[60] Hill, *Western Pilgrims*, 262-6.
[61] Hill, *Quakers and Puritans*, 257-8.
[62] Hill, *Western Pilgrims*, 28; *Great Migration* 6:497 (Rowland Stebbins, who relocated from Roxbury to Springfield); *Torrey's New England Marriages*, 256, 661; and *Hampshire Records* (from NEHGS, on-line), 1687.

died in 1690. He and his wife relocated from Roxbury to Springfield, where he became the Clerk of the Writts. They had several children, including [probably] Sarah, born 1621, who married (1) Judah Gregory and (2) HENRY WAKELEE; Henry [II], whose descendants continued to live in Springfield; and Abigail, who married (1) Francis Ball, (2) Benjamin Munn, and (3) Thomas Stebbins, in Springfield

Henry BURT = Eulalia MARCHE (prob. parents of Sarah BURT)
Henry WAKELEE = Sarah BURT, widow of Judah GREGORY
Jacob WAKELEE = _____ (_____) WALLIS
Henry WAKELEE = Sarah FROST
Benajah MALLORY = Elizabeth WAKELEE, married (1) _____ CRANE
Isaac HILL [Jr.] = Eunice MALLORY
Ephraim HILL = Charlotte PRINCE
William Prince HILL = Sarah P. "Sally" HERRICK
Charles W. HILL = Adelia Catharine "Delia" RILEY
George J. HILL = Jessie Fidelia STOCKWELL

BENJAMIN BUTTERFIELD

BENJAMIN BUTTERFIELD[63] was probably born in England; died at Chelmsford, Mass., 2 March 1687/8. He must have emigrated to Massachusetts on or before 1638. He was a selectman of Chelmsford, and he held other appointments in the colony. He married (1), probably in England, **ANN _____**, who died 19 May 1660; he married (2), **Mrs. Hannah (___) WHITTEMORE**.

Benjamin BUTTERFIELD = Ann _____
Nathaniel BUTTERFIELD = Deborah UNDERWOOD
Nathaniel BUTTERFIELD Jr. = Sarah FLETCHER
Lieut. Joseph MOORS = Esther BUTTERFIELD
Simeon MOORS = Joanna THORNDIKE
Jeduthan WARREN = Joanna MOORS
Jesse WARREN = Betsy JACKSON
Herbert Marshall WARREN = Eliza Caroline COPP
William Toy SHOEMAKER = Mabel WARREN

ANN (_____) BUTTERFIELD

ANN _____ married **BENJAMIN BUTTERFIELD**, probably in England. They came to Massachusetts on or before 1638, at which time he was recorded in Charlestown. They had two children who were born in England, and three more, born in Woburn, Mass. She died 1 May 1660 (see preceding).

JOHN CADWALADER

JOHN CADWALADER[64] is said to have been born in 1645 in Radnorshire, Wales; died at Goshen Twp., Chester Co., Pa., and was buried there on 30 December 1742. He probably came with others from Wales between 1682 and 1700 and settled on what was then known as the Welsh tract. Cadwalader was a given name in Wales, but it became a surname in Pennsylvania. He married, perhaps in 1667 or 1670, **SARAH ROBERTS**; born say 1650; died in Goshen Twp., Pa., and was buried there, 10 October 1737.

John CADWALADER = Sarah ROBERTS
Rev. John CADWALADER = Mary CASSELL (aka CASTLE)
Robert COMLY = Jane CADWALADER
Robert COMLY = Sarah JONES
Ezra COMLY = Hannah IREDELL
Charles SHOEMAKER = Rachel COMLY
Julien SHOEMAKER = Hannah Ann HESTER
William Toy SHOEMAKER = Mabel WARREN

---

[63] Hill, *Quakers and Puritans*, 156-8.
[64] Hill, *Quakers and Puritans*, 37-43.

THOMAS CANFIELD

THOMAS CANFIELD[65] married **PHEBE ____**. They were early settlers of Milford, Conn., in 1656, perhaps emigrating there from England. Their daughter, Phebe Canfield, was born at Milford, 8 May 1656; died 3 May 1730; married, at Milford, Conn., 23 January 1672/3, JOHN SMITH, a wheelwright.

Thomas CANFIELD = Phebe _____
John SMITH = Phebe CANFIELD
John SMITH = Ruth BRISCOE
Caleb SMITH = Abigail CLARK
John OVIATT = Abigail SMITH
Edward Howell PRINCE = Huldah OVIATT
Ephraim HILL = Charlotte PRINCE
William Prince HILL = Sarah P. "Sally" HERRICK
Charles W. HILL = Adelia Catherine RILEY
George J. HILL = Jessie Fidelia STOCKWELL

PHEBE (_____) CANFIELD

PHEBE _____, who married **THOMAS CANFIELD**, was an early settler of Milford, Conn. She and her husband arrived there in about 1656, perhaps emigrating from England (see preceding).

ALEXANDER CARPENTER

ALEXANDER CARPENTER,[66] of Wrington, co. Somerset, England, was born in, say, 1551; died, probably, sometime before 1644, perhaps in the Netherlands. He was one of the 300 members of the Ancient Brethren, who moved to the Netherlands to find freedom of religion that was impossible in Elizabethan England. He married **Priscilla DILLEN** in about 1583 in Bath, England. They had five daughters, all of whom came to Plymouth Colony, New England: Juliana, Agnes, Alice, Mary, and Priscilla. Juliana married GEORGE MORTON and is an ancestor of George J. Hill, the Iowa Pioneer. Alice married (2) as his second wife, Governor WILLIAM BRADFORD, and she, too, may be an ancestor of George Hill. Agnes married Samuel Fuller, brother of MATTHEW FULLER. Mary died a spinster. Priscilla married (1) William Wright; and (2) John Cooper, but has no descendants.

ALICE CARPENTER

ALICE CARPENTER,[67] third of the five daughters of Alexander Carpenter, was born say 1590 in co. Somerset, England; died at Plymouth, Mass., 26 March 1670. She married (1) in Leyden, 28 May 1613, **Edward SOUTHWORTH**, a say-weaver, who came from a titled family in England. He died in 1623. They had two sons (Constant and Thomas), who came to America. She married (2), as his second wife, **Governor WILLIAM BRADFORD**, who she met in the Netherlands and was a neighbor of GEORGE MORTON, who was married to her sister Juliana. William and Alice (Carpenter) (Southworth) Bradford had three children. His son and namesake, Maj. William Bradford, may be an ancestor of George J. Hill (see WILLIAM BRADFORD).

JULIANA CARPENTER

JULIANA CARPENTER,[68] eldest of the five daughters of Alexander Carpenter, was born say 1584; christened in Bath, co. Somerset, 17 March 1584; died at Plymouth Colony, Mass., 19 February 1664/5. She married (1) in Leyden, the Netherlands, 23 July 1612, **GEORGE MORTON,** probably son of

---

[65] Hill, *Western Pilgrims*, 141.
[66] Hill, *Western Pilgrims*, 165-9.
[67] Hill, *Western Pilgrims*, 165-9. The descent to George J. Hill depends on the assumption that Jerusha P., wife of Rufus Herrick (III), was Jerusha Pierce. See discussion of this question in *Western Pilgrims*, 45 (Herrick Family.)
[68] Hill, *Western Pilgrims*, 165-9.

George and Catherine (Boun) Morton; born about 1585 in Bawtry, co. York; died in 1664 in Plymouth Colony. They had three daughters and two sons. She married (2) **Manasseh KEMPTON**, without issue. She is an ancestor of George J. Hill, the Iowa Pioneer (see GEORGE MORTON).

JAMES CASE

JAMES CASE[69] was probably of Rhode Island in the mid-17th century, and he was likely an immigrant. He married **ANNA** _____. They were of Little Compton, R.I., when their daughter, Penelope, was married, on 11 February 1714, at Little Compton, R.I., to Joseph Lake; born at Dartmouth, Mass., or Little Compton, R.I., 17 July 1686, and died before 1766. James and Anna Case may be ancestors of Sarah D. Rundall (also see JOHN TOMPKINS).

James CASE = Anna _____

Joseph LAKE = Penelope CASE

Daniel LAKE = Sarah "Sally" _____

Bartholomew TOMPKINS = [unmarried] Martha LAKE (possibly daughter of Daniel Lake)

Reuben John RUNDALL = Martha TOMPKINS

Silas William RUNDALL = Rachel MANLY

William Henry "Will" THOMPSON = Sarah D. "Sadie" RUNDALL

JOHANNES PETER CASSEL

JOHANNES PETER CASSEL,[70] second son and second child of Yelles and Mary Kasel, was born at Kriegsheim, Alzey-Worms, Lower Palitanate, 17 April 1639; died at Germantown, Philadelphia Co., Pa., 17 April 1691. He was born into a prominent Mennonite family. He came to America on the *Jeffries*, arriving 20 March 1685/6 and settled at Germantown. He was a weaver in Germany and America. He married, in Kriegsheim, 20 December 1659, **MARY OP den GRAEFF**, who was probably a child of *ISAAC OP DEN GRAEFF*; born about 1642. Johannes and Mary (Op den Graeff) Cassel had five children.

Johannes Peter CASSEL = Mary Op den GRAEFF

Rev. John CADWALADER = Mary CASSELL (aka CASTLE)

Robert COMLY = Jane CADWALADER

Robert COMLY = Sarah JONES

Ezra COMLY = Hannah IREDELL

Charles SHOEMAKER = Rachel COMLY

Julien SHOEMAKER = Hannah Ann HESTER

William Toy SHOEMAKER = Mabel WARREN

MARGARET CHANDLER

MARGARET CHANDLER,[71] daughter of Tobias and Johan (Momford) Chandler of Bishop's Stortford, co. Hertford, England, was born there, 13 October 1577; died at Roxbury, Mass., 3 February 1645/6. She married (1) **Henry MONK**. She married (2) 7 November 1603, **Mr. WILLIAM DENISON**, maltster, son of John and Agnes (Willie) Denyson; baptized 1571/2; died at Roxbury, Mass., 25 January 1653. They had seven children. Her son Maj. Gen. Daniel Denison married Patience, daughter of **Governor Thomas Dudley**. By her youngest son, Capt. George Denison, she is an ancestor of George J. Hill.

SAMUEL CHAPIN

Deacon SAMUEL CHAPIN,[72] probably the son of John and Philipe (Easton) Chapin who was christened 8 October 1598 in Devonshire, England; died at Springfield, Mass., 11 November 1675. He

---

[69] Hill, *Fundy to Chesapeake*, 229-32. See HENRY LAKE for speculation on the possible ancestry of Martha Lake.

[70] Hill, *Quakers and Puritans*, 44-8.

[71] Hill, *Western Pilgrims*, 65.

[72] Hill, *Western Pilgrims*, 203-5.

came to America in 1638, and was admitted to the Roxbury church. His descendants include **Presidents Grover Cleveland** and **William Howard Taft,** and the **abolitionist, John Brown.** He married, probably 9 February 1628, **CICELY PENNY**, daughter of Henry and Jane (Dabinott) Penny who was christened 21 February 1601; died in Springfield, 3 February 1682/3. The Penny family were probably Huguenots.

Deacon Samuel CHAPIN = Cicely (aka Cisely) PENNY

Josiah CHAPIN = Mrs. Lydia (poss. née PRATT) BROWN

Cornet John HOLBROOK = Hannah CHAPIN

Lt. Aaron HOLBROOK = Hannah PARTRIDGE

Ebenezer STOCKWELL = Abi HOLBROOK

Joseph H. STOCKWELL = Anna Maria SAXE

Benajah Flavel STOCKWELL = Emily Lodiweska (Emma F.) HYDE

George J. HILL = Jessie Fidelia STOCKWELL

ELIZABETH CHARD

ELIZABETH CHARD[73] was born probably in co. Dorset. She married (1) **Aaron COOKE**, and with him had a son, Aaron Cooke, Jr. She married (2), in co. Dorset, 19 June 1616, as his first wife, **THOMAS FORD**, with whom she had five more children. They came to America on the *Mary and John* in 1630 and relocated to Windsor, Conn.; she died on 18 April 1643. Her daughter married Capt. ROGER CLAPP and is an ancestor of Jessie F. Stockwell.

CHARLEMAGNE

CHARLEMAGNE, **Emperor**,[74] son of Pepin the Short and Bertrada of Laon, was born in what is now Germany or Belgium on 2 April 742 (or 747); died at Aachen, now in Germany, 28 January 814. He was the descendant of royalty extending back to Merovee, who founded the Merovingian Dynasty. He was King of the Franks in 768, and the Pope crowned him Holy Roman Emperor in 800. His family life was complicated, with his first marriage annulled, followed by marriage to a girl named **Hildegard** from Swabia. He probably fathered children by other wives and mistresses. He founded the Carolingian Dynasty, and his progeny soon occupied most of the thrones in Europe. It has become a tradition in genealogy to search for a "Gateway" ancestor, who is an immigrant to America from Europe who is known to be a descendant of the Emperor. The first that I discovered was Thomas Trowbridge, who is an ancestor of both me and my wife, Helene. Others in our ancestry who are descended from Charlemagne include John Thorndike, who is an ancestor of my wife; and Edward Howell, who is my ancestor.

WILLIAM CHESEBROUGH

WILLIAM CHESEBROUGH,[75] blacksmith, of Boston, co. Lincoln, was born about 1595; died at Stonington, Conn., 9 June 1667. He married 15 December 1620, **ANN STEVENSON**, daughter of Peter Stephenson; born about 1598; died at Stonington, 9 June 1667. They had eight children in England. He came to America in 1630, perhaps with his mother, for a woman named Sarah Chesebrough appears on the roll of the First Church of Boston, Mass. He was Deputy from Boston to the General Court, and later Deputy to the General Court in Connecticut.

William CHESEBROUGH = Ann STEVENSON

Capt. Samuel CHESEBROUGH = Abigail _____

John AVERY = Abigail CHESEBROUGH

Capt. William DENISON = Mary AVERY

Edward HERRICK = Mary DENNISON

Col. Rufus HERRICK = Miss _____ GIBBS, prob. Myra (Mary) GIBBS

Capt. Rufus HERRICK, Jr. = Lydia NEWMAN

---

[73] Hill, *Western Pilgrims*, 339-40

[74] Hill, *Western Pilgrims*, 29-30 (Trowbridge), 144-56 (Howell), 344-6 (Allyn), 242-3 (Bowen); and *Quakers and Puritans*, 137-8 (Thorndike), and 236-9 (Trowbridge).

[75] Hill, *Western Pilgrims*, 77-9.

Rufus HERRICK [III] = Jerusha P._____ (prob. PIERCE)
William Prince HILL = Sarah P. "Sally" HERRICK
Charles W. HILL = Adelia Catharine "Delia" RILEY
George J. HILL = Jessie Fidelia STOCKWELL

FRANCES CHICHESTER

FRANCES CHICHESTER,[76] daughter of Amias Chichester, Esq., and his wife Joan (or Jane) Giffard, married before 1584, **John WYATT (or WYOTT),** Gent., of Braunton, Devon, baptized at Braunton, 11 November 1557. Frances Chichester is a descendant of **Charlemagne** in the line of Alice of Normandy and other Royal ancestors. John and Frances (Chichester) Wyatt had two sons and four daughters. Their daughter MARGARET WYATT married MATTHEW ALLYN and is an ancestor of Jessie F. Stockwell.

Amias CHICHESTER = Joan GIFFARD
John WYATT = Frances CHICHESTER
Matthew ALLYN = Margaret WYATT
(see MATTHEW ALLYN and MARGARET WYATT)

ROGER CLAPP

Captain ROGER CLAPP,[77] son of William and Jone (Channon) Clapp (aka Clap), was born at Salcombe Regis, co. Devon, 2 April 1609; died at Boston, Mass., 2 February 1690/1. He came to America in 1630 in the *Mary and John* and settled at Dorchester, Mass. He was appointed Captain of the Castle of Boston. His handwritten memoir was published in 1731. He married, at Dorchester, 6 November 1633, **Joanna FORD,** daughter of THOMAS FORD and his wife ELIZABETH CHARD, widow of Aaron Cooke; born about 1617 in Bridport; died at Dorchester, 29 June 1695.

Roger CLAPP = Joanna FORD
Preserved CLAPP = Sarah NEWBERRY
Abraham MILLER = Hannah CLAPP
Samuel ALLEN = Hannah MILLER
Corporal Jabez WARD = Jemima ALLEN
Private Henry HYDE = Thyrina (Therina) WARD
Luther HYDE = Phoebe GIDDINGS
Harvey HYDE = Fidelia Gadcourt POTTER
Benajah Flavel STOCKWELL = Emily Lodiweska (Emma F.) HYDE
George J. HILL = Jessie Fidelia STOCKWELL

ELIZABETH CLARK

ELIZABETH CLARK[78] died in 1683. She married, in 1642, probably in Dedham, Mass., **GEORGE BARBOUR,** born in England in 1615, who came to America in 1635 and was a townsman of Dedham in 1640. He was a captain in the Ancient and Honorable Artillery Company. They had nine children. By her daughter Mary, who married Jonathan Morse, she is an ancestor of Jessie F. Stockwell.

GEORGE CLARK

GEORGE CLARK,[79] whose origin is unknown, married **MARY COLEY.** They are the parents of Abigail Clark, who married, at Milford, Conn., 26 April 1728, Caleb Smith.

George CLARK = Mary COLEY
Caleb SMITH = Abigail CLARK
John OVIATT = Abigail SMITH
Edward Howell PRINCE = Huldah OVIATT

---

[76] Hill, *Western Pilgrims*, 346; and Richardson, *Royal Ancestry*, 1:114.
[77] Hill, *Western Pilgrims*, 337-9.
[78] Hill, *Western Pilgrims*, 210.
[79] Hill, *Western Pilgrims*, 142.

Ephraim HILL = Charlotte PRINCE
William Prince HILL = Sarah P. "Sally" HERRICK
Charles W. HILL = Adelia Catharine "Delia" RILEY
George J. HILL = Jessie Fidelia STOCKWELL

AGNES CLARKE

AGNES CLARKE,[80] daughter of John and Ann (Macye) Clarke, of Colyton, co. Devon; died in September 1630, at about the same time as her husband. She married **Richard CONANT**, son of John Conant. Richard and Agnes (Clarke) Conant had eight children, one of whom was the father of Rev. John Conant, D.D., Vice Chancellor of Oxford University. Their youngest child, ROGER CONANT, became the governor of the Beverly Colony, and then Delegate from Salem to the Massachusetts General Court.

Richard CONANT =Agnes CLARKE
Roger CONANT = Sarah HORTON
(see ROGER CONANT)

WILLIAM CLARKE

Lieut. **WILLIAM CLARKE**[81], born about 1609, first appeared in Dorchester, Mass., about 1635; died 10 July 1681. It appears that he may have first arrived in 1630 or 1633, and then returned in 1636 with his wife. He married (1) **SARAH ___** (possibly **STRONG** or **HOLTON**). They were members of the Dorchester church in 1636. He relocated to Northampton, where he was Deputy to the General Court. His house was burned in a fire set by a Negro named Jack, and for this mischief Jack was hanged and burned. He married (2) **Mrs. Sarah COOPER**, whose husband was killed by Indians at Springfield in 1675. He had ten children with his first wife.

Lieutenant William CLARKE = Sarah ____ (poss. STRONG or HOLTON)
Israel RUST = Rebecca CLARK
Deacon Samuel ALLEN = Sarah RUST
Samuel ALLEN = Hannah MILLER
Corporal Jabez WARD = Jemima ALLEN
Private Henry HYDE = Thyrina (Therina) WARD
Luther HYDE = Phoebe GIDDINGS
Harvey HYDE = Fidelia Gadcourt POTTER
Benajah Flavel STOCKWELL = Emily Lodiweska (Emma F.) HYDE
George J. HILL = Jessie Fidelia STOCKWELL

SARAH (_____) CLARKE

SARAH _____, whose origin is unknown, but whose maiden name has been suggested as either Strong or Holton, married **WILLIAM CLARKE** soon after he arrived in Dorchester, Mass. They moved to Northampton, where she died on 6 September 1675. She and her husband made the arduous trek from Boston to Northampton in 1659. At age 50, he walked ahead of her, while she, on horseback, carried two boys in baskets, with another on her lap (see preceding).

ANN CLIBBEN

ANN CLIBBEN,[82] daughter of William Clibborn, was born in 1630 at Cowley, co. Durham, England. She married, probably in about 1654, **JOHN MILLER**, a Quaker, born at Kerbywilk, Yorkshire, who came with her to Pennsylvania from Ireland, where he was a planter. They had two sons, both of whom may be ancestors of Sarah Rundall.

---

[80] Hill, *Quakers and Puritans*, 245.
[81] Hill, *Western Pilgrims*, 334-5.
[82] Hill, *Fundy to Chesapeake*, 268. This genealogy is based on the probability that Rachel Jackson is the daughter of John Jackson, Jr.

GEORGE CLIFFORD

GEORGE CLIFFORD,[83] whose origin is unknown, appeared in Massachusetts in 1643, where he was a servant to Tomas Buttall. He was a drummer in the Ancient and Honorable Artillery Company. His grandson's wife, Ann Smith, was involved with the sad case of "Goody" Cole, who was accused of witchcraft, but who died without punishment in Hampton, N.H. He married (1) _____ _____.

George CLIFFORD = _____ _____
John CLIFFORD = Sarah _____
Israel CLIFFORD = Ann SMITH
Joshua PRESCOTT = Sarah CLIFFORD (prob. dau. of Israel Clifford)
Joshua PRESCOT = Abigail AMBROSE
William PUTNAM = Dorothy "Dolly" PRESCOTT
William ARCHIBALD = Susannah "Susan" PUTNAM
Joseph Scott THOMPSON = Ruth E. ARCHIBALD
James Everett THOMPSON = Jane GRANT
William Henry "Will" THOMPSON = Sarah D. "Sadie" RUNDALL

_____ (_____) CLIFFORD

_____ _____ may have come to America with her husband, **GEORGE CLIFFORD,** or she may have died before he arrived in 1643. Their first known child was born about 1614 (see preceding).

[_____ "GOODMAN" CLOSE]

[_____ **"Goodman" CLOSE**[84] was an early settler of Fairfield, Conn., where he died by 1653. He married, as her first husband, **Elizabeth** _____, who died at Stamford, 4 September 1656. "Goodman" (whose first name is unknown) and Elizabeth Close had four children, two of whom had descendants. Sarah D. Rundall is not their direct descendant, but *Fundy to Chesapeake* shows some of the relationships that exist between the sixteen men and women named Close in the Rundall genealogy.]

RICE COLE

RICE COLE[85], whose origin is unknown, died at Charlestown, Mass., 15 May 1646. He came to Massachusetts in 1630 and was admitted to the Boston church sometime in 1631. He was on the committee to divide the common in Charlestown. He married, by about 1616, **[H]ARRALD** _____, who died at Charlestown in 1661. One of his sons was a servant of Samuel Fuller of Plymouth. His daughter Elizabeth married Sergeant Thomas Pierce and may be an ancestor of George J. Hill.

Rice COLE = [H]Arrald _____ (assuming that she was the mother of all of his children)
Sgt. Thomas PIERCE Jr. = Elizabeth COLE
Thomas PIERCE = Eliza _____
Judge Timothy PIERCE = Lydia SPAULDING
Nathaniel PIERCE = Elizabeth STEVENS
Willard PIERCE = Jerusha PELLET
Rufus HERRICK [III] = Jerusha P. _____ (prob. PIERCE)
William Prince HILL = Sarah P. "Sally" HERRICK
Charles W. HILL = Adelia Catharine "Delia" RILEY
George J. HILL = Jessie Fidelia STOCKWELL

[H]ARRALD (_____) COLE

[H]ARRALD _____, wife of **Rice COLE,** died at Charlestown, Mass., in 1661. She was the mother of five children, and probably is an ancestor of George J. Hill (see above).

---

[83] Hill, *Fundy to Chesapeake*, 105.
[84] Hill, *Fundy to Chesapeake*, 153.
[85] Hill, *Western Pilgrims*, 84; caution noted in footnote on p.83; it assumes that Jerusha P. is Jerusha Pierce.

MARY COLEY

MARY COLEY,[86] whose origin is unknown, married **GEORGE CLARK.** They are the parents of Abigail Clark, baptized at First Church, Milford, Conn., 1 April 1711, who married, at Milford, 26 April 1728, Caleb Smith. She is an ancestor of George J. Hill, the Iowa Pioneer.

JOHN COLLER

JOHN COLLER,[87] born in about 1632, took the oath of fidelity at Watertown, Mass., in 1652. He removed to Sudbury, Mass., after 1657. He married **Hannah CUTLER**, daughter of JAMES CUTLER and his wife ANN; born at Watertown, Mass., 26 July 1638. They had three children.

John COLLER = Hannah CUTLER
James CUTTING = Hannah COLLER
David CUTTING = Elizabeth WALES
David CUTTING = Sarah EDMUNDS
Sheriff Joseph SCOTT = Sarah CUTTING
James THOMPSON Sr. = Hannah ____, prob. Hannah SCOTT
Joseph Scott THOMPSON = Ruth E. ARCHIBALD
James Everett THOMPSON = Jane GRANT
William Henry "Will" THOMPSON = Sarah D. "Sadie" RUNDALL

BARTHOLOMEW COLLINRIDGE

BARTHOLOMEW COLLINRIDGE[88] farmed on the manor of Medmenham, Buckinghamshire, in 1397. He married *Alice ARUNDEL*, daughter and heiress of Ralph de Arundel, a descendant of the Fitz Alan family, with ancestors that include **William the Conqueror**, French royalty; two **Sureties of the Magna Charta**; of Geoffrey V Plantagenet; and of Richard "Strongbow" de Clare.

Bartholomew COLLINRIDGE = Alice ARUNDEL
William COLLINRIDGE = Sarah _____
Geoffrey DORMER, Sr. = Alice COLLINRIDGE
Thomas CROKER = Alice DORMER
Edward HAWTEN, Gent. = Margery CROKER
Henry HOWELL = Margaret HAWTEN
Mr. Edward HOWELL, Lord of the Manor of Westbury = *Frances PAXTON*
(See EDWARD HOWELL)

JOHN COLVIN

JOHN COLVIN[89] appears in the records of America with the birth of his child, Anna Colvin, at Dartmouth, Mass., 26 March 1679. He died before 1729, probably in Rhode Island. He married, perhaps in England, **DOROTHY ____ (?ALLEN)**; died between 1723-1728; mother of his nine children.

John COLVIN = Dorothy _____ (?ALLEN)
James COLVIN = Mary (or possibly Ann) LIPPIT
Benjamin COLVIN = Eleanor BURLINGAME
Capt. Oliver POTTER = Mary COLVIN
Capt. Freeborn POTTER = Dolly IRISH
Harvey HYDE = Fidelia Gadcourt POTTER
Benajah Flavel STOCKWELL = Emily Lodiweska (Emma F.) HYDE
George J. HILL = Jessie Fidelia STOCKWELL

---

[86] Hill, *Western Pilgrims*, 142.
[87] Hill, *Fundy to Chesapeake*, 45. For the question of Hannah ___ (?SCOTT), see discussion on pp. 3-4.
[88] Hill, *Western Pilgrims*, 153-4 (Collinridge), and 144-52 (Howell).
[89] Hill, *Western Pilgrims*, 318-20.

DOROTHY (_____) COLVIN

DOROTHY _____ **(?ALLEN)** married **JOHN COLVIN**, perhaps in England. She is said by some to have been the daughter of Matthew Allen. Her first child was born in Dartmouth, Mass., in 1679. She probably died in Providence, R.I., between 1723 and 1728 (see preceding).

DAVID COMEE

DAVID COMEE[90] was born in Scotland; died at Sudbury, Mass., 21 April 1676. He fought for King Charles II at the Battle of Worcester, 11 November 1651, at which time Oliver Cromwell's forces prevailed. He was then sent as a prisoner to America. He arrived in Massachusetts by 1662 and was killed at the Sudbury Fight, 21 April 1676. He married (1) **ELIZABETH** _____, who died at Concord, 4 March 1671; and (2) **Esther** _____, with whom he had two more children.

David COMEE = Elizabeth ____
John COMEE = Martha MUNROE
Jonas PIERCE = Abigail COMEE
John PEIRCE = Abigail BEARD
Oliver JACKSON = Mary PEIRCE
Jesse WARREN = Betsy JACKSON
Herbert Marshall WARREN = Eliza Caroline COPP
William Toy SHOEMAKER = Mabel WARREN

ELIZABETH (_____) COMEE

ELIZABETH ____ married **DAVID COMEE**, who fought on the losing side at the Battle of Worcester and was sent to America as a prisoner. He achieved freedom in Concord, Mass. They had five children. She died in 1671, and he remarried, having two more children before he was killed (see preceding).

HENRY COMLY

HENRY COMLY,[91] weaver, son of Henry Comly, was born in England, 25 January 1615; died in Pennsylvania, 13 May 1684. He married (1) **Judith** _____, in England; they had four children. He married (2) in England, 25 December 1673, **JOAN TYLER**, born at Bristol, 1630; buried at Middletown, Pa., 20 December 1689. They came with their son Henry Jr. in November 1683 in *Samuel and Mary*.

Henry COMLY = Joan TYLER
Henry COMLY, Jr. = Agnes HEATON
Robert COMLY = Jane CADWALADER
Robert COMLY, Jr. = Sarah JONES
Ezra COMLY = Hannah IREDELL
Charles SHOEMAKER = Rachel COMLY
Julien SHOEMAKER = Hannah Ann HESTER
William Toy SHOEMAKER = Mabel WARREN

ROGER CONANT

ROGER CONANT,[92] youngest child of Richard and Agnes (Clarke) Conant, was baptized at East Budleigh, co. Devon, 9 April 1592; died at Beverly, Mass., 19 November 1679. He was known as a "salter of London." He came to New England in 1623, probably in the *Anne*. He soon settled at Nantasket (Hull), and in the following year, 1624, he and several others landed at Gloucester. He became the Governor of the Beverly Colony, which later merged with the Massachusetts Bay Colony. He married, at London, 11 November 1618, **SARAH HORTON**, daughter of Thomas and Catherine (Satchfield) Horton; she died between 1660 and 1677. They had ten children.

---

[90] Hill, *Quakers and Puritans*, 228-9.
[91] Hill, *Quakers and Puritans*, 29-30.
[92] Hill, *Quakers and Puritans*, 246-9.

Roger CONANT = Sarah HORTON
Lot CONANT = Elizabeth WALTON
John CONANT = Bethiah MANSFIELD
John DARBY Jr. = Deborah CONANT
Andrew "Miller" DARBY = Elizabeth PATCH
Sgt. Josiah JACKSON = Mary DARBY
Oliver JACKSON = Mary PEIRCE
Jesse WARREN = Betsy JACKSON
Herbert Marshall WARREN = Eliza Caroline COPP
William Toy SHOEMAKER = Mabel WARREN

[CONSTABLE OF HALSHAM]

[*CONSTABLE of HALSHAM*[93] was proposed by J. G. Hunt to be an ancestor of GEORGE MORTON. His research was based on an imagined connection. See discussion in the Notes for *Western Pilgrims*, summarized below in *WILLIAM SKIPWITH*. Also see *WILLOUGHBY D'ERESBY.*]

SUSANNA COOK

SUSANNA COOK,[94] born say 1616; died at Haverhill, 11 April 1682; married, probably in Newbury, Mass., in about 1638-9, **RICHARD SINGLETARY**, born say 1599; died at Haverhill, Mass., 25 October 1687. He may be the young heir to the Dunham (aka Donham) estate, who was kidnapped and sent to America. She is an ancestor of **President Barack Obama** and of Jessie F. Stockwell.

ELIZABETH COOKE

ELIZABETH COOKE[95] was the daughter of William and Martha (White) Cooke; she died in 1682. She married, at Holy Trinity, Dorchester, co. Dorset, 10 April 1627, **Rev. WILLIAM WALTON**, born in England in about 1602; died of apoplexy at Marblehead, Mass., 9 November 1668. They came to New England in 1635, and then to Marblehead in 1638. They had seven children and are ancestors of Mabel Warren.

[JOHN COOLIDGE]

[**JOHN COOLIDGE**[96] is mentioned here because Grace (neé Ravens) (Sherman) (Rogers) Porter called him "brother" in her will, and this would imply that her maiden name was Coolidge. In fact, he was her brother-in-law (see GRACE RAVENS).]

ELIZA CAROLINE COPP

ELIZA CAROLINE COPP,[97] daughter of James John and Caroline (Bigwood) Copp, was born at Bath, England, 14 December 1828; died at West Newton, Mass., 29 March 1879. The Copp and Bigwood families had long lived in the southwestern part of England. Her father was a prosperous baker, with a shop near the Anglican Church of St. Swithin's. Eliza's father was a parishioner of St. Swithin's at the time that the Rev. George Austen, father of Jane Austen, returned to Bath, and it is likely that the Copps and the Austens were acquainted. Eliza's father was a non-conformist and she became a member of the Church of the New Jerusalem – the Swedenborgian Church. She married, in St. Louis, Missouri, **Herbert Marshall WARREN**, son of Jesse and Betsey (Jackson) Warren; born at West Dedham, Mass., 16 January 1827; died on Long Island Sound when the *Narragansett* burned and sank, 11 June 1880.

Herbert Marshall WARREN = Eliza Caroline COPP
William Toy SHOEMAKER = Mabel WARREN

---

[93] Hill, *Western Pilgrims*, 704.
[94] Hill, *Western Pilgrims*, 183-4.
[95] Hill, *Quakers and Puritans*, 250.
[96] Hill, *Quakers and Puritans*, 256.
[97] Hill, *Quakers and Puritans*, 188.

BARTHOLOMEW COPPOCK

BARTHOLOMEW COPPOCK, Sr.,[98] was born at Saltney, Cheshire, England; died at Marple, Chester Co., Pa., 20 December 1718. He came early to Pennsylvania, probably in 1681/2. He was a commissioner of the Court of Equity, and a member of the Provincial Council. He married, in England, **MARGARET YARWOOD**, 4 mo. 1678; she died in 7 mo. 1735. They had five children.

Bartholomew COPPOCK = Margaret YARWOOD
Bartholomew COPPOCK, Jr. = Mrs. Phebe (née TAYLOR) MASSEY
Daniel SHARPLES = Sarah COPPOCK
Solomon MERCER = Abigail SHARPLES
William WALTER = Phebe MERCER
William H. MANLY = Sarah D. WALTER
Silas William RUNDALL = Rachel MANLY
William Henry "Will" THOMPSON = Sarah D. "Sadie" RUNDALL

ELIZABETH CORNELL

ELIZABETH CORNELL,[99] probably born between 1675 and 1679, married, in about 1700, **Nathaniel TOMPKINS [II]**, grandson of JOHN TOMPKINS of Westchester Co., N.Y.; born at Eastchester, 20 September 1678; died at Yorktown, N.Y., 15 February 1731/2. Her ancestry is unknown. She could be either a woman whose birth name was Elizabeth Cornell, or, less likely, a widow, still young, of a man named Cornell. The prominent Cornell family, which includes Hon. Ezra Cornell, for whom Cornell University is named, is said to descend from the emigrant Thomas Cornell, of Massachusetts, New York, and Rhode Island. I cannot find her in the family of this Thomas Cornell, or in any others with the Cornell family name. She is an ancestor of Sarah D. Rundall.

THOMAS CROASDALE

THOMAS CROASDALE,[100] perhaps born at Waddington, Yorkshire, England, 20 May 1644; died at Neshaminy Creek, Bucks Co., Pa., 2 November 1684. He came to Pennsylvania with his wife and six children in 1682, to occupy a grant of 1000 acres that he had purchased from William Penn. He married, in England, **AGNES HATHORTHWAITE**, daughter of William Hawthornthwaite of Swarthmore, Lancashire; born about 1633; died at her home on the Neshaminy Creek, Bucks Co., Pa., 8mo. 20, 1684.

Thomas CROASDALE = Agnes HATHORTHWAITE
David POTTS = Alice CROASDALE
John POTTS = Elizabeth McVAUGH
Isaac SHOEMAKER, Jr. = Elizabeth POTTS
Jonathan SHOEMAKER, Esq. = Hannah LUKENS
Charles SHOEMAKER = Rachel COMLY
Julien SHOEMAKER = Hannah Ann HESTER
William Toy SHOEMAKER = Mabel WARREN

THOMAS CROKER

THOMAS CROKER[101] was of Ffaringdon, co. Barks, England. He married *Alice DORMER*, daughter of Geoffrey Dormer, of Thame, co. Oxford; she died in 1513. Alice Dormer was of **Royal descent**, descended from Ralph de Arundel, father-in-law of *BARTHOLOMEW COLLINRIDGE*.

Thomas CROKER = Alice DORMER
John CROKER = Isabell SKINNER
Edward HAWTEN = Margery CROKER

---

[98] Hill, *Fundy to Chesapeake*, 299-301.
[99] Hill, *Fundy to Chesapeake*, 209-10.
[100] Hill, *Quakers and Puritans*, 83-5.
[101] Hill, *Western Pilgrims*, 155.

Henry HOWELL = Margaret HAWTEN
Mr. Edward HOWELL, Lord of the Manor of Westbury = *Frances PAXTON*
(See EDWARD HOWELL)

ROBERT CROSS

ROBERT CROSS,[102] yeoman, born about 1612; died after April 1695. He was admitted to the church at Ipswich, Mass., before 1658. He owned the islands called Dafeadownedilla near Ipswich. He married (1), in Ipswich, 20 August 1635, **Anna JORDAN**, daughter of STEPHEN JORDAN; born about 1615 in England; died at Ipswich 29 October 1677. They had eight children. He married (2) **Mary _____.**

Robert CROSS(E) = Anna JORDAN
Ephraim "of Beverly" HERRICK = Mary CROSS(E)
Lieutenant Stephen HERRICK = Elizabeth TRASK
Edward HERRICK = Mary DENISON
Col. Rufus HERRICK = Miss _____ GIBBS, prob. Myra "Mary" GIBBS
Rufus HERRICK [III] = Jerusha P. _____ (prob.) PIERCE
William Prince HILL = Sarah P. "Sally" HERRICK
Charles W. HILL = Adelia Catharine "Delia" RILEY
George J. HILL = Jessie Fidelia STOCKWELL

JAMES CUTLER

JAMES CUTLER,[103] planter, was born in about 1606, probably in England; died at Lexington, Mass., 17 July 1694. He first appeared in Watertown, Mass., in 1635, where he became surveyor of highways. He married (1), by 1635, **ANN _____**, who was buried at Watertown, 30 September 1644.

James CUTLER = Ann _____
John COLLER = Hannah CUTLER
James CUTTING = Hannah COLLER
David CUTTING = Elizabeth WALES
David CUTTING = Sarah EDMUNDS
Sheriff Joseph SCOTT = Sarah CUTTING
James THOMPSON Sr. = Hannah _____, prob. Hannah SCOTT
Joseph Scott THOMPSON = Ruth E. ARCHIBALD
James Everett THOMPSON = Jane GRANT
William Henry "Will" THOMPSON = Sarah D. "Sadie" RUNDALL

ANN (_____) CUTLER

ANN ___ was of Watertown, Mass., when she married, by 1635, as his first wife, **JAMES CUTLER**, planter, born about 1606; died at Lexington, Mass., 17 July 1694 (see preceding).

RICHARD CUTTING

RICHARD CUTTING,[104] wheelright, son of Richard and Susan (Stone) Cutting, was baptized at Great Bromley, co. Essex, 6 February 1621/2; died at Watertown, Mass., 21 March 1695/6. At age eleven, he was enrolled on 30 April 1634, on the *Elizabeth*. He owned a "great Bible" and wheelright tools at the time of his death. He married, in say 1644, **SARAH __**; born about 1625; died at Watertown, 4 November 1685. Their son James married Hannah Coller and is probably an ancestor of William H. Thompson.

Richard CUTTING = Sarah _____
James CUTTING = Hannah COLLER
David CUTTING = Elizabeth WALES

---

[102] Hill, *Western Pilgrims*, 302.
[103] Hill, *Fundy to Chesapeake*, 45. For the question of Hannah ___ (?SCOTT), see *Fundy to Chesapeake*, 3-4.
[104] Hill, *Fundy to Chesapeake*, 41. For the question of Hannah ___ (?SCOTT), see *Fundy to Chesapeake*, 3-4.

David CUTTING = Sarah EDMUNDS
Sheriff Joseph SCOTT = Sarah CUTTING
James THOMPSON Sr. = Hannah _____, prob. Hannah SCOTT
Joseph Scott THOMPSON = Ruth E. ARCHIBALD
James Everett THOMPSON = Jane GRANT
William Henry "Will" THOMPSON = Sarah D. "Sadie" RUNDALL

SARAH (_____) CUTTING

SARAH ___ was born about 1625, probably in England. She was of Watertown, Mass., when she married, in say 1644, **RICHARD CUTTING**. Their first child was born in say 1645 (see preceding).

JOHN DARBY

JOHN DARBY,[105] fisherman, died at Marblehead, Mass., in about 1689-90. He owned a house and lot in Marblehead, and he appeared as a creditor to the estate of John Clay, fisherman. He left only a small estate, totaling £5.7s.9d, to his widow and five children. He married, in about 1678, **ALICE _____**, who died after having eight children by her second husband, John Woodbury, a widower.

John DARBY = Alice _____
John DARBY, Jr. = Deborah CONANT
Andrew "Miller" DARBY = Elizabeth PATCH
Sgt. Josiah JACKSON = Mary DARBY
Oliver JACKSON = Mary PEIRCE
Jesse WARREN = Betsy JACKSON
Herbert Marshall WARREN = Eliza Caroline COPP
William Toy SHOEMAKER = Mabel WARREN

ALICE (_____) DARBY

ALICE ____ was of Marblehead, Mass., when she first appeared in the records. She married (1) **JOHN DARBY**, with whom she had five children, born between 1679 and 1687. He died in 1689-90, leaving a meagre estate and some debts. She promptly, and understandably, married again. She married (2), as his second wife, **John WOODBURY**, son of Humphrey and grandson of the emigrant John Woodbury. John Woodbury had several living children by his first marriage, which lasted 44 years. The Woodburys and those to whom they were related were prominent in the affairs of Beverly and Salem. Alice (___) (Darby) Woodbury bore eight children by her second husband. She raised a total of 13 children by her two marriages. Salem court records show that she was a contentious woman (see preceding).

AARON DAVIS

Rev. **AARON DAVIS**,[106] a mason, died at Dartmouth, Mass., in about 1713 or soon thereafter. He first appeared in the public records in Newport, R.I., on 25 February 1673, when he and his wife **MARY _____** sold a house and 15 acres. He was a Baptist minister, and served the First Baptist Church at Dartmouth.

Aaron DAVIS = Mary _____
Aaron DAVIS, Jr. = Mary _____
William ALLEBY = Sarah DAVIS
Jesse IRISH = Mary ALLEBEE
William IRISH = Dolly _____
Capt. Freeborn POTTER = Dolly IRISH
Harvey HYDE = Fidelia Gadcourt POTTER
Benajah Flavel STOCKWELL = Emily Lodiweska (Emma F.) HYDE
George J. HILL = Jessie Fidelia STOCKWELL

---

[105] Hill, *Quakers and Puritans*, 216-8.
[106] Hill, *Western Pilgrims*, 355-6.

MARY (_____) DAVIS

MARY _____ married the **Rev. AARON DAVIS**, an ordained Baptist minister. They lived a simple life in Dartmouth, Mass., and in Tiverton and Little Compton, R.I.   They are ancestors of Jessie F. Stockwell (see preceding).

ABRAHAM DAWES

ABRAHAM DAWES,[107] maltster, said to have come from London, England, to Pennsylvania; died about May 1731 at Whitemarsh, Philadelphia Co. He was at Whitemarsh as early as 1713, and he had a large estate at his death. He left 125 acres in Chestnut Hill to his son, and he owned 418 acres in Whitpain. He married **EDITH _____**, with whom he had four children.

Abraham DAWES = Edith _____
Samuel SPENCER = Mary DAWES
Joseph LUKENS = Elizabeth SPENCER
Jonathan SHOEMAKER, Esq. = Hannah LUKENS
Charles SHOEMAKER = Rachel COMLY
Julien SHOEMAKER = Hannah Ann HESTER
William Toy SHOEMAKER = Mabel WARREN

EDITH (_____) DAWES

EDITH _____ married, perhaps in England, **ABRAHAM DAWES**, maltster, who came to Pennsylvania in about 1713. Her husband was a Quaker businessman, and he left a large estate (see preceding).

FRANCOIS DU PUY

FRANCOIS DU PUY,[108] (aka De Pui, De Puy) of Calais, Province of Artois, France, was a Huguenot emigrant to America. He married, in the Dutch Reformed Church of New Amsterdam, 26 September 1661, **GEERTRUY WILLEMS**, of Amsterdam, the Netherlands.

Francois DE PUI (or Du Puy) = Geertruy WILLEMS
William DE PUY (or Du Puy) = Elizabeth WEDT
Pierre FORSHAY = Abigail De PEW (aka DuPuis, Du Puy)
Nathaniel TOMPKINS [III] = Mary FORSHAY
Nathaniel TOMPKINS [IV] = Elizabeth "Polly" OAKLEY
Bartholomew TOMPKINS = [unmarried] Martha LAKE (possibly daughter of Daniel Lake)
Reuben John RUNDALL = Martha TOMPKINS
Silas William RUNDALL = Rachel MANLY
William Henry "Will" THOMPSON = Sarah D. "Sadie" RUNDALL

WILLIAM DENISON

Mr. WILLIAM DENISON,[109] son of John and Agnes (Willie) Denyson, was baptized 3 February 1571/2 at Bishop's Stortford, co. Hertford; died at Roxbury, Mass., 25 January 1653/4. He came on the *Lion* in 1631. He was one of the five wealthiest men in Roxbury in 1642. He married, at Bishop's Stortford, Herts, 7 November 1603, as her second husband, **MARGARET CHANDLER,** who married (1) Henry Monk. She was the daughter of Tobias and Johan (Momford) Chandler, born 13 October 1577; died at Roxbury, Mass., 3 February 1645/6.

Mr. William DENISON = Margaret CHANDLER
Capt. George DENISON, gent. = Ann BORODELL
Capt. John Borodell DENISON = Phebe LAY
Capt. William DENISON = Mary AVERY

---

[107] Hill, *Quakers and Puritans*, 74.
[108] Hill, *Fundy to Chesapeake*, 226.
[109] Hill, *Western Pilgrims*, 65-9.

Edward HERRICK = Mary DENISON
Col. Rufus HERRICK = Miss _____ GIBBS, prob. Myra "Mary" GIBBS
Capt. Rufus HERRICK Jr. = Lydia NEWMAN
Rufus HERRICK [III] = Jerusha P. _____ (prob.) PIERCE
William Prince HILL = Sarah P. "Sally" HERRICK
Charles W. HILL = Adelia Catharine "Delia" RILEY
George J. HILL = Jessie Fidelia STOCKWELL

WILLIAM DEREHAUGH

WILLIAM DEREHAUGH,[110] of Badingham, co. Suffolk, son of John and Agnes (Thurston) Derehaugh; born about 10 February 1559; buried at Badingham, 4 September 1610. He married, about 1578, **Mary WRIGHT**, daughter of Edmund Wright, a descendant of **John "Lackland," King of England**.

William DEREHAUGH = Mary WRIGHT
John SRATTON, Gent. = Anne DEREHAUGH
Mr. John THORNDIKE = Elizabeth STRATTON
(see JOHN THORNDIKE and ELIZABETH STRATTON)

ALICE DICKINSON

ALICE DICKINSON[111] was born in about 1699 in England; died in Pennsylvania between 29 March 1727 and 2 October 1738. She came to America on *Submission*, and arrived in December 1682 in Bucks County, Pa. She married, before 1702, **EDMOND McVAUGH**, born 1664; died before 3 November 1739. She is an ancestor of **President Theodore Roosevelt** and of Dr. William T. Shoemaker.

JOHN GEORGE DIPPOLT

JOHN GEORGE DIPPOLT[112] is said to have been born in Hesse-Kassel in about 1750, but perhaps was born in New Jersey in 1745. He was probably a Hessian soldier, who fought on the British side in the Revolutionary War. Nothing is known of his wife, but he is known to have had at least three children. His daughter Mary, born say 1773 in Germany, probably joined him after the war.

John George DIPPOLT = _____
Jacob HESTER = Mary DIPPOLT
John Dippolt HESTER = Rhoda "Rhody" KNOWLES
Julien SHOEMAKER = Hannah Ann HESTER
William Toy SHOEMAKER = Mabel WARREN

WILLIAM DIXEY

Capt. **WILLIAM DIXEY**,[113] presumably born in England in about 1607, died between 1688 and 1690, probably at Beverly, Mass. He was a man of substance in Salem, and captain of the Beverly Foot Company. He married **ANN _____**, who is presumed to be the mother of all of his children.

Capt. William DIXEY = Ann _____
Sergeant Samuel MORGAN = Elizabeth DIXEY
Hezekiah OBER = Ann (Anna) MORGAN
James THORNDIKE = Anna OBER
Simeon MOORS = Joanna THORNDIKE
Jeduthan WARREN = Joanna MOORS
Jesse WARREN = Betsy JACKSON
Herbert Marshall WARREN = Eliza Caroline COPP
William Toy SHOEMAKER = Mabel WARREN

---

[110] Hill, *Quakers and Puritans*, 148. Richardson, *Royal Ancestry*, "Derehaugh," 2:439-40.
[111] Hill, *Quakers and Puritans*, 87.
[112] Hill, *Quakers and Puritans*, 27-28.
[113] Hill, *Quakers and Puritans*, 181-2.

ANN (_____) DIXEY

ANN _____, wife of **Capt. WILLIAM DIXEY**, and probably the mother of all of his children, appeared in the record of Salem in 1636 when she and her husband became members of the church. They probably came earlier, for he was recorded as a freeman in 1634. She had six children (see preceding).

HENRY DIXON

HENRY DIXON,[114] born say about 1633 at Sego Parish, co. Armagh, Ireland, died between 1667 and 1687, probably at New Castle Co., Delaware. The family was probably Scottish. He came to New Castle before 1690, at which time he is recorded as an innkeeper. He married, in Ireland, in about 1660, **ROSE _____ (?)HARLAN**, born say about 1637, probably in co. Armagh ; died about 1687 at Kennett Twp., Chester Co., Pa. They are ancestors of **President Richard M. Nixon**.

Henry DIXON = Rose _____ (?) HARLAN
William DIXON = Ann GREGG
William DIXON the Younger = Hannah HOLLINGSWORTH
Jacob DIXON = Esther PHILLIPS
James WALTER = Sarah DIXON (prob. daughter of Jacob Dixon)
William WALTER = Phebe MERCER
William H. MANLY = Sarah D. WALTER
Silas William RUNDALL = Rachel MANLY
William Henry "Will" THOMPSON = Sarah D. "Sadie" RUNDALL

ROSE (?HARLAN) DIXON

ROSE _____ (?) HARLAN, born say about 1637, probably in co. Armagh, Ireland, died about 1687 in Kennett Twp., Chester Co., Pa. She married, in Ireland in about 1660, **HENRY DIXON**, with whom she had three children. The eldest, born in Ireland, is an ancestor of Sarah D. Rundall (see preceding).

MARY DOLBERE

MARY DOLBERE (aka DOLBAIR),[115] daughter of Rawkey and Mary (Michell) Dolbere, was christened 7 June 1607 at Colyton, co. Devon, England; died at Windsor, Hartford Co., Conn., 5 Jan 1685/6. On 29 March 1634, at Colyton, she married **JONATHAN GILLETT**, son of the Rev. William Gyllett; born say 1610; died at Windsor, Conn., 23 August 1677. They are ancestors of George J. Hill.

GEOFFREY DORMER

GEOFFREY DORMER,[116] merchant, married (1) *Margery _____*, by whom he had 13 children: five sons and eight daughters. He married (2) *Alice COLLINRIDGE*, daughter of William and granddaughter of Bartholomew Collinridge. His second wife was of **Royal descent**.

Geoffrey DORMER, Sr. = Alice COLLINRIDGE
Thomas CROKER = Alice DORMER
Edward HAWTEN, Gent. = Margery CROKER
Henry HOWELL = Margaret HAWTEN
Mr. Edward HOWELL, Lord of the Manor of Westbury = *Frances PAXTON*
(see EDWARD HOWELL)

---

[114] Hill, *Fundy to Chesapeake*, 334-6.
[115] Hill, *Western Pilgrims*, 118-26.
[116] Hill, *Western Pilgrims*, 154-5.

ANNE DOVER

ANNE DOVER,[117] born at Crewkerne, co. Somerset, in 1610, married there, 14 November 1626, as his second wife, **WILLIAM PHELPS**; born about 1593; died at Windsor, Conn., 14 July 1672. She came to New England with her husband in 1630 and died in 1689. She is an ancestor of George J. Hill.

SAMUEL DUNCAN

SAMUEL DUNCAN (aka DUNKIN), Sr.,[118] originally a servant, and later husbandman and planter, was perhaps from co. Kent, born in say 1619; died in Massachusetts, probably Roxbury, after 24 March 1680/1. He came in 1634/5 with Comfort Starr. He later owned the modern equivalent of 9-15 city blocks on the "Muddy River," now the border between Roxbury and Brookline. He married, by about 1645, probably in Boston or Roxbury, **MARY _____**, who died between 1655 and 1672.

Samuel DUNCAN = Mary _____

John SCOTT = Hannah DUNCAN

Joseph SCOTT = Hannah PRIOR

Lieut. Joseph SCOTT = Mary EDMANDS

Sheriff Joseph SCOTT = Sarah CUTTING

James THOMPSON Sr. = Hannah _____, prob. Hannah SCOTT

Joseph Scott THOMPSON = Ruth E. ARCHIBALD

James Everett THOMPSON = Jane GRANT

William Henry "Will" THOMPSON = Sarah D. "Sadie" RUNDALL

MARY (_____) DUNCAN

MARY _____, probably an immigrant to Massachusetts, who married there, by 1645, **Samuel DUNCAN**. He had come in 1634/5 as a servant and after release from servitude, began to acquire a considerable amount of land along the "Muddy River," now Roxbury (see preceding).

[ELNATHAN DUNKLEE]

[ELNATHAN DUNKLEE[119] appears in *Western Pilgrims* as an ancestor of George J. Hill, the Iowa Pioneer, but this is incorrect. Silence Dunklee appears in *Western Pilgrims*, p. 225, as the wife of Caleb Putnam, and it is said there that Silence Dunklee was a descendant of the Rev. John Lothrop. Later, by the time I wrote *Fundy to Chesapeake*, I had discovered that the full name of Caleb Putnam's wife was Silence (Phillips) Dunklee. She married (1) to _____ Dunklee; and (2) to Caleb Putnam. The Dunklee line would connect with the Rev. John Lothrop, but not the line of Phillips. The comments about the Lothrop, Learned, Dunklee families in *Western Pilgrims*, Chapter 43, p. 225, are therefore no longer relevant. Her birth name was Silence Phillips, and she was not a descendant of the Rev. John Lothrop.]

WILLIAM EAGER

WILLIAM EAGER,[120] probably the son of William Eager, who is said to have been born in England and died at Dublin in 1695. The father, William Eager, came from a family that had owned a large amount of land in co. Kerry for 200 years. William Eager, the son, probably arrived in Plymouth, Mass., in about 1630. He can be followed with certainty from the time of his marriage, in Malden, Mass., in December 1659, until his death in 1690. He was one of the owners of the six thousand-acre Ockoocanganset Plantation. He was not recorded to be a citizen, perhaps because he was a Presbyterian. On 7 December 1659, at Malden, Mass., he married (1) **Ruth HILL**, daughter of ABRAHAM HILL and

---

[117] Hill, *Western Pilgrims*, 21.

[118] Hill, *Fundy to Chesapeake*, 30-31. The line of descent for Samuel Duncan depends on the assumption that Hannah ___, who married James Thompson, Sr., is Hannah Scott, daughter of Joseph Scott, as discussed on pp.3-4.

[119] Hill, *Fundy to Chesapeake*, 75; and *Western Pilgrims*, 60, 225.

[120] Hill, *Western Pilgrims*, 325-7.

SARAH LONG; born at Malden, 20 June 1641; died at Cambridge, 6 January 1679; eight children. He married (2) in 1680, **Lydia (BARRETT) COLE**, a widow, and had six more children with her.

William EAGER = Ruth HILL
Abraham EAGER = Lydia WOODS
Jabez WARD = Phebe EAGER
Corporal Jabez WARD = Jemima ALLEN
Private Henry HYDE = Thyrina (Therina) WARD
Luther HYDE = Phoebe GIDDINGS
Harvey HYDE = Fidelia Gadcourt POTTER
Benajah Flavel STOCKWELL = Emily Lodiweska (Emma F.) HYDE
George J. HILL = Jessie Fidelia STOCKWELL

WILLIAM EDMONDS/EDMANDS

WILLIAM EDMONDS, Senior,[121] tailor and keeper of an inn and tavern, was born in about 1610; died, probably at Lynn, Mass., between 15 June 1681 and 8 September 1693. He came to Massachusetts in about 1634. He married (1), by 1638, **MARY _____**, who died at Lynn, 2 March 1657, having borne four children. He married (2), in 1657, a "healer" or "doctor woman," **Ann (_____) MARTIN**.

William EDMONDS = Mary _____
John EDMONDS = Mary (_____) GEORGE
Joseph EDMANDS = Mary PRATT
Lieut. Joseph SCOTT = Mary EDMANDS   David CUTTING = Sarah EDMUNDS
Sheriff Joseph SCOTT [Jr.] = Sarah CUTTING
James THOMPSON Sr. = Hannah _____, prob. Hannah SCOTT
Joseph Scott THOMPSON = Ruth E. ARCHIBALD
James Everett THOMPSON = Jane GRANT
William Henry "Will" THOMPSON = Sarah D. "Sadie" RUNDALL

MARY (_____) EDMONDS/EDMANDS

MARY _____, first wife of **WILLIAM EDMONDS, Senior**, a prosperous innkeeper and tavern operator, was probably an immigrant to Massachusetts in the early 1630s. She was married by 1638 and had the first of her four children in that year, having confessed "her sin before the congregation" on 26 June 1638, presumably for having sexual relations before marriage. Her husband married again in 1657, so Mary probably lived for several years after the birth of her last child in say 1650 (see preceding).

ANN EVANS

ANN EVANS,[122] daughter of Rowland Evans of co. Wicklow, Ireland, married, at Oldcastle, co. Meath, 2mo. 29, 1696, **ISAAC JACKSON**, son of Anthony Jackson; born in 1665; died in Pennsylvania in the fall of 1750. They came to America in 1725. Isaac and Ann (Evans) Jackson had ten children. She died in 1731 or 1732. She is an ancestor of Sarah D. Rundall.

ROBERT EVANS

ROBERT EVANS,[123] second son of Evan "Lloyd" ap Evan (i.e., Robert, son of Evan "Lloyd," son of Evan), was born about 1658 in Wales; died at Gwynedd Twp., Montgomery Co., Pa., 1 mo. 1738. He was one of the four Evans brothers who emigrated from Pennlyn, Merionethshire, Wales, to Pennsylvania in 1698. He owned more than 1000 acres in what is now Lower Gwynedd Township. He married **Ellen _____**. They are presumed to be the parents of Gaynor Evans who married Peter Lukens.

---

[121] Hill, *Fundy to Chesapeake*, 32-3. See also pp. 3-4 for discussion about whether Hannah _____ is the daughter of Joseph Scott.
[122] Hill, *Fundy to Chesapeake*, 262.
[123] Hill, *Quakers and Puritans*, 69-71.

Robert EVANS = Ellen _____
Peter LUKENS = Gaynor EVANS
Joseph LUKENS = Elizabeth SPENCER
Jonathan SHOEMAKER Esq. = Hannah LUKENS
Charles SHOEMAKER = Rachel COMLY
Julien SHOEMAKER = Hannah Ann HESTER
William Toy SHOEMAKER = Mabel WARREN

ELLEN (_____) EVANS

ELLEN ____was the wife of **ROBERT EVANS**, son of Evan "Lloyd" ap Evan, who came from Wales. She probably had eight children, born in a house that was still standing in 1927 (see preceding).

JOHN EYRE

JOHN EYRE,[124] of Wedhamptom and Northcombe, Wiltshire, England, was probably born in the latter part of the 14th century. He married *Ellen CROKER*, daughter and heir of John Croker, gent., of Erchefount, Wiltshire. They are ancestors of Anne Eyre, who married William Howell, Lord of the Manor of Westbury Manor, Bucks, whose grandson, Mr. EDWARD HOWELL, was an immigrant to America.

John EYRE, Esq. = Ellen CROKER
Symon EYRE, Esq. = _____
Thomas EYRE = _____
William EYRE = _____
William HOWELL, Lord of the Manor of Westbury = Ann EYRE
Mr. Henry HOWELL, Lord of the Manor of Westbury = Margaret HAWTEN
Mr. Edward HOWELL, Lord of the Manor of Westbury = *Frances PAXTON*
(see EDWARD HOWELL)

VAN THOMAS FARRINGTON

VAN THOMAS FARRINGTON,[125] born at Flushing, Long Island (now Queens Co., N.Y.), in 1645; died at Westchester Co., in 1697. He married in 1670, **MARY PANTON**, born at Flushing in about 1648.

Van Thomas FARRINGTON = Mary PANTON
Thomas OAKLEY = Abigail FARRINGTON
Elisha OAKLEY = Elizabeth YEOMANS
Nathaniel TOMPKINS [IV] = Elizabeth "Polly" OAKLEY
Bartholomew TOMPKINS = [unmarried] Martha LAKE (possibly daughter of Daniel Lake)
Reuben John RUNDALL = Martha TOMPKINS
Silas William RUNDALL = Rachel MANLY
William Henry "Will" THOMPSON = Sarah D. "Sadie" RUNDALL

JUDITH FEAKE

JUDITH FEAKE,[126] daughter of James and Awdrey (Crompton) Feake, Jr., was born in England in about 1621; died at Greenwich, Fairfield Co., Conn., in 1667-1668. Her father and paternal grandfather were goldsmiths of London. Her brother, Capt. Tobias Feake, R.N., came to Flushing, L.I., where he was *schout*. Judith's uncle, Lieut. Robert Feake, was the second husband of Elizabeth (Fones) Winthrop, known as "The Winthrop Woman." Judith Feake married (1), in about 1637, **Lieut. WILLIAM PALMER.** They had seven children. She married (2), **Jeffrey FERRIS**, and (3), **Capt. John**

---

[124] Hill, *Western Pilgrims*, 145.
[125] Hill, *Fundy to Chesapeake*, 227-8.
[126] Hill, *Fundy to Chesapeake*, 141-4.

39

BOWERS, who married, after Judith died, the widow Hannah (Close) Knapp. Judith Feake is an ancestor of Sarah D. Rundall (see WILLIAM PALMER).

SARAH FENNER

SARAH FENNER,[127] daughter of Arthur and Sarah (Browne) Fenner, was born at Horley, co. Surrey, England, 26 November 1615; died at Saybrook, Conn., 25 May 1676. She married (1) **John TULLY**, born 1613; died in 1644. She came to America with his son, John Tully. She married (2), at Saybrook, in December 1647, **ROBERT LAY,** Deputy to the General Court. She is an ancestor of George J. Hill.

ANTHONY FISHER

ANTHONY FISHER, Sr.,[128] son of Anthony and Mary (Fiske) Fisher, was baptized at Syleham, co. Suffolk, 23 April 1591; died at Dorchester, Mass., 18 April 1671. He probably came in the ship *Rose*, which arrived Boston on 26 June 1637. He was a member of the Ancient and Honorable Artillery Company and a Deputy to the General Court. His "proud and haughty spirit" caused a delay in his admission to the church. He married (1), after 1663, **MARY**____, with whom he had five children. He married (2) **Isabel (____) BRECK**, without additional progeny.

Anthony FISHER, Sr. = Mary _____
Daniel MORSE = Lydia FISHER
Jonathan MORSE = Mary Marie BARBOUR
Jonathan MORSE (Jr.) = Jane WHITNEY
Joseph PARTRIDGE = Eunice MORSE
Lt. Aaron HOLBROOK = Hannah PARTRIDGE
Ebenezer STOCKWELL = Abi HOLBROOK
Joseph H. STOCKWELL = Anna Maria SAXE
Benajah Flavel STOCKWELL = Emily Lodiweska (Emma F.) HYDE
George J. HILL = Jessie Fidelia STOCKWELL

MARY (_____) FISHER

MARY _____ married **ANTHONY FISHER**, who came to Boston in 1637. They were married in Syleham, co. Suffolk, and the first of their five children were born there. She was admitted to the church in Dedham in 1642, but he was "not comfortably received" for three more years. She died before 1663; her sons had agreed to give bond to pay her £10 per year until she died (see preceding).

EDWARD FISHER

EDWARD FISHER[129] came to Portsmouth, R.I., before 1655. He married **JUDITH** _____, with whom he had at least two children.

Edward FISHER = Judith ____
John POTTER = Ruth FISHER
John POTTER = Jane BURLINGAME
William POTTER = Martha TILLINGHAST
Capt. Oliver POTTER = Mary COLVIN
Capt. Freeborn POTTER = Dolly IRISH
Harvey HYDE = Fidelia Gadcourt POTTER
Benajah Flavel STOCKWELL = Emily Lodiweska (Emma F.) HYDE
George J. HILL = Jessie Fidelia STOCKWELL

---

[127] Hill, *Western Pilgrims*, 71.
[128] Hill, *Western Pilgrims*, 209.
[129] Hill, *Western Pilgrims*, 256.

JUDITH (_____) FISHER

JUDITH _____ married **EDWARD FISHER** and had at least two children with him. They are ancestors of Jessie F. Stockwell in the line of Potters of Rhode Island and Vermont (see preceding).

JOHN FISHER

JOHN FISHER,[130] linen weaver, was born at Londonderry, Northern Ireland, 2 December 1675; died at Londonderry, N.H. He married, in Ireland, in about 1700, **SARAH _____**; born in Londonderry, Ireland, about 1675; died in Londonderry, N.H. Their son William James Fisher relocated to Colchester Co., Nova Scotia, in the depths of winter, December 1762, with his wife and nine children, while she was pregnant with her tenth child. William James Fisher represented Truro in the Nova Scotia Assembly.

John FISHER = Sarah _____
William James FISHER = Eleanor ARCHIBALD
Lt. Col. John ARCHIBALD 2nd = Margaret FISHER
William ARCHIBALD = Susannah "Susan" PUTNAM
Joseph Scott THOMPSON = Ruth E. ARCHIBALD
James Everett THOMPSON = Jane GRANT
William Henry "Will" THOMPSON = Sarah D. "Sadie" RUNDALL

SARAH (_____) FISHER

SARAH _____ was born in Londonderry, Ireland, in about 1675; died in Londonderry, N.H. She married, in Ireland, in about 1700, **JOHN FISHER**, born in Ireland and returned from New Hampshire to marry her. They had one son. They settled in Derry in what is now New Hampshire (see preceding).

NATHAN FISKE

NATHAN FISKE, Sr.,[131] son of Geoffrey and Mary (Cooke) Fiske, was born at St. James, South Elmham, co. Suffolk, probably about 1592; died in New England, probably at Watertown, Mass., 21 June 1676. He was a yeoman and selectman, who married, probably in England, **SUSANNA _____**; five children, born at Watertown. He was first recorded when his son, Nathan, was born, 17 October 1642.

Nathan FISKE = Susanna _____
Abraham GALE = Sarah FISKE
Ebeneezer GALE = Elizabeth GREEN
Ebeneezer GALE, Jr. = Elizabeth KENNEY
Benajah STOCKWELL = Hannah GALE
Ebenezer STOCKWELL = Abi HOLBROOK
Joseph H. STOCKWELL = Anna Maria SAXE
Benajah Flavel STOCKWELL = Emily Lodiweska (Emma F.) HYDE
George J. HILL = Jessie Fidelia STOCKWELL

SUSANNA (_____) FISKE

SUSANNA _____ came to America with her husband, **NATHAN FISKE**, who was first recorded in Watertown in 1642. She had five children. Nathan was "very crazy in his memory" (see preceding).

MARGARET FLEMING

MARGARET FLEMING,[132] daughter of Henry and Alice (Dawkin) Fleming, married, in 1627, GRIFFITH BOWEN, gent., son of Francis and Ellen (Franklyn) Bowen, of an ancient family of Oxwich,

---

[130] Hill, *Fundy to Chesapeake*, 54-5.
[131] Hill, *Western Pilgrims*, 192.
[132] Hill, *Western Pilgrims*, 242-3. The line from Alice ferch John to Griffith Bowen is shown in Roberts, *600 Immigrants*, 485-6; and Weis, *Ancestral Roots*, 8th ed., 170-1.

Wales. He was born about 1600; died probably at London in about 1675. She and her husband came to America in about 1638 with several of their children. She had more children in Massachusetts, eventually having a total of ten. They returned to Wales, and then to London, where she probably died. Their surviving children remained in America. She is an ancestor of Jessie F. Stockwell.

ROBERT FLETCHER

ROBERT FLETCHER,[133] was born in about 1592, perhaps in Yorkshire; died at Concord, Mass., 3 April 1677. He is said by Pope to have arrived in Concord in 1635. He held public office only as the constable of Concord from 1637 to 1639, and he was discharged from office with the dubious distinction of "not being found faulty." Robert Fletcher had a daughter and four sons; one of the sons died in his thirties, unmarried, but the others married, had children, and all were uncommonly successful. He married, in say 1617, _____; she came to America with him, and died, probably in Concord or Chelmsford, Mass., sometime after he made his will in 1672. Robert Fletcher and his unnamed wife are ancestors of Mabel Warren through two lines in descent from their son William, and they are also probably ancestors of George J. Hill, in the line of their daughter, Grissell.

Robert FLETCHER = _____
Ensign William FLETCHER = Lydia BATES
Lieut. William FLETCHER = Sarah RICHARDSON
Josiah FLETCHER = Joanna SPALDING   Nathaniel BUTTERFIELD Jr. = Sarah FLETCHER
Capt. Joseph WARREN = Joanna FLETCHER   Lieut. Joseph MOORS = Esther BUTTERFIELD
Simeon MOORS = Joanna THORNDIKE
Jeduthan WARREN = Joanna MOORS
Jesse WARREN = Betsy JACKSON
Herbert Marshall WARREN = Eliza Caroline COPP
William Toy SHOEMAKER = Mabel WARREN

Robert FLETCHER = _____
Thomas JEWELL = Grissell "Cary" FLETCHER
Joseph SPALDING = Mercy JEWELL
Judge Timothy PIERCE = Lydia SPAULDING
Nathaniel PIERCE = Elizabeth STEVENS
Willard PIERCE = Jerusha PELLET
Rufus HERRICK [III] = Jerusha P._____ (prob. PIERCE)
William Prince HILL = Sarah P. "Sally" HERRICK
Charles W. HILL = Adelia Catharine "Delia" RILEY
George J. HILL = Jessie Fidelia STOCKWELL

_____ (_____) FLETCHER

_____, whose name is unknown, married, in say 1617, **ROBERT FLETCHER,** in England, probably Yorkshire, and came with him to America. She bore three or four children in England and one or two in Massachusetts, and she survived her husband, but then disappeared again from the record. She was truly a *femme covert*, yet four of her five children survived (see preceding).

JOHN FOLGER

JOHN FOLGER,[134] of Norwich, co. Norfolk, England; died at Martha's Vineyard, Mass., in 1664. He was a widower when he crossed the Atlantic in 1635. He settled at Watertown, and he later owned a

---

[133] Hill, *Quakers and* Puritans, 133-6; and *Western Pilgrims*, 90-1; caution noted in footnote on p.83; it assumes that Jerusha P., who married Rufus Herrick [III], is Jerusha Pierce.
[134] Hill, *Fundy to Chesapeake*, 43-4. For the question of Hannah ___ (?SCOTT), see discussion on pp. 3-4.

house and meadow land at Martha's Vineyard. John Folger married (1) _____ _____. He married (2) **MERIBAH GIBBS**, daughter of John Gibbs of Freudes Hall, Diss, co. Norfolk; she died after 1664. They had one child, Peter Folger, who was the grandfather of **Benjamin Franklin.**

John FOLGER = Meribah GIBBS
Peter FOLGER = Mary MORRILL
Joseph PRATT = Dorcas FOLGER
Joseph EDMANDS = Mary PRATT
Lieut. Joseph SCOTT = Mary EDMANDS
Sheriff Joseph SCOTT = Sarah CUTTING
James THOMPSON Sr. = Hannah _____, prob. Hannah SCOTT
Joseph Scott THOMPSON = Ruth E. ARCHIBALD
James Everett THOMPSON = Jane GRANT
William Henry "Will" THOMPSON = Sarah D. "Sadie" RUNDALL

THOMAS FORD

THOMAS FORD,[135] of co. Dorset, England, was born about 1591; died at Northampton, Mass., 28 November 1676. He came with his wife and five children on the *Mary and John* in 1630, and he served as Deputy to the Connecticut General Court from Windsor. He married (1), in Bridport, co. Dorset, 19 June 1616, as her second husband, **ELIZABETH CHARD**, widow of Aaron Cooke; she died 18 April 1643 in Windsor, Conn. He married (2), in Hartford, Conn., 7 November 1644, **Mrs. Ann SCOTT**, with whom he had a daughter.

Thomas FORD = Elizabeth CHARD (widow of Aaron Cooke)
Captain Roger CLAP = Joanna FORD
Preserved CLAPP = Sarah NEWBERRY
Abraham MILLER = Hannah CLAPP
Samuel ALLEN = Hannah MILLER
Corporal Jabez WARD = Jemima ALLEN
Private Henry HYDE = Thyrina (Therina) WARD
Luther HYDE = Phoebe GIDDINGS
Harvey HYDE = Fidelia Gadcourt POTTER
Benajah Flavel STOCKWELL = Emily Lodiweska (Emma F.) HYDE
George J. HILL = Jessie Fidelia STOCKWELL

JAN Le FAUCHEUR (aka FORSHAY)

JAN (JEAN) LeFAUCHEUR,[136] a Huguenot, was born about 1650 in France; died in New York. He married, probably in France, **JUDITH _____**. His brother André Fourche, born about 1647, was "of the landed gentry of France." They had at least two sons, with whom they migrated to America in 1695.

Jan LeFAUCHEUR = Judith _____
Pierre FOSHAY = Abigail DuPUY
Nathaniel TOMPKINS [III] = Mary FORSHAY
Nathaniel TOMPKINS [IV] = Elizabeth "Polly" OAKLEY
Bartholomew TOMPKINS = [unmarried] Martha LAKE (possibly daughter of Daniel Lake)
Reuben John RUNDALL = Martha TOMPKINS
Silas William RUNDALL = Rachel MANLY
William Henry "Will" THOMPSON = Sarah D. "Sadie" RUNDALL

JUDITH (_____) FAUCHEUR (aka FORSHAY)

JUDITH _____ married, in France, in say 1674, **Jan LeFAUCHEUR**, a Huguenot. They had at least two sons, with whom they emigrated to New York in 1695, with other members of her husband's family. The family name was normalized later as Forshay (see preceding).

---

[135] Hill, *Western Pilgrims*, 339-40.
[136] Hill, *Fundy to Chesapeake*, 224.

JOANE FOWLE

JOANE FOWLE,[137] daughter of Richard and Mary (Filkes) Fowle, was born say 1604 in co. Kent, England; died at Portsmouth, R.I., 15 July 1688. Her Fowle line (spelled variously) can be traced for four previous generations in co. Kent. She married, at Headcorn, co. Kent, 28 September 1625, **RICHARD BORDEN**, son of Thomas Borden of Headcorn; baptized there, 22 February 1595/6; died at Portsmouth, R.I., 25 May 1671. Her husband held many public offices in Rhode Island. They had twelve children. Their daughter Sarah Borden married Capt. Jonathan Holmes and is an ancestor of Jessie F. Stockwell.

JOHN FREDD

JOHN FRED[138] **(or FREDD)** was born in Ireland; died at Birmingham, Chester Co., Pa., in 1719/20. John Fred(d) and his family came to America sometime in the first decade of the eighteenth century. A Quaker record places John Fred in Ireland in 1706, although his daughter Mary is said to have died in Pennsylvania in 1704. John Fred was married at Belturbet, co. Cavan, 11 Mo. 6, 1685, to **CATHERINE STARKEY**, of co. Cavan; she died at Birmingham, Chester Co., Pa., in the fall of 1723.

John FRED(D) = Catherine STARKEY
James MILLER = Rachel FRED
John JACKSON Sr. = Sarah MILLER
John JACKSON Jr. = Susanna JACKSON [not a relative]
William MANLY = Rachel JACKSON (prob. daughter of John Jackson, Jr.)
William H. MANLY = Sarah D. WALTER
Silas William RUNDALL = Rachel MANLY
William Henry "Will" THOMPSON = Sarah D. "Sadie" RUNDALL

WILLIAM FRENCH

Captain WILLIAM FRENCH,[139] brother of John French, who emigrated to America by 1637, was born in England in about 1604; died at Billerica, Mass., 20 November 1681. He was trained as a tailor in England, and he embarked from London in July 1635 with his wife and four children. They came on the *Defence* and arrived at Cambridge. He was an original settler of the town of Billerica. He married, in England, **ELIZABETH _____**; born in England in about 1603-5; died at Billerica, 31 March 1668. He married (2), **Mrs. Mary (LOTHROP) STEARNS**.

Captain William FRENCH = Elizabeth _____ (perhaps GODFREY)
Sergeant Jonathan HYDE = Mary FRENCH
Jonathan HYDE Jr. = Dorothy KIDDER
John WOODWARD = Hannah HYDE   James HYDE = Mary UTTER
Henry BACON = Hannah WOODWARD
Hannah BACON = Jabez HYDE
Private Henry HYDE = Thyrina (Therina) WARD
Luther HYDE = Phoebe GIDDINGS
Harvey HYDE = Fidelia Gadcourt POTTER
Benajah Flavel STOCKWELL = Emily Lodiweska (Emma F.) HYDE
George J. HILL = Jessie Fidelia STOCKWELL

ELIZABETH (_____? GODFREY) FRENCH

ELIZABETH _____ (?GODFREY) married, in England, **Captain WILLIAM FRENCH**, with whom she had nine children, three of whom were born in England. She came to America with her husband and three children in 1635. They settled in Billerica, Mass., where she died in 1668 (see preceding).

---

[137] Hill, *Western Pilgrims*, 284-9.
[138] Hill, *Fundy to Chesapeake*, 274. This line assumes that Rachel Jackson is the daughter of John Jackson, Jr.
[139] Hill, *Western Pilgrims*, 223-5.

WILLIAM FROST

WILLIAM FROST[140] of Fairfield, Conn., came from Notts, England; died in 1645, leaving a will; five children are known. He devolved his estate in England to his daughter Mary Riley and her children. He presumably immigrated after some of his children were of age, and his wife may not have come with him. His eldest son, Daniel, was living in 1670, with eight children, including Joseph, who died about 1707.

William FROST = _____
Daniel FROST = Elizabeth BARLOW
Joseph FROST = Elizabeth HUBBELL
Henry WAKELEE = Sarah FROST
Benajah MALLORY = Elizabeth WAKELEE, married (1) _____ CRANE
Isaac HILL [Jr.] = Eunice MALLORY
Ephraim HILL = Charlotte PRINCE
William Prince HILL = Sarah P. "Sally" HERRICK
Charles W. HILL = Adelia Catharine "Delia" RILEY
George J. HILL = Jessie Fidelia STOCKWELL

EDWARD FULLER

EDWARD FULLER,[141] elder son of Robert and Frances Fuller, was baptized at Redenhall parish, co. Norfolk, 4 September 1575. He and his wife, whose name is unknown, came on the *Mayflower* to Plymouth, in 1620, with their son, Samuel. An older son, Matthew, stayed in England and came later to Plymouth. Both Edward and "Mrs. Fuller" died between 11 January and 10 April 1621.

Edward FULLER = _____
Dr. Matthew FULLER = Frances _____ possibly IYDE
Dr. John FULLER = Hannah MORTON
Captain John PRINCE = Reliance FULLER
Samuel PRINCE = Abigail HOWELL
Edward Howell PRINCE = Huldah OVIATT
Ephraim HILL = Charlotte PRINCE
William Prince HILL = Sarah P. "Sally" HERRICK
Charles W. HILL = Adelia Catherine RILEY
George J. HILL = Jessie Fidelia STOCKWELL

_____ (_____) FULLER

_____, who came on the *Mayflower* with her husband, **EDWARD FULLER**, one of her two sons, and her brother-in-law and his family, is known only as "Mrs. Fuller." She died in the winter of 1620-1621, probably in the first months of 1621, and was buried with others who died in that winter (see preceding).

REBECCA FURBURST

REBECCA FURBURST[142] married, as his second wife, 12 May 1692, **SAMUEL HARDY**. Their daughter, Hannah Hardy, born 6 July 1693, married Samuel Rundle, and is an ancestor of Sarah D. Rundall.

RICHARD GALE

RICHARD GALE,[143] yeoman, first appears as the purchaser of a "homestall" of six acres in Watertown, Mass., in 1640; died in Watertown, 22 March 1678/9. He was the owner of one of the finest tracts of land in Watertown. He married **MARY** _____. They were probably married in England and came to America together. She died before he wrote his will on 25 February 1678/9.

---

[140] Hill, *Western Pilgrims*, 28, 638-9.
[141] Hill, *Western Pilgrims*, 157-60.
[142] Hill, *Fundy to Chesapeake*, 120, 145, 623.
[143] Hill, *Western Pilgrims*, 191-3.

Richard GALE = Mary _____
Abraham GALE = Sarah FISKE
Ebeneezer GALE = Elizabeth GREEN
Ebeneezer GALE, Jr. = Elizabeth KENNEY
Benajah STOCKWELL = Hannah GALE
Ebenezer STOCKWELL = Abi HOLBROOK
Joseph H. STOCKWELL = Anna Maria SAXE
Benajah Flavel STOCKWELL = Emily Lodiweska (Emma F.) HYDE
George J. HILL = Jessie Fidelia STOCKWELL

MARY (_____) GALE

MARY _____ married **RICHARD GALE** and came with him to Watertown, Mass., in 1640. She bore five children between 1641 and about 1673, and died before her husband (see preceding).

JOHN GALLEY

JOHN GALLEY,[144] planter, of Salem, Mass., was born about 1605; died in Massachusetts in 1683. He first appeared when he received 20 acres at Salem in the division of 1636. His estate inventory totaled £202, of which £182 was real estate, with a home lot of 20 acres. He married **FLORENCE** ____, who died at Beverly, 23 December 1686. They had three daughters, including Dorcas, who was probably conceived before they were married. Dorcas later became infamous for organizing a burglary ring in Salem. Their daughter Elizabeth married **OSMOND TRASK** and is an ancestor of George J. Hill.

John GALLEY = Florence _____
Osmond TRASK = Elizabeth GALLEY
Lieutenant Stephen HERRICK = Elizabeth TRASK
Edward HERRICK = Mary DENNISON
Col. Rufus HERRICK = Miss _____ GIBBS, prob. Myra (Mary) GIBBS
Capt. Rufus HERRICK Jr. = Lydia NEWMAN
Rufus HERRICK [III] = Jerusha P. _____ (prob.) PIERCE
William Prince HILL = Sarah P. "Sally" HERRICK
Charles W. HILL = Adelia Catharine "Delia" RILEY
George J. HILL = Jessie Fidelia STOCKWELL

FLORENCE (_____) GALLEY

FLORENCE _____, born say 1606; died at Beverly, Mass., 23 December 1686, "aged about eighty years." She married **JOHN GALLEY**, born about 1605; died in Salem or Beverly, Mass., in 1683. He was fined 20s. in 1634 or 1635 for "knowing his wife carnally before marriage. Her eldest daughter, Dorcas, married William Hoare and organized her own daughters and a neighboring maidservant into a burglary ring (see preceding).

ROBERT GAMLIN

ROBERT GAMLIN, Sr.,[145] planter, was born about 1585 in England; buried at Concord, Mass., 7 September 1642. He embarked on *William & Francis*, 7 March 1631/2, with two children. His wife had presumably died, for her passage was not recorded. He came to Roxbury and was admitted to the church as member #10. He relocated to Concord and died there.

Robert GAMLIN, Sr. = _____
Thomas BACON = Mary GAMLIN
Joseph BACON = Margaret BOWEN
Henry BACON = Hannah WOODWARD
Jabez HYDE = Hannah BACON
Private Henry HYDE = Thyrina (Therina) WARD

---

[144] Hill, *Western Pilgrims*, 62-3. Anderson, *Great Migration Begins*, v.3 (G-H), 1-4, on line from NEHGS.
[145] Hill, *Western Pilgrims*, 239.

Luther HYDE = Phoebe GIDDINGS
Harvey HYDE = Fidelia Gadcourt POTTER
Benajah Flavel STOCKWELL = Emily Lodiweska (Emma F.) HYDE
George J. HILL = Jessie Fidelia STOCKWELL

JOHN GEORGE

JOHN GEORGE,[146] of Boston, a chimney cleaner and possibly earlier an apprentice in 1641 to Governor John Winthrop, was a founding member of the First Baptist Church at Boston. He was baptized there as an adult, on 28 May 1665. As a result, he was accused of attending a church other than the Puritan church and was arrested. He was harshly treated and died on 12 September 1666, soon after he was released from prison. He married **ELIZABETH _____**, who survived him.

John GEORGE = Elizabeth _____
William MUNROE = Martha GEORGE
John COMEE = Martha MUNROE
Jonas PEIRCE = Abigail COMEE
John PEIRCE = Abigail BEARD
Oliver JACKSON = Mary PEIRCE
Jesse WARREN = Betsy JACKSON
Herbert Marshall WARREN = Eliza Caroline COPP
William Toy SHOEMAKER = Mabel WARREN

ELIZABETH (_____) GEORGE

ELIZABETH _____ was the wife of **JOHN GEORGE**. They had five daughters and one son. He was accused in 1665-6 of "meeting in opposition to the ordinances of Christ" and was imprisoned. He died from his harsh treatment, and she married again, to a **Mr. HARBOUR**. She died sometime after two of her children were baptized as adults, on 15 July 1677 (see preceding).

ISRAEL GIBBS

ISRAEL GIBBS[147] was living in Providence, Providence Co., R.I., in 1747, and in a two-person household in Rhode Island in 1774 (one man, one woman, over the age of 16); supposedly died in 1780. He may have moved to Canterbury, Conn. His wife's name is unknown. He is believed to have had one child.

Israel GIBBS = _____
Josiah GIBBS = Mary _____
Col. Rufus HERRICK = Miss _____ GIBBS, prob. Myra (Mary) GIBBS
Capt. Rufus HERRICK Jr. = Lydia NEWMAN
Rufus HERRICK [III] = Jerusha P. _____ (prob.) PIERCE
William Prince HILL = Sarah P. "Sally" HERRICK
Charles W. HILL = Adelia Catharine "Delia" RILEY
George J. HILL = Jessie Fidelia STOCKWELL

_____ (_____) GIBBS

_____, of whom nothing else is known, married **ISRAEL GIBBS**. They were living in Providence, R.I., in 1747. She had at least one child, and is probably an ancestor of George J. Hill, although the evidence for this is rather weak (see preceding).

---

[146] Hill, *Quakers and Puritans*, 233-5.
[147] Hill, *Western Pilgrims*. The confusing story of the Gibbs family in America is discussed on pp. 80-4.

MERIBAH GIBBS

MERIBAH GIBBS,[148] daughter of John Gibbs of Freudes Hall, Diss, co. Norfolk, and second wife of **JOHN FOLGER**, came to America in 1635 with her husband and their son, Peter, then about 18. They settled first at Watertown, and then at Martha's Vineyard, where she died sometime after her husband died in 1664. She was a great-grandmother of **Benjamin Franklin** and perhaps also an ancestor of William H. Thompson.

GEORGE GIDDINGS

GEORGE GIDDINGS,[149] yeoman, son of John Giddings, husbandman, and his wife Joan Purrier, was baptized at Clapham, Bedfordshire, 24 September 1609; died at Ipswich, Mass., 1 June 1676. He married, at St. Albans, Hertfordshire, 20 February 1633/4, **JANE LAWRENCE**, daughter of Thomas and Joan (Antrobus) Lawrence; born about 1614; died at Ipswich, Mass., 2 March 1680/[?1]. They enrolled at London on the *Planter* for New England on 2 April 1635. Jane Lawrence is of **Royal descent**.

George GIDDINGS = Jane LAWRENCE
Lieut. John GIDDINGS = Sarah ALCOCK
Thomas GIDDINGS = Sarah ANDREWS
Joseph GIDDINGS = Eunice ANDREWS
Benjamin GIDDINGS = Martha SEELEY
Luther HYDE = Phoebe GIDDINGS
Harvey HYDE = Fidelia Gadcourt POTTER
Benajah Flavel STOCKWELL = Emily Lodiweska (Emma F.) HYDE
George J. HILL = Jessie Fidelia STOCKWELL

JONATHAN GILLETT

JONATHAN GILLETT,[150] son of the Rev. William Gyllett of co. Somerset, England, was born say 1609; died at Windsor, Conn., 29 August 1677. He emigrated in 1633, but he returned to England and was married there on 29 March 1634. He was granted four acres at Windsor in 1639. He married **MARY DOLBERE**, daughter of Rawkey and Mary (Michell) Dolbere; baptized 1607; died 5 January 1685.

Jonathan GILLETT = Mary DOLBERE
Joseph GILLETT = Elizabeth HAWKES
Nathaniel GILLETT = Sarah CULVER
Mr. Nathaniel GILLETT Jr. = Mercy SMITH
Lieut. John GILLETT = Abigail HOUGH
Lieut. Joseph GILLETT = Katherine "Catherine" HUNT
Simeon RILEY = Katharine "Catherine" GILLETT
Charles W. HILL = Adelia Catharine "Delia" RILEY
George J. HILL = Jessie Fidelia STOCKWELL

RICHARD GODFREY

RICHARD GODFREY,[151] born perhaps about 1631, or earlier, in England; died, probably at Taunton, Mass., 16 October 1691. He first appeared in Taunton in 1651 in the part of that town called Squawbetty, "near the old forge, now Raynham," and proably had an interest in the iron works there. He married (1), about 1650, **Jane TURNER**, daughter of John and Jane Turner, and granddaughter of JOHN TURNER, born about 1632; died before 9 March 1670/1, with whom he had six children.

---

[148] Hill, *Fundy to Chesapeake*, 43-4. For the question of Hannah ___ (?SCOTT), see discussion on pp. 3-4.

[149] Hill, *Western Pilgrims*, 293-8. Jane Lawrence, with her husband, George Giddings, is in the 19th generation of descent from Alice of Normandy, sister of William I, the Conqueror (Richardson, *Royal Ancestry*, 3:552). She was, like her brother, a child of Robert I of France, and thus a descendant of Charlemagne (Richardson, *RA*, 1:xxv, and 5:481 (Appendix A).

[150] Hill, *Western Pilgrims*, 118-26.

[151] Hill, *Western Pilgrims*, 196-7.

Richard GODFREY = Jane TURNER
Deacon Peter HOLBROOK = Alice GODFREY
Cornet John HOLBROOK = Hannah CHAPIN
Lt. Aaron HOLBROOK =Hannah PARTRIDGE
Ebenezer STOCKWELL = Abi HOLBROOK
Joseph H. STOCKWELL = Anna Maria SAXE
Benajah Flavel STOCKWELL = Emily Lodiweska (Emma F.) HYDE
George J. HILL = Jessie Fidelia STOCKWELL

GOODSPEED

____*GOODSPEED*,[152] perhaps *WILLIAM*, son of James and Alice Goodspeed of Wingrave, Bucks, England, died before 1524-5. His widow *Alice (____) GOODSPEED*, was taxed on goods valued at £3 in the subsidy of 1524-5. They had two children, William, who is an ancestor of Margaret Goodspeed, mother of JOHN PUTNAM, who emigrated to Salem; and Nicholas, who is the ancestor of most of those named Goodspeed in America. *Goodspeed* of Buckinghamshire is an ancestor of three U.S. Presidents: **Gerald R. Ford, Calvin Coolidge,** and **Herbert Hoover**; and of William H. Thompson.

_____ *GOODSPEED = Alice* _____
William GOODSPEED = Anna _____
John GOODSPEED = Elizabeth _____
Nicholas PUTNAM of Stutely = Margaret GOODSPEED
John PUTNAM Sr. = Priscilla GOULD
(see JOHN PUTNAM)

PRISCILLA GOULD

PRISCILLA GOULD,[153] daughter of Richard and Elizabeth (Coleman) Gould of co. Herts, England, was baptized in about 1585; died at Salem Village, 30 December 1662. She was admitted a member of the church at Salem in 1641. She married, at Bovington in 1611, **JOHN PUTNAM**, son of Nicholas and Margaret (Goodspeed) Putnam. They had seven children. She is an ancestor of William H. Thompson.

CHRISTOPHER GRANT

CHRISTOPHER GRANT,[154] a glazier, was born about 1610; died at Watertown, Mass., in September 1685. He came to New England in 1634 and was paid for mending the windows of the meeting house in 1648. Christopher Grant married, in 1633-4, **MARY** _____; died at Watertown, before 25 January 1692.

Christopher GRANT = Mary _____
Daniel SMITH Jr. = Mary GRANT
John PEIRCE = Elizabeth SMITH
Jonas PEIRCE = Abigail COMEE
John PEIRCE =Abigail BEARD
Oliver JACKSON = Mary PEIRCE
Jesse WARREN = Betsy JACKSON
Herbert Marshall WARREN = Eliza Caroline COPP
William Toy SHOEMAKER = Mabel WARREN

MARY (_____) GRANT

MARY ____, married **CHRISTOPHER GRANT** in 1634. She came with him to New England after they were married, perhaps when she was pregnant with the first of her nine children (see preceding).

---

[152] Hill, *Fundy to Chesapeake*, 70.
[153] Hill, *Fundy to Chesapeake*, 72-4.
[154] Hill, *Quakers and Puritans*, 253.

WILLIAM GRANT

WILLIAM GRANT,[155] a shoemaker, was born in say 1795. He was probably born in Inverness, Scotland, and he probably came to Nova Scotia when he was young. He married, at St. Margaret's Anglican Church, Halifax, 3 April 1819, **Margaret BOYD**, daughter of ERROLL BOYD and his wife JEAN WILSON. His cousin James Grant, son of his uncle Alexander Grant, married Mary Jane Archibald, daughter of John Archibald, a descendant of ROBERT ARCHIBALD.

William GRANT = Margaret BOYD
James Everett THOMPSON = Jane GRANT
William Henry "Will" THOMPSON = Sarah D. "Sadie" RUNDALL

ANDREW GREELEY

ANDREW GREELEY[156] was an early settler in Salisbury, Mass. He was born, probably in England, in about 1617, he died in Salisbury, 30 June 1697. He first appears in the town records in "16-9-1640" in connection with a planting lot lying near the mill, known as Greely's Mill. He was very active in town affairs, and later in Haverhill, Mass. In 1642, he married **Mary MOYSE**, daughter of JOSEPH MOYSE and his wife HANNAH, probably at Salisbury, Mass.; she died at Salisbury, 24 December 1703.

Andrew GREELEY, Sr. = Mary MOYSE
Andrew GREELEY, Jr. = Sarah BROWN
John SINGLETARY = Mary GREELEY
Ebenezer STOCKWELL = Mary SINGLETARY
Benajah STOCKWELL = Hannah GALE
Ebenezer STOCKWELL = Abi HOLBROOK
Joseph H. STOCKWELL = Anna Maria SAXE
Benajah Flavel STOCKWELL = Emily Lodiweska (Emma F.) HYDE
George J. HILL = Jessie Fidelia STOCKWELL

THOMAS GREENWOOD

THOMAS GREENWOOD, Esq.,[157] weaver, son of Thomas Greenwood of Heptonstall, co. York, was born in England, probably near the ancient family estate, Greenwood Lee, in about 1643; died at Newton, Mass., 1 September 1693. He came first to Boston, Mass., in 1665. He then removed to Cambridge Village, now Newton, by 1667. He was elected constable in 1679, and he was probably also the first town clerk. He left a large estate. He married (1), at Newton, 8 July 1670, **Hannah WARD**, daughter of Ensign John and Hannah (Jackson) Ward, of Newton, and granddaughter of Deacon WILLIAM WARD; born at Newton, about 1651; died before 1687.

Thomas GREENWOOD = Hannah WARD
John GREENWOOD, Esq. = Hannah TROWBRIDGE
Isaac JACKSON = Ruth GREENWOOD
Sgt. Josiah JACKSON = Mary DARBY
Oliver JACKSON = Mary PEIRCE
Jesse WARREN = Betsy JACKSON
Herbert Marshall WARREN = Eliza Caroline COPP
William Toy SHOEMAKER = Mabel WARREN

WILLIAM GREGG

WILLIAM GREGG, Jr.,[158] son of William Gregg, Sr., was born in about 1642 at Glenorchy, Argyllshire, Scotland, or Glenarm Barony, co. Antrim, Ireland; died 1 September 1687 at Christiana

---

[155] Hill, *Fundy to Chesapeake*, 108.
[156] Hill, *Western Pilgrims*, 188-90.
[157] Hill, *Quakers and Puritans*, 219-27.
[158] Hill, *Fundy to Chesapeake*, 337.

Hundred, New Castle Co., Pa. (now Delaware). He is said to have come to America in the ship *Caledonia* with William Hoge sometime after 1682. He built a log cabin on Stand Milas (aka Strand Millas) in 1684. He married, at Antrim Meeting, co. Antrim, Ireland, 11 mo. 5, 1702, **ANN WILKINSON**, of Antrim, born say 1646, in Ireland; died at Christiana Hundred, New Castle Co., Pa. (now Delaware), in January 1692.

William GREGG, Jr. = Ann WILKINSON
William DIXON = Ann GREGG
William DIXON the Younger = Hannah HOLLINGSWORTH
Jacob DIXON = Esther PHILLIPS
James WALTER = Sarah DIXON (prob. daughter of Jacob Dixon)
William WALTER = Phebe MERCER
William H. MANLY = Sarah D. WALTER
Silas William RUNDALL = Rachel MANLY
William Henry "Will" THOMPSON = Sarah D. "Sadie" RUNDALL

ROBERT HALE

Deacon **ROBERT HALE**,[159] probably born in England about 1607; died 16, 5th mo. 1659, Charlestown, Mass.; came in the Winthrop Fleet, 1630; member of Ancient and Honorable Artillery Company, 1644; married **JOANNA** _____ [sometimes said to be Cutter]. His son, Rev. John Hale, was an interrogator in the early days of the Salem witchcraft delusion. He is an ancestor of the Patriot **Nathan Hale**.

Deacon Robert HALE = Joanna _____ (?CUTLER or CUTTER)
John LARKIN = Joanna HALE
Capt. John THORNDIKE = Joanna LARKIN
James THORNDIKE = Anna OBER
Simeon MOORS = Joanna THORNDIKE
Jeduthan WARREN = Joanna MOORS
Jesse WARREN = Betsy JACKSON
Herbert Marshall WARREN = Eliza Caroline COPP
William Toy SHOEMAKER = Mabel WARREN

JOANNA (_____ [?CUTLER]) HALE

JOANNA ____, whose maiden name may have been Cutler or Cutter, married **Deacon ROBERT HALE** and came with him to America in 1630. She was admitted to the Boston church as a founding member in that year. She had five children with him, all born in Massachusetts. After he died she married (2) **Richard JACOB** of Ipswich, who she also survived. She died in 1681 (see preceding).

[JOHN HALLOCK]

[**JOHN HALLOCK**,[160] who married **Abigail** ____, was the father of Catherine Hallock. She is said in hundreds of Ancestry.com websites to have married Thomas Willits and had a daughter, Catherine Martha Willet, who married, in 1701, John[3] Townsend. I believe this is incorrect (see discussion).]

THOMAS HALSEY

THOMAS HALSEY,[161] son of Robert and Dorothy (Downes) Halsey, was baptized at Great Gaddesden, co. Herts, 2 January 1592; died at Southampton, Long Island, 27 August 1678. He married (1) **ELIZABETH WHEELER**, born about 1604 in Cranfield, Bedford, England; murdered by Indians in Southampton, L.I., in 1649. They had six children. He married (2) **Mrs. Ann JONES**, without issue.

Thomas HALSEY = Elizabeth "Phoebe" WHEELER
Richard HOWELL = Elizabeth HALSEY

---

[159] Hill, *Quakers and Puritans*, 169.
[160] Hill, *Fundy to Chesapeake*, 313-7; and Appendix, 541-2, for discussion of the Townsend-Willet question.
[161] Hill, *Western Pilgrims*, 150.

Richard HOWELL = Sarah SCOTT
Edward HOWELL = Abigail SANFORD
Samuel PRINCE = Abigail HOWELL
Edward Howell PRINCE = Huldah OVIATT
Ephraim HILL = Charlotte PRINCE
William Prince HILL = Sarah P. "Sally" HERRICK
Charles W. HILL = Adelia Catherine RILEY
George J. HILL = Jessie Fidelia STOCKWELL

[RICHARD HARCOURT]

[**RICHARD HARCOURT**,[162] who married **Elizabeth POTTER**, was the father of Susanna Harcourt, born at Oyster Bay, L.I., in 1692. She was thought to have married, in 1670, John Townsend, son of John and Elizabeth (Montgomery) Townsend. Instead, it has been found that she married his cousin, James[3] (James[2], John[1]) Townsend. She is not an ancestor of Sarah D. Rundall (see JOHN TOWNSEND).]

SAMUEL HARDY

SAMUEL HARDY,[163] of Greenwich, Conn., married (1) **Rebecca HOBBY**, daughter of JOHN HOBBY; and (2), on 12 May 1692, **REBECCA FURBURST**. Their daughter Hannah Hardy, born 6 July 1693, married Samuel Rundle, and is an ancestor of Sarah D. Rundall. The genealogy of the Hardy family was inadvertently omitted from *Fundy to Chesapeake*.

Samuel HARDY = Rebecca FURBURST
Samuel RUNDLE Sr. = Hannah HARDY
Reuben RUNDLE Sr. = Amy HOBBY
Shadrack RUNDALL Sr. = Phebe BROWN
Reuben John RUNDALL = Martha TOMPKINS
Silas William RUNDALL = Rachel MANLY
William Henry "Will" THOMPSON = Sarah D. "Sadie" RUNDALL

MARGARET HARVEY

MARGARET HARVEY,[164] daughter of James Harvey of Ilkeson, Derbyshire, married (1), by 1633, **WILLIAM WILCOCKSON (aka WILCOX)**. They had nine children. She married (2) **William HAYDEN**, and was a patient of John Winthrop, Jr., in 1657. She is an ancestor of George J. Hill.

AGNES HATHORNTHWAITE

AGNES HATHORNTHWAITE,[165] presumably the daughter of William Hawthornthwaite of Swarthmore, Lancashire, was born about 1633-43; died at her home on the Neshaminy Creek, Middletown Twp., Bucks Co., Pa., 8mo. 20, 1684. Agnes came with her husband and their children to America in 1682 in the *Lamb*. She married, 3mo. 1, 1664, **THOMAS CROASDALE**, perhaps born at Waddington, Yorkshire, 20 May 1644; died at Nishaminy Creek, Bucks Co., Pa., 2 November 1684. Their daughter Alice Crosdale married DAVID POTTS and is an ancestor of William T. Shoemaker.

EDWARD HAWTEN

EDWARD HAWTEN,[166] son of Edward and Elizabeth (Pierson) Hawten, of The Ley, co. Oxford, was born about 1525 in Swalcliffe, Epwell, co. Oxford; died at The Ley, before 14 October 1594. He married,

---

[162] Hill, *Fundy to Chesapeake*, Appendix, 534-6.
[163] Hill, *Fundy to Chesapeake*, 120, 145, 623.
[164] Hill, *Western Pilgrims*, 24, calls her Margaret (___) HARVEY, and little more. Her full name appears in *Great Migration* 7:396-401 (WILLIAM WILCOCKSON) as MARGARET HARVEY, along with other information.
[165] Hill, *Quakers and Puritans*, 82-3.
[166] Hill, *Western Pilgrims*, 155-6.

about 1550, *Margery CROKER*, daughter of John Croker, Esq., and his wife Isabell Skinner; probably born at Hook Norton, co. Oxford, after 14 October 1594. In about 1556 she was accused of adultery and conspiracy to murder her husband, but the Star Chamber concluded that the principal witness lied. She was of **Royal Descent**, from Ralph de Arundel, father-in-law of Bartholomew Collinridge (q.v.) They are ancestors of the immigrant, Edward Howell.

Edward HAWTEN = *Margery CROKER*

Henry HOWELL = *Margaret HAWTEN*

Mr. Edward HOWELL, Lord of the Manor of Westbury = *Frances PAXTON*

(See EDWARD HOWELL)

MARY HAYES

MARY HAYES, [167] sister of Johnathan Hayes of Cheshire, England, died in Pennsylvania on 4-11-1728. Her brother came to Pennsylvania, where he was a Justice and Assemblyman. She married (1), in about 1663, **ROBERT TAYLOR**, yeoman, of Clatterwick, Cheshire, England, son of Thomas and Mary (Barrow) Taylor; born at Great Budworth, co. Cheshire; baptized there, 12-15-1633; died at Springfield, Chester Co., Pa., in about 1695. Robert and Mary (Hayes) Taylor had nine children who were born at Great Budworth between 1665 and 1681; a tenth child was born in Pennsylvania. She came with her children on the *Endeavor* in 1683. Two of the children are ancestors of Sarah D. Rundall. Mary (Hayes) Taylor married (2) **Joseph SELBY**, without further issue (see ROBERT TAYLOR).

[HAYWARD]

[Several men and women with the surname Hayward are shown in Part I of *Western Pilgrims*. In the Holbrook family, there are Susannah, Mary, and Jonathan Hayward, and his son William. In the family of Abraham Hill there is Hannah Hayward. None are ancestors of George J. Hill, the Iowa Pioneer.[168]]

MARY HEATH

MARY HEATH,[169] daughter of William Heath, was baptized at Ware, Herts, England, 24 March 1593/4; buried there, 15 May 1629. She married there, 21 September 1613, as his first wife, **Capt. JOHN JOHNSON**, born about 1590; died at Roxbury, Mass., 30 September 1659. He immigrated in 1630 to New England and settled at Roxbury, Mass. Mary Heath and John Johnson had ten children. Their son Isaac died in the Great Swamp Fight. She is an ancestor of Jessie F. Stockwell.

ROBERT HEATON

ROBERT HEATON,[170] yeoman, perhaps son of Richard and Hester (Pearson) Heaton, was born at Settle, co. York, 2 June 1637; died in Bucks Co., Pa., on 10 July 1717. He married **ALICE ___** and came to America in 1682 on *The Lamb*. Robert Heaton Sr. owned a large tract of land on Neshaminy Creek.

Robert HEATON Sr. = Alice _____

Henry COMLY Jr. = Agnes HEATON

Robert COMLY = Jane CADWALADER

Robert COMLY, Jr. = Sarah JONES

Ezra COMLY = Hannah IREDELL

Charles SHOEMAKER = Rachel COMLY

Julien SHOEMAKER = Hannah Ann HESTER

William Toy SHOEMAKER = Mabel WARREN

---

[167] Hill, *Fundy to Chesapeake*, 302-3.

[168] Hill, *Western Pilgrims*, 196-7, 325.

[169] Hill, *Western Pilgrims*, 246-7.

[170] Hill, *Quakers and Puritans*, 114-5.

ALICE (_____) HEATON

ALICE _____, a Quaker, came with her husband **ROBERT HEATON** and children to Pennsylvania on *The Lamb* in 1682. She was born in about 1645; died in Bucks Co., Pa., in 1727 (see preceding).

JAMES HEDGE

JAMES HEDGE,[171] of East Barholt, co. Suffolk, England; died after 13 February 1533/4. He married *Elizabeth _____*, who died after March 1566/7. They are the grandparents of Elizabeth Hedge, who married the Rev. Richard Ravens. Their daughter, GRACE RAVENS, emigrated to America and was, by her first husband, John Sherman, an ancestor of **Roger Sherman, Signer of the Declaration of Independence**. By her second husband, THOMAS ROGERS, she is an ancestor of Mabel Warren.

James HEDGE = Elizabeth _____
Nicholas HEDGE = Alice BURROUGH
Rev. Richard RAVENS = Elizabeth HEDGE
Thomas ROGERS = Grace RAVENS
(see THOMAS ROGERS and GRACE RAVENS)

PATRICK HENDERSON

Dr. PATRICK HENDERSON,[172] born say 1650 in Antrim, Ireland; died 17 August 1702 in Kennett, Chester Co., Pennsylvania. He married, in 1676, in Ireland, **KATHERINE _____**; born in Ireland; died in Pennsylvania. He was called "Doctor," meaning an eminent teacher, but probably not a physician. Their child, Margaret Henderson, married Gayen Miller and may be an ancestor of Sarah D. Rundall.

Dr. Patrick HENDERSON = Katherine _____
Gayen MILLER = Margaret HENDERSON
James MILLER = Rachel FRED
John JACKSON Sr. = Sarah MILLER
John JACKSON Jr. = Susanna JACKSON [not a relative]
William MANLY = Rachel JACKSON (prob. daughter of John Jackson, Jr.)
William H. MANLY = Sarah D. WALTER
Silas William RUNDALL = Rachel MANLY
William Henry "Will" THOMPSON = Sarah D. "Sadie" RUNDALL

KATHERINE (_____) HENDERSON

KATHERINE _____, wife of **Dr. PATRICK HENDERSON**, died in Pennsylvania. (see preceding).

SARAH HENDRICHS

SARAH HENDRICHS[173] is presumed to be the maiden name of Sarah Shoemaker, who married *GEORGE SHOEMAKER* in say 1662, in Kriegsheim, Rhineland Palitanate (now Germany). He died on the passage to America in 1685, but she landed in Pennsylvania with her children and was the matriarch of a successful family. She was born in about 1641 and died after 1708. Known in America as "Sarah Shoemaker," she is the ancestor of Dr. William T. Shoemaker.

ISAIAH HENDRYX

Sergeant ISAIAH J. HENDRYX,[174] who may have been the son of William and Eunice (Thorp) Hendryx, was born at Redding, Conn., 1 December 1756; died at Troy, N.Y., 30 November 1835. He participated in the ill-fated invasion of Quebec, and was at Fort Ticonderoga, White Plains, and

[171] Hill, *Quakers and Puritans*, 257-8.
[172] Hill, *Fundy to Chesapeake*, 273. This line assumes that Rachel Jackson is the daughter of John Jackson, Jr.
[173] Hill, *Quakers and Puritans*, 6.
[174] Hill, *Western Pilgrims*, 12.

Bennington. He married **Esther JACKSON**, daughter of Michael and Susannah (Wilcox) Jackson, and granddaughter of JOSEPH JACKSON. She was born 23 May 1758 and died sometime after 1 July 1837, after receiving a widow's pension for a Revolutionary War soldier.

William HENDRYX = Eunice THORP
Sergeant Isaiah J. HENDRYX (perhaps son of William) = Esther JACKSON
Josiah (Isaiah) RILEY = Susannah HENDRYX
Simeon RILEY = Katharine "Catherine" GILLETT
Charles W. HILL = Adelia Catharine "Delia" RILEY
George J. HILL = Jessie Fidelia STOCKWELL

HENRY HERRICK

HENRY HERRICK[175] was born in England, probably about 1598, perhaps in Leicestershire; died in Essex County, Mass., probably in Salem, between 24 November 1670 and 28 March 1671. For many years Henry Herrick of Salem was believed to be the son of Sir William and Lady Joan (May) Herrick, but Henry Herrick of Salem was a different man. He may have come on the *Lyon* in 1629, but the first certain reference to Henry Herrick of Salem appears on 19 October 1630, when he requested admittance as a freeman of Salem. He married, in about 1636, **Editha LASKIN**, daughter of HUGH LASKIN and his wife ALICE, in Salem; born in England, 1612; died in Essex County, Mass., 23 November 1672.

Henry HERRICK = Editha LASKIN
Ephraim "of Beverly" HERRICK = Mary CROSS(E)
Lieutenant Stephen HERRICK = Elizabeth TRASK
Edward HERRICK = Mary DENNISON
Col. Rufus HERRICK = Miss _____ GIBBS, prob. Myra (Mary) GIBBS
Capt. Rufus HERRICK Jr. = Lydia NEWMAN
Rufus HERRICK [III] = Jerusha P. _____ (prob.) PIERCE
William Prince HILL = Sarah P. "Sally" HERRICK
Charles W. HILL = Adelia Catharine "Delia" RILEY
George J. HILL = Jessie Fidelia STOCKWELL

JACOB HESTER

JACOB HESTER[176] was a prominent citizen of Trenton, New Jersey, in the first half of the nineteenth century; he died at Trenton, 9 September 1841. He came to America after the Revolutionary War, arriving in 1786. He was born in 1770 in what is now the republic of Germany, perhaps in Hesse-Kassel. He was the owner of Lamb's Tavern, and was a vestryman at St. Michael's Church. He married, at Trenton, N.J., 28 April 1790, **Mary DIPPOLT**, probably daughter of JOHN GEORGE DIPPOLT.

Jacob HESTER = Mary DIPPOLT
John Dippolt HESTER = Rhoda "Rhody" KNOWLES
Julien SHOEMAKER = Hannah Ann HESTER
William Toy SHOEMAKER = Mabel WARREN

ABRAHAM HILL

ABRAHAM HILL, Sr.,[177] was born in England in about 1615; died at Charlestown, Mass., 1 February 1669/70. He arrived in Charlestown in about 1636 and was admitted as a freeman there in 1640. He was a tavern keeper in Malden in 1657. He married, in about 1640, **Sarah LONG**, daughter of ROBERT LONG and Sarah Taylor; born in England, 13 October 1616; died in Massachusetts after 1656/7.

Abraham HILL Sr. = Sarah LONG
William EAGER = Ruth HILL
Abraham EAGER = Lydia WOODS

---

[175] Hill, *Western Pilgrims*, 45-8.
[176] Hill, *Quakers and Puritans*, 23.
[177] Hill, *Western Pilgrims*, 325.

Jabez WARD = Phebe EAGER
Corporal Jabez WARD = Jemima ALLEN
Private Henry HYDE = Thyrina (Therina) WARD
Luther HYDE = Phoebe GIDDINGS
Harvey HYDE = Fidelia Gadcourt POTTER
Benajah Flavel STOCKWELL = Emily Lodiweska (Emma F.) HYDE
George J. HILL = Jessie Fidelia STOCKWELL

LUKE HILL

LUKE HILL, Sr.,[178] a ferryman, was probably born in England in about 1613; died between 9 May 1695 and the end of the year 1696, probably in Simsbury, Hartford Co. He married, in Windsor, Hartford Co., Conn., 6 May 1651, **MART HOUT**, whose origin is unknown. She was probably born no later than 1634. They had two sons and five daughters. Two sons of Luke Hill are ancestors of the parents of George J. Hill of Wright County, Iowa; one is agnate, and the other is cognate, through female lines to his mother.

Luke HILL, Sr. = Mary HOUT

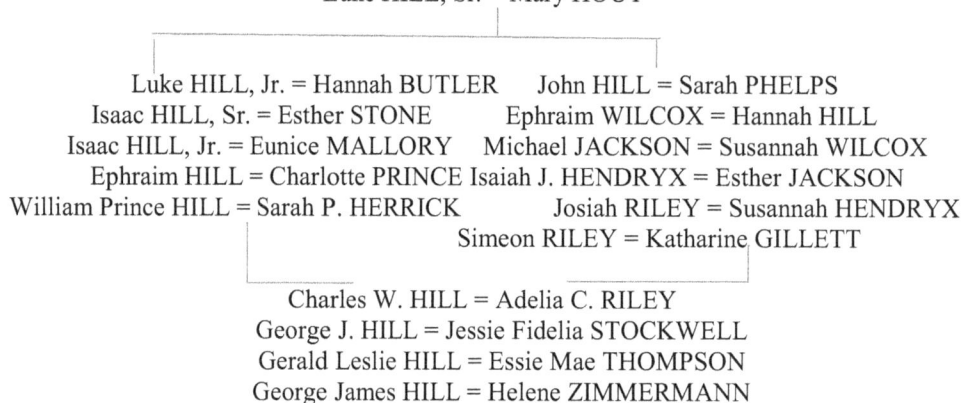

Luke HILL, Jr. = Hannah BUTLER   John HILL = Sarah PHELPS
Isaac HILL, Sr. = Esther STONE   Ephraim WILCOX = Hannah HILL
Isaac HILL, Jr. = Eunice MALLORY   Michael JACKSON = Susannah WILCOX
Ephraim HILL = Charlotte PRINCE   Isaiah J. HENDRYX = Esther JACKSON
William Prince HILL = Sarah P. HERRICK   Josiah RILEY = Susannah HENDRYX
Simeon RILEY = Katharine GILLETT

Charles W. HILL = Adelia C. RILEY
George J. HILL = Jessie Fidelia STOCKWELL
Gerald Leslie HILL = Essie Mae THOMPSON
George James HILL = Helene ZIMMERMANN

THOMAS HINE

THOMAS HINE[179] was born in 1638; died at Milford, Conn., in 1698. His son John married, as her second husband Mary (Fenn) Lane. Further study of the Hine and Fenn families remains to be completed.

Thomas HINE = _____
John HINE = Mary FENN, widow of ____ LANE
John OVIATT = Susanna HINE
John OVIATT = Abigail SMITH
Edward Howell PRINCE = Huldah OVIATT
Ephraim HILL = Charlotte PRINCE
William Prince HILL = Sarah P. "Sally" HERRICK
Charles W. HILL = Adelia Catherine RILEY
George J. HILL = Jessie Fidelia STOCKWELL

JOHN HOBBY

JOHN HOBBY,[180] born about 1632, probably in England; died in Greenwich, Fairfield Co., Conn., in May 1707. He first appeared in the records of New England on 11 October 1659, when he gave testimony before the Magistrate's Court in New Haven. He was one of the original patentees of

---

[178] Hill, *Hill: The Ferry Keeper's Family*, 1-8; Hill, *Western Pilgrims*, 1-4. Many communications have been received which support the conclusions in these books. Furthermore, in recent years, I have found a Y-DNA in common with a previously unknown male cousin, who is believed to be a descendant of another one of Luke Hill's sons; this is reassuring to both of us, for we are thus likely to be descendants of the immigrant, Luke Hill, Sr.

[179] Hill, *Western Pilgrims*, 140.

[180] Hill, *Fundy to Chesapeake*, 145.

Greenwich in May 1665. He married in about 1655 and had ten children with a wife whose name is unknown.

John HOBBY = _____ _____
Jonathan HOBBY Sr. = Sarah MEAD
Jonathan HOBBY Jr. = Deborah LYON
Reuben RUNDLE Sr. = Amy HOBBY
Shadrack RUNDALL Sr. = Phebe BROWN
Reuben John RUNDALL = Martha TOMPKINS
Silas William RUNDALL = Rachel MANLY
William Henry "Will" THOMPSON = Sarah D. "Sadie" RUNDALL

_____ (_____) HOBBY

_____ _____ was the wife of **JOHN HOBBY**, immigrant to America, probably from England. He was born about 1632, and she was probably born a year or two later. They were married in about 1655 and she had the first of their ten children before they emigrated in about 1659 (see preceding).

JOHN HODGES

Captain **JOHN HODGES**,[181] of Wapping, Middlesex, England, was born by about 1610, or earlier; died between 10 October 1654 and 3 January 1654/5, when his widow **MARY MILLER** remarried. He was a mariner who arrived in Charlestown by 1633, and was captain of the *Rebecca*. He is probably the father of Mary Hodges, who married ROBERT TAYLOR of Newport.

Capt. John HODGES = Mary MILLER
Robert TAYLOR = Mary HODGES (prob. dau. of Capt. John Hodges)
John TAYLOR = Abigail _____
Jonathan IRISH = Mary TAYLOR
Jesse IRISH = Mary ALLEBEE
William IRISH = Dolly _____
Capt. Freeborn POTTER = Dolly IRISH
Harvey HYDE = Fidelia Gadcourt POTTER
Benajah Flavel STOCKWELL = Emily Lodiweska (Emma F.) HYDE
George J. HILL = Jessie Fidelia STOCKWELL

THOMAS HOLBROOK

THOMAS HOLBROOK,[182] possibly the son of William Holbrook, was born about 1589, probably in Glastonbury, co. Somerset, England; died presumably in Massachusetts, probably in Weymouth, between 31 December 1673 (date of codicil to his will) and 20 March 1676/7 (date of inventory). Thomas Holbrook was enrolled at age 34 as a passenger for New England on the *Marygould* from Weymouth, on 20 March 1634/5, with his wife, **JANE POWYS**. In 1651, he had a Great Lot at Weymouth. Their eldest son, Capt. John Holbrook, is an ancestor of **President James A. Garfield.**

Thomas HOLBROOK = Jane POWYS
Thomas HOLBROOK [II] = Joan KINGMAN
Deacon Peter HOLBROOK = Alice GODFREY
Cornet John HOLBROOK = Hannah CHAPIN
Lt. Aaron HOLBROOK = Hannah PARTRIDGE
Ebenezer STOCKWELL = Abi HOLBROOK
Joseph H. STOCKWELL = Anna Maria SAXE
Benajah Flavel STOCKWELL = Emily Lodiweska (Emma F.) HYDE
George J. HILL = Jessie Fidelia STOCKWELL

---

[181] Hill, *Western Pilgrims*, 359-60. The Ahnentafel of *Western Pilgrims*, xxvi, shows John TAYLOR = Abigail HODGES. This is erroneous. Abigail's surname is unknown, as shown in the text on p.360.
[182] Hill, *Western Pilgrims*, 194.

VALENTINE HOLLINGSWORTH

VALENTINE HOLLINGSWORTH,[183] son of Henry and Catharine Hollingsworth, was born at Belleniskcrannell, co. Armagh, Ireland, in August 1632; died at Newark, New Castle Co., Del. He was married in 1655 to **Ann REE**, also of co. Armagh. They had four children, born between 1656 and 1663. Ann (Ree) Hollingsworth died in 1671, and while their children were still very young, he began to have problems as a Quaker. He married again in 1672, to **Ann CALVERT**, daughter of Thomas Calvert, of co. Armagh. They were probably members of the Calvert family that included the Lords Baltimore and Proprietors of Maryland. Valentine Hollingsworth came to the Delaware in the *Antelope*, which arrived at the Delaware on 9-10 December 1682. He was accompanied by his second wife, Ann née Calvert.

Valentine HOLLINGSWORTH = Ann REE
Thomas HOLLINGSWORTH = Grace COOK
William DIXON the Younger = Hannah HOLLINGSWORTH
Jacob DIXON = Esther PHILLIPS
James WALTER = Sarah DIXON (prob. daughter of Jacob Dixon)
William WALTER = Phebe MERCER
William H. MANLY = Sarah D. WALTER
Silas William RUNDALL = Rachel MANLY
William Henry "Will" THOMPSON = Sarah D. "Sadie" RUNDALL

OBADIAH HOLMES

Rev. OBADIAH HOLMES,[184] son of Robert and Katherine (Johnson) Hulme, was born, probably in Reddish, co. Lancaster, England, and was baptized at Didsbury, 18 March 1609/10; died at Newport, R.I., 15 October 1682. He learned to be a glassmaker before he came to America in 1638. He was constable of Salem in 1642, and he then became a Baptist and went to Newport, R.I. He was whipped for preaching without permission in Boston, and he was an early property owner in New Jersey. He married, in Manchester, co. Lancaster, 20 November 1630, **KATHERINE HYDE**, who died after 1682.

Rev. Obadiah HOLMES = Katherine HYDE
Captain Jonathan HOLMES = Sarah BORDEN
Phillip TILLINGHAST, J.P. = Martha HOLMES
William POTTER = Martha TILLINGHAST
Capt. Oliver POTTER = Mary COLVIN
Capt. Freeborn POTTER = Dolly IRISH
Harvey HYDE = Fidelia Gadcourt POTTER
Benajah Flavel STOCKWELL = Emily Lodiweska HYDE
George J. HILL = Jessie Fidelia STOCKWELL

ALICE HONOR

ALICE HONOR,[185] daughter of Ambrose Honor of Blewberry, Berks, England, died at Hull, Mass., in 1668. She married, as his first wife, at Watertown, Mass., in May 1637, **Elder JOHN PRINCE**; born at Oxford, England, in 1610; died at Hull, Mass., 16 August 1676. Her husband studied at Oxford, but did not receive a degree because he was a dissenter. She is an ancestor of George J. Hill, the Iowa Pioneer.

SARAH HORTON

SARAH HORTON,[186] daughter of Thomas and Catherine (Satchfield) Horton; died between November 1660 and 1 March 1677. She married, at St. Ann's Blackfriars, London, England, 11 November 1618,

[183] Hill, *Fundy to Chesapeake*, 339-40.
[184] Hill, *Western Pilgrims*, 277-8. At the time *Western Pilgrims* was published, I noted that this genealogy depends on the likely assumption that Oliver Potter is the son of William and Mary (Tillinghast) Potter. Since then, this has been confirmed by research conducted for me by the New England Historic Genealogical Society.
[185] Hill, *Western Pilgrims*, 130.
[186] Hill, *Quakers and Puritans*, 246.

ROGER CONANT, son of Richard and Agnes (Clarke) Conant, who was baptized at East Budleigh, co. Devon, 9 April 1592; died at Beverly, Mass., 19 November 1679. He became Governor of the Beverly Colony in what is now Massachusetts. They had ten children. She is an ancestor of Mabel Warren.

ABIGAIL HOUGH

ABIGAIL HOUGH,[187] whose ancestry has not yet been traced, was of Canaan, Conn., when she was married, at Salisbury, Conn., 17 November 1754, **Lieut. John GILLETT**, son of Nathaniel and Mercy (Smith) Gillett, and great-great-grandson of JONATHAN GILLETT; born at Litchfield, Conn., 19 February 1733; died after 1800 in Canaan, Columbia Co., or Steuben Co., N.Y. He was a soldier in the French and Indian War, and the Revolutionary War. She is an ancestor of George J. Hill.

MARY HOUT

MARY HOUT,[188] whose ancestry is unknown, married, in Windsor, Conn., 6 May 1651, **LUKE HILL**, a ferryman of the town. She was probably born between 1623 and 1634. Her surname is a common Dutch family name. Her husband died in 1696, and she lived for several years thereafter. Two of her sons, Luke and John, are ancestors of George J. Hill, the Iowa Pioneer.

JOHN HOW

JOHN HOW,[189] of Littleham by Exmouth, co. Devon, England, married *Mary DIDO*, 11 September 1741. They had two children, baptized at Littleham by Exmouth.
John HOW = Mary DIDO
John THORN(E)= Mary HOW
Josiah COPP Sr. = Elizabeth (Betty or Bettey) THORN
James John COPP = Caroline BIGWOOD
Herbert Marshall WARREN = Eliza Caroline COPP
Dr. William Toy SHOEMAKER =Mabel WARREN

NATHANIEL HOWARD

NATHANIEL HOWARD,[190] born 1642 or 1643 and died at Chelmsford, Mass., 24 January 1709/10. It is likely that he was the son of Nathaniel Howard, who was at Dorchester, Mass., by 1641, and was a member of the Ancient and Honorable Artillery Company. He married (1) 2 July 1666, at Charlestown, Mass., **Sarah WILLARD**, daughter of Major SIMON WILLARD and MARY SHARPE; born 1642; died 22 January 1677/8. He married (2) **Sarah PARKER**, daughter of JACOB PARKER.
Nathaniel HOWARD = Sarah WILLARD
Benjamin PARKER = Sarah HOWARD
Joseph WARREN Jr. = Tabitha PARKER
Capt. Joseph WARREN = Joanna FLETCHER
Jeduthan WARREN = Joanna MOORS
Jesse WARREN = Betsy JACKSON
Herbert Marshall WARREN = Eliza Caroline COPP
William Toy SHOEMAKER = Mabel WARREN

EDWARD HOWELL

Mr. EDWARD HOWELL,[191] Lord of the Manor of Marsh Gibbon, co. Bucks, was son of Henry and Margaret (Hawten) Howell. The Hawtens and their ancestors are descendants of **Royalty**. He was

---

[187] Hill, *Western Pilgrims*, 123.
[188] Hill, *Western Pilgrims*, 3. Her name has often been written, incorrectly, as "Mary Hoyt."
[189] Hill, *Quakers and Puritans*, 195.
[190] Hill, *Quakers and Puritans*, 176-7.
[191] Hill, *Western Pilgrims*, 147ff.

baptized 26 July 1584; died at Southampton, Long Island, N.Y., October 1655. He took the oath as a freeman in Boston in 1638. He led a group from Lynn, Mass., who settled on Long Island. His first wife, *Frances PAXTON*, died in England in 1630. He came to America with his second wife.

Mr. Edward HOWELL = *Frances PAXTON*
Richard HOWELL = Elizabeth HALSEY
Richard HOWELL = Sarah SCOTT
Edward HOWELL = Abigail SANFORD
Samuel PRINCE = Abigail HOWELL
Edward Howell PRINCE = Huldah OVIATT
Ephraim HILL = Charlotte PRINCE
William Prince HILL = Sarah P. "Sally" HERRICK
Charles W. HILL = Adelia Catherine RILEY
George J. HILL = Jessie Fidelia STOCKWELL

SIMON HOYT

SIMON HOYT[192] was born about 1593, probably in West Hatch, Somersetshire, England; died in Stamford, Conn., 1 September 1657. His first wife died in about 1625. He emigrated in 1629 with three surviving sons. After he arrived in America, he married (2) **SUSANNAH** ____, and had seven more children. He appeared in Charlestown in 1629. By 1633 he removed to Dorchester.

Simon HOYT = Susannah _____ (sometimes said to be SMITH)
Thomas LYON, Sr. = Mary HOYT
Thomas LYON, Jr. = Abigail OGDEN
Jonathan HOBBY Jr. = Deborah LYON
Reuben RUNDLE Sr. = Amy HOBBY
Shadrack RUNDALL Sr. = Phebe BROWN
Reuben John RUNDALL = Martha TOMPKINS
Silas William RUNDALL = Rachel MANLY
William Henry "Will" THOMPSON = Sarah D. "Sadie" RUNDALL

SUSANNAH (_____) HOYT

SUSANNAH _____ married, in America, as his second wife, **SIMON HOYT**. She married (2) **Robert BATES**, and died at Stamford. Her estate was distributed on 1, 12mo 1675/5. (see preceding).

AARON HUNT

AARON HUNT[193] was born 7 April 1745 in Wyoming, Wyoming Co., N.Y. died there after 1778. In 1767, he married **KATHERINE JOHNSON**, born 12 April 1751 in Wyoming, N.Y.; died after 1778.

Aaron HUNT = Katherine JOHNSON
Joseph GILLETT = Katherine "Catherine" HUNT
Simeon RILEY = Katharine "Catherine" GILLETT
Charles W. HILL = Adelia Catharine "Delia" RILEY
George J. HILL = Jessie Fidelia STOCKWELL

ROBERT HUSTED

ROBERT HUSTED (aka HUESTIS)[194] was born about 1595, probably in Dorsetshire, England; died at Stamford, Conn., in 1654. He came to America in 1635 on the *Marygould*. His first residence in America was in Boston and he settled for a time at Mount Wollaston, Mass. He married (1) at Bridport, Dorsetshire, 6 April 1616, **Anne MOON**, who died in January 1621/2. They had three children. He married (2), in England, in 1622-1623, **ELIZABETH** ___, who died in 1654. They had three children.

---

[192] Hill, *Fundy to Chesapeake*, 161-2.
[193] Hill, *Western Pilgrims*, 124.
[194] Hill, *Fundy to Chesapeake*, 205-6; Jacobus proposed Angel HUSTED to be the father-in-law of Edward JESSUP.

Robert HUSTED (aka HUESTIS) = Elizabeth _____
Angel HUSTED = _____
Edward JESSUP = [possible unnamed daughter] HUSTED
Jonathan JESSUP = Sarah _____
David BROWN = Deborah JESSUP
Shadrack RUNDALL Sr. = Phebe BROWN
Reuben John RUNDALL = Martha TOMPKINS
Silas William RUNDALL = Rachel MANLY
William Henry "Will" THOMPSON = Sarah D. "Sadie" RUNDALL

ELIZABETH (_____) HUSTED

ELIZABETH ____ married, in England, in 1622-3, as his second wife, **ROBERT HUSTED**, and had three children. She died in Stamford, Conn., in 1654, in the same year as her husband (see preceding).

JONATHAN HYDE

Sergeant **JONATHAN HYDE**[195] was born about 1626; died in Newton, Middlesex County, Mass., 5 October 1711. He came to America on the *Jonathan* in 1639. He married (1) in Cambridge, Mass., in 1650, **Mary FRENCH** (1632-1672), daughter of Captain WILLIAM FRENCH.

Sergeant Jonathan HYDE = Mary FRENCH
Jonathan HYDE Jr. = Dorothy KIDDER
John WOODWARD = Hannah HYDE   James HYDE = Mary UTTER
Henry BACON = Hannah WOODWARD
Hannah BACON = Jabez HYDE
Private Henry HYDE = Thyrina (Therina) WARD
Luther HYDE = Phoebe GIDDINGS
Harvey HYDE = Fidelia Gadcourt POTTER
Benajah Flavel STOCKWELL = Emily Lodiweska (Emma F.) HYDE
George J. HILL = Jessie Fidelia STOCKWELL

KATHERINE HYDE

KATHERINE HYDE[196] married in Manchester, co. Lancaster, at the Collegiate Church, 20 November 1630, **Rev. OBADIAH HOLMES**, son of Robert and Katherine (Johnson) Hulme; baptized at Didsbury, 18 March 1609/10; died at Newport, R.I., 15 October 1682. He became a Baptist minister and went to Newport, R.I. He was whipped for preaching without permission in Boston, and he was an early property owner in New Jersey. They had 10 children. She died in 1684. She is an ancestor of Jessie Stockwell.

THOMAS IREDELL

THOMAS IREDELL[197] son of Robert and Ellinor (Jackson) Iredell, was born at Rigg Bank, co. Cumberland, England, in 1676; died in Pennsylvania. He received a certificate from the Monthly Meeting at Pardsay Cragg, Cumberland, on 27, 6mo. 1700. He married, 3 mo. 9, 1705, at Friends Meeting House, Philadelphia, **REBECCA WILLIAMS**. They had one child.

Thomas IREDELL = Rebecca WILLIAMS
Robert IREDELL = Hannah LUKENS
Ezra COMLY = Hannah IREDEL
Charles SHOEMAKER = Rachel COMLY
Julien SHOEMAKER = Hannah Ann HESTER
William Toy SHOEMAKER = Mabel WARREN

---

[195] Hill, *Western Pilgrims*, 227.
[196] Hill, *Western Pilgrims*, 277-8. At the time *Western Pilgrims* was published, I noted the likely assumption that Oliver Potter is the son of William and Mary (Tillinghast) Potter. This has now been confirmed by the NEHGS.
[197] Hill, *Quakers and Puritans*, 67.

JOHN IRISH

JOHN IRISH,[198] said to be of Clisdon, Somersetshire, England, was born by about 1611; died at Duxbury, Plymouth Colony, by 5 March 1677/8. He came to Plymouth Colony with John Bradford in 1629, where he was an indentured servant of Timothy Hatherly, a feltmaker in England and merchant in America. Irish originally settled at Plymouth and later relocated to Duxbury. He was initially a laborer and was later a roper, and he eventually became a planter and surveyor. He married, by about 1644, **ELIZABETH _____,** said without proof to be Elizabeth Risley; she died 28 August 1687.

John IRISH = Elizabeth _____

John IRISH = Elizabeth _____ possibly SAVORY

Jonathan IRISH = Mary TAYLOR

Jesse IRISH = Mary ALLEBEE

William IRISH = Dolly _____

Capt. Freeborn POTTER = Dolly IRISH

Harvey HYDE = Fidelia Gadcourt POTTER

Benajah Flavel STOCKWELL = Emily Lodiweska (Emma F.) HYDE

George J. HILL = Jessie Fidelia STOCKWELL

ELIZABETH (_____) IRISH

ELIZABETH _____ married, by 1644, **JOHN IRISH,** supposedly of co. Somerset, England, who came to Plymouth Colony in 1629. They had four children. Their son John married (2) Priscilla (Southworth) Talbot, daughter of Edward Southworth. He was the first husband of ALICE CARPENTER, who married (2) Governor WILLIAM BRADFORD (see preceding).

EDWARD JACKSON

EDWARD JACKSON, Esq.,[199] tailor, son of Christopher and Susan (Johnson) Jackson, was baptized at St. Dunstan's Church, Stepney, London, 3 February 1604; died at Newton, Mass., 17 July 1681. He came to New England with his first wife, Frances, and several of their children, arriving between 20 February 1642/3 and 17 October 1643. He was admitted freeman in 1644, and he rose to become a prominent citizen in both the town and the colony. He married (1), in England, **FRANCES _____.** She died at Cambridge, Mass., in about 1648. They had nine children. Their son Sebas, who married Sarah Baker, and their daughter Hannah, who married John Ward, are ancestors of Mabel Warren. Edward Jackson married (2) at Cambridge, Mass., 14 March 1648/9 **Elizabeth (NEWGATE) OLIVER,** daughter of John Newgate and his first wife, Lydia ___, and widow of John Oliver; baptized at St. Olaves Southwark, Surrey; died at Newton, Mass., 30 September 1709. They had six children.

Edward JACKSON Esq. = Frances _____

Sebas "Seaborn" JACKSON = Sarah BAKER   Ens. John WARD = Hannah JACKSON

Edward JACKSON = Mary _____   Thomas GREENWOOD, Esq. = Hannah WARD

Sgt. Josiah JACKSON = Mary DARBY   John GREENWOOD, Esq. = Hannah TROWBRIDGE

Isaac JACKSON = Ruth GREENWOOD

Sgt. Josiah JACKSON = Mary DARBY

Oliver JACKSON = Mary PEIRCE

Jesse WARREN = Betsy JACKSON

Herbert Marshall WARREN = Eliza Caroline COPP

William Toy SHOEMAKER = Mabel WARREN

FRANCES (_____) JACKSON

FRANCES _____ married, as his first wife, **EDWARD JACKSON, Esq.** (1604-81), son of Christopher and Susan (Jackson) Jackson. She died at Cambridge, Mass., 5 October 1648. (see above).

---

[198] Hill, *Western Pilgrims*, 347. Anderson, *Great Migration Begins*, 1-3:1065-7.
[199] Hill, *Quakers and Puritans*, 201, 259.

EPHRAIM JACKSON

EPHRAIM JACKSON,[200] born at Macclesfield, Cheshire, England, 3mo. 1658; died at Edgemont, Chester Co., Pa., 1mo. 11, 1698. He arrived in this country in December 1684 as a servant of Jacob Hall of Macclesfield. He was clerk of Chester Monthly Meeting of Friends. He married, at Concord Monthly Meeting, 12-10-1695, **Rachel NEWLIN**, daughter of NICHOLAS NEWLIN and his wife ELIZABETH; born at Mountmellick, Ireland, in about 1674; died in Edgemont, Chester Co., Pa., in 1742.

Ephraim JACKSON = Rachel NEWLIN
Joseph JACKSON = Susanna MILLER
John JACKSON Jr. = Susanna JACKSON
William MANLY = Rachel JACKSON (prob. daughter of John Jackson, Jr.)
William H. MANLY = Sarah D. WALTER
Silas William RUNDALL = Rachel MANLY
William Henry "Will" THOMPSON = Sarah D. "Sadie" RUNDALL

ISAAC JACKSON

ISAAC JACKSON,[201] son of Anthony Jackson, was born in 1665, probably at co. Cavan, Ireland; died in Pennsylvania, in the fall of 1750. He emigrated with his wife and all but two of their surviving children to Pennsylvania. They left Dublin and reached New Castle, Delaware, on 11, 9mo. 1725. He married at Oldcastle, co. Meath, 2mo. 29, 1696, **ANN EVANS**, daughter of Rowland Evans; she died in 1731-32.

Isaac JACKSON = Ann EVANS
John JACKSON Sr. = Sarah MILLER
John JACKSON Jr. = Susanna JACKSON
William MANLY = Rachel JACKSON (prob. daughter of John Jackson, Jr.)
William H. MANLY = Sarah D. WALTER
Silas William RUNDALL = Rachel MANLY
William Henry "Will" THOMPSON = Sarah D. "Sadie" RUNDALL

JOSEPH JACKSON

JOSEPH JACKSON[202] is said to have been born in Ireland in 1685 and died in Connecticut in 1738, and that he married in Aston by Sutton, Cheshire, England, 25 July 1710, **ESTHER NORMAN**; born 1690; died 22 March 1741.

Joseph JACKSON = Esther NORMAN
Michael JACKSON = Susannah WILCOX
Sergeant Isaiah J. HENDRYX = Esther JACKSON
Josiah (Isaiah) RILEY = Susannah HENDRYX
Simeon RILEY = Katharine "Catherine" GILLETT
Charles W. HILL = Adelia Catharine "Delia" RILEY
George J. HILL = Jessie Fidelia STOCKWELL

ELIZABETH JASPER

ELIZABETH JASPER,[203] daughter of Lancelot Jasper, a husbandman, and his wife Rose, was of co. Suffolk, England; baptized at Redgrave, Suffolk, 30 January 1579/80; died at Medfield, Mass., 20 June 1655. She married **SAMUEL MORSE**, probably the son of the Rev. Thomas Morse of co. Suffolk; died

---

[200] Hill, *Fundy to Chesapeake*, 276. This genealogy is based on the probability that Rachel Jackson is the daughter of John Jackson, Jr. Also see JOHN MILLER for relationships between Sarah and Susanna Miller.
[201] Hill, *Fundy to Chesapeake*, 262. This genealogy is based on the probability that Rachel Jackson is the daughter of John Jackson, Jr. Also see JOHN MILLER for relationships between Sarah and Susanna Miller.
[202] Hill, *Western Pilgrims*, 10.
[203] Hill, *Western Pilgrims*, 208.

at Medfield, Mass., 5 December 1654. They had eight children, of whom several accompanied them to New England. She is an ancestor of Jessie F. Stockwell.

HENRY JEFTS

HENRY JEFTS[204] was born, probably in England, in about 1606, given his age at death "about 94" on 24 May 1700, at Billerica, Mass. He was first recorded as a proprietor of Woburn, Mass., in 1640. Little is known about him except for his four marriages. An interesting story is told about the first husband of his third wife, Mary (___) Bird. Her first husband, Simon Bird, was excommunicated "for filthy unclean dalliances with his maid servant." In 1657, Jefts became an incorporator of Billerica. He had five children by his second wife, **HANNAH BIRTHS**, who died 15 September 1662.

Henry JEFTS = Hannah BIRTHS
Deacon Andrew SPALDING = Hannah JEFTS
Josiah FLETCHER = Joanna SPALDING
Capt. Joseph WARREN = Joanna FLETCHER
Jeduthan WARREN = Joanna MOORS
Jesse WARREN = Betsy JACKSON
Herbert Marshall WARREN = Eliza Caroline COPP
William Toy SHOEMAKER = Mabel WARREN

JOHN JESSUP

JOHN JESSUP,[205] possibly the son of Francis and Frances (White) Jessup, and grandson of Richard and Ann (Swift) Jessup, of Broom Hall, Sheffield, Yorkshire, but whose origin is unproved, died, early in 1638, probably at Wethersfield or Hartford, Conn. He apparently came to America with a substantial amount of money. He was first recorded in New England in December 1637. John Jessup married, probably before he came to America, **JOANNA _____**. When he died, John Jessup left three small children, or more, and his widow, Joanna (_____) Jessup, soon remarried.

John JESSUP = Joanna ____
Edward JESSUP = Elizabeth _____
Edward JESSUP = [possible unnamed daughter] HUSTED
Jonathan JESSUP = Sarah _____
David BROWN = Deborah JESSUP
Shadrack RUNDALL Sr. = Phebe BROWN
Reuben John RUNDALL = Martha TOMPKINS
Silas William RUNDALL = Rachel MANLY
William Henry "Will" THOMPSON = Sarah D. "Sadie" RUNDALL

JOANNA (_____) JESSUP

JOANNA _____, wife of **JOHN JESSUP**, was probably born in England and came with him to America in about 1637. They had three small children when he died a year later. She remarried, but her second husband, **John WHITMORE**, was killed by Indians in 1648, leaving her again a widow. She raised her children alone in Stamford, Conn., with the wealth left to her by John Jessup (see preceding).

THOMAS JEWELL

THOMAS JEWELL[206] married, as her first husband, in about 1640, **Grissell FLETCHER**, daughter and eldest child of ROBERT FLETCHER. She was born in England, perhaps Yorkshire, say 1618-1619; died at Chelmsford, Mass., 9 July 1669. He was given a land grant in Braintree for three heads that year.

---

[204] Hill, *Quakers and Puritans*, 154.

[205] Hill, *Fundy to Chesapeake*, 198, 205-6. This line depends on Donald Lines Jacobus' suggestion that Angel HUSTED is the father of _____ HUSTED, who m. Edward JESSUP.

[206] Hill, *Western Pilgrims*, 91; additional details in Notes, 670. Caution noted in footnote on p.83; it assumes that Jerusha P. is Jerusha Pierce.

With Grissell Fletcher, he had at least four, or perhaps six, children. Thomas Jewell made his will, 10 April 1654, proved 21 July 1654, giving her all his estate as long as she remained a widow.

Thomas JEWELL = Grissell "Cary" FLETCHER
Joseph SPALDING = Mercy JEWELL
Judge Timothy PIERCE = Lydia SPAULDING
Nathaniel PIERCE = Elizabeth STEVENS
Willard PIERCE = Jerusha PELLET
Rufus HERRICK [III] = Jerusha P._____ (prob. PIERCE)
William Prince HILL = Sarah P. "Sally" HERRICK
Charles W. HILL = Adelia Catharine "Delia" RILEY
George J. HILL = Jessie Fidelia STOCKWELL

JOHN JOHNSON

Captain JOHN JOHNSON[207] was born in England in about 1588; died at Roxbury, Mass., 30 September 1659. He came to America in 1630. He was first elected as a Deputy to the General Court in 1634. He married (1) at Ware, Hertfordshire, 21 September 1613, *Mary HEATH*, buried at Ware, 15 May 1629. Their eldest son, Isaac, was killed while leading his company in the Great Swamp Fight in 1675. Their son Humphrey is an ancestor of **President Franklin D. Roosevelt.**

Capt. John JOHNSON = *Mary HEATH*
Capt. Isaac JOHNSON = Elizabeth PORTER
Lieut. Henry BOWEN = Elizabeth JOHNSON
Joseph BACON = Margaret BOWEN
Henry BACON = Hannah WOODWARD
Jabez HYDE = Hannah BACON
Private Henry HYDE = Thyrina (Therina) WARD
Luther HYDE = Phoebe GIDDINGS
Harvey HYDE = Fidelia Gadcourt POTTER
Benajah Flavel STOCKWELL = Emily Lodiweska (Emma F.) HYDE
George J. HILL = Jessie Fidelia STOCKWELL

KATHERINE JOHNSON

KATHERINE JOHNSON[208] married, in 1767, **AARON HUNT**, born 7 April 1745 in Wyoming, Wyoming Co., N.Y.; died there after 1778. She was probably not an immigrant, but her origin has not been determined. She is an ancestor of George J. Hill, the Iowa Pioneer.

THOMAS JONES

THOMAS JONES, gentleman,[209] aka Thomas ap John, son of John Thomas "of Llaithgwm" and his first wife, Ann Lloyd, was born before August 1665, in Wales, probably at Penllyn, Merionethshire, near Lake Bala; died at Merion, Montgomery Co., Pa., 6 August 1727. He came in *Morning Star* in 1683 with his step-mother, Katherine Roberts, and her children, known in America as Jones. He probably married (1), on 11, 4 mo. 1686, **LOWRY JONES**, widow of Thomas Lloyd, born 1666; died about 1701.

Thomas JONES, aka Thomas ap John = Lowry JONES, aka. Lowry ferch John
Thomas JONES [II] = Katherine ARETS
John JONES = Rebecca HEAD
Robert COMLY, Jr. = Sarah JONES
Ezra COMLY = Hannah IREDELL
Charles SHOEMAKER = Rachel COMLY
Julien SHOEMAKER = Hannah Ann HESTER
William Toy SHOEMAKER = Mabel WARREN

[207] Hill, *Western Pilgrims*, 243.
[208] Hill, *Western Pilgrims*, 124.
[209] Hill, *Quakers and Puritans*, 92-3. Thomas Jones' mother, Ann Lloyd, was the sister of Dr. Edward Jones.

STEPHEN JORDAN

STEPHEN JORDAN[210] was born 1590; died at Newbury, Mass., 8 February 1670. He came to America in the *Mary and John* in 1634 and owned land in Ipswich. He married (1) _____, who died after 1626.

Stephen JORDAN = _____
Robert CROSS(E) = Anna\Hannah JORDAN
Ephraim "of Beverly" HERRICK = Mary CROSS(E)
Lieutenant Stephen HERRICK = Elizabeth TRASK
Edward HERRICK = Mary DENNISON
Col. Rufus HERRICK = Miss _____ GIBBS, prob. Myra (Mary) GIBBS
Capt. Rufus HERRICK Jr. = Lydia NEWMAN
Rufus HERRICK [III] = Jerusha P. _____ (prob.) PIERCE
William Prince HILL = Sarah P. "Sally" HERRICK
Charles W. HILL = Adelia Catharine "Delia" RILEY
George J. HILL = Jessie Fidelia STOCKWELL

THOMAS JORDAN

THOMAS JORDAN,[211] of co. Dorset England, had a daughter, Cecily Jordan. She married 18 September 1580 or 1581, Robert Fitzpen als Fippen; their son DAVID PHIPPEN emigrated to Massachusetts, and is an ancestor of Jessie F. Stockwell.

Thomas JORDAN = _____
Robert FITZPEN als FIPPEN = Cecily JORDAN
David PHIPPEN = Sarah _____
(see DAVID PHIPPEN).

EVA KATHERINE KELLENBENZ

JOHANN MICHAEL KELLENBENZ,[212] son of Johann Georg Kellenbenz, and his wife Anna Maria Clement, was born at Kleineislingen, Württemberg, 26 February 1825; died at Göppengen, Württemberg, 31 July 1888. He married, 18 May 1853, **Clara GRÖZINGER**. born at Ottenbach, Württemberg, 29 July 1828; died at Kleineislingen, 9 November 1889. They had 16 children. **EVA KATHERINE KELLENBENZ**, daughter of Johann Michael and Clara (Grözinger) Kellenbenz, came to Philadelphia with her uncle Gottlieb in about 1867. She married there, 15 October 1885, **JOHN ZIMMERMANN**.

Johannes KELLENBENZ = _____
Georg KELLENBENZ = _____
Sebastian KELLENBENZ = _____
Johann Jacob KELLENBENZ = _____
Dr. Gottlieb KELLENBENZ = _____
Dr. Gottlieb (II) KELLENBENZ = Dr. Jakobine SCHRAG
Johann Jacob KELLENBENZ = Christina SILLER
Johann Georg KELLENBENZ = Anna Maria CLEMENT
Johann Michael KELLENBENZ = Clara GRÖZINGER
John ZIMMERMANN = Eva Katherine KELLENBENZ
Albert Walter ZIMMERMANN = Barbara SHOEMAKER

JAMES KIDDER

Ensign JAMES KIDDER[213] is probably the James Kidder who was the son of James Kidder of Grinstead, co. Sussex. He appeared in Cambridge, Mass., in 1649, where he married **Anna MOORE**,

---

[210] Hill, *Western Pilgrims*, 302. The Ahnentafel for Stephen Jordan erroneously shows his wife as Susannah Peabody. Susanna (Peabody) Merrill was his second wife, and not the mother of Anna, who married Robert Cross.
[211] Hill, *Western Pilgrims*, 309.
[212] Hill, *American Dreams*, 49-65, 75-96.
[213] Hill, *Western Pilgrims*, 235.

daughter of Elder FRANCIS MOORE and his wife KATHERINE, born in England in 1630. He was commander of the garrison-house in Billerica during King Philip's War. James and Anna have two lines of descent to Jessie Stockwell.

Ensign James KIDDER = Anna MOORE
Jonathan HYDE Jr. = Dorothy KIDDER
John WOODWARD = Hannah HYDE James HYDE = Mary UTTER
Henry BACON = Hannah WOODWARD
Hannah BACON = Jabez HYDE
Private Henry HYDE = Thyrina (Therina) WARD
Luther HYDE = Phoebe GIDDINGS
Harvey HYDE = Fidelia Gadcourt POTTER
Benajah Flavel STOCKWELL = Emily Lodiweska (Emma F.) HYDE
George J. HILL = Jessie Fidelia STOCKWELL

HENRY KINGMAN

HENRY KINGMAN[214] was born about 1594; died at Weymouth, Mass., 5 June 1667. He enrolled at Weymouth, England, on 20 March 1634/5 on *Marygould*, bound for New England, with his wife, four children, and a servant, John Ford. Henry Kingman was Deputy to the Massachusetts Bay Court. He married, in England, **JOAN ___**; born about 1596; died at Weymouth, 11 April 1659.

Henry KINGMAN = Joan _____
Thomas HOLBROOK [II] = Joan KINGMAN
Deacon Peter HOLBROOK = Alice GODFREY
Cornet John HOLBROOK = Hannah CHAPIN
Lt. Aaron HOLBROOK = Hannah PARTRIDGE
Ebenezer STOCKWELL = Abi HOLBROOK
Joseph H. STOCKWELL = Anna Maria SAXE
Benajah Flavel STOCKWELL = Emily Lodiweska (Emma F.) HYDE
George J. HILL = Jessie Fidelia STOCKWELL

JOAN (_____) KINGMAN

JOAN _____, born in England in about 1596; died at Weymouth, Mass., 11 April 1659, came to Massachusetts in 1634/5 with her husband **HENRY KINGMAN** and their children (see preceding).

ROBERT KINSMAN

ROBERT KINSMAN,[215] born in England about 1605; died at Ipswich, Mass., 28 January 1664/5. He came on the *Mary and John* in 1634 and was a glazier at Ipswich, Mass. He acquired a considerable amount of real estate. He had six children, by a wife whose name is unknown. They were probably married in about 1629-30; she died before 1664.

Robert KINSMAN = _____
Daniel RINDGE = Mary KINSMAN
Joseph ANDREWS = Sarah RINDGE
John ANDREWS = Elizabeth WALLIS   Thomas GIDDINGS = Sarah ANDREWS
Capt. Joseph GIDDINGS = Eunice ANDREWS
Benjamin GIDDINGS = Martha SEELEY
Luther HYDE = Phoebe GIDDINGS
Harvey HYDE = Fidelia Gadcourt POTTER
Benajah Flavel STOCKWELL = Emily Lodiweska (Emma F.) HYDE
George J. HILL = Jessie Fidelia STOCKWELL

---

[214] Hill, *Western Pilgrims*, 195.
[215] Hill, *Western Pilgrims*, 305.

_____ (_____) KINSMAN

_____ _____, born in England, married **ROBERT KINSMAN** in about 1629-30, and came with him to Massachusetts in 1634. She raised six children in Ipswich and died before 1664 (see preceding).

NICHOLAS KNAPP

NICHOLAS KNAPP[216] was born about 1606; died at Stamford, Conn., in 1670. He first appears in the records of Watertown in 1630. At that time, he was "fined £5 for taking upon him to cure the scurvy by a water of no worth nor value." His later profession was that of a weaver. Nicholas Knapp married, by 1631, (1) **ELINOR _____**; died at Stamford, 16 August 1658. She was the mother of his 10 children.

Nicholas KNAPP = Elinor _____
Caleb KNAPP = Hannah ?SMITH
Ebenezer MEAD, J.P. = Sarah KNAPP
Jonathan HOBBY Sr. = Sarah MEAD
Jonathan HOBBY Jr. = Deborah LYON
Reuben RUNDLE Sr. = Amy HOBBY
Shadrack RUNDALL Sr. = Phebe BROWN
Reuben John RUNDALL = Martha TOMPKINS
Silas William RUNDALL = Rachel MANLY
William Henry "Will" THOMPSON = Sarah D. "Sadie" RUNDALL

ELINOR (_____) KNAPP

ELINOR _____ married **NICHOLAS KNAPP**, either in England or shortly after he arrived in America in about 1630. They lived in Watertown, Mass., and later in Stamford, Conn. She bore 10 children and died at Stamford in 1658 (see preceding).

HENRY KNOWLES

HENRY KNOWLES,[217] who may be the Henry Knowles who was born about 1609 near Hull, co. York, England, and who came to New England in 1635 in the *Susan and Ellen*, died in January 1670 at Warwick or Kingston, R.I. He was licensed to keep a tavern. He married _____, who died about 2 January 1670 in Kingston, R.I. His daughter Mary has two lines of descent to Jessie F. Stockwell.

Henry KNOWLES = _____ _____
Moses LIPPITT = Mary KNOWLES

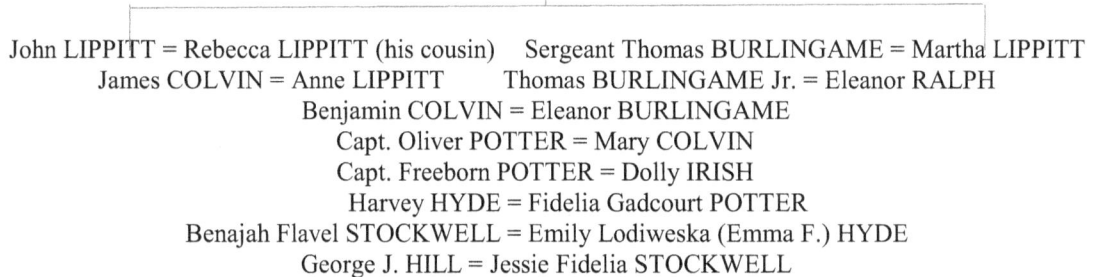

John LIPPITT = Rebecca LIPPITT (his cousin)   Sergeant Thomas BURLINGAME = Martha LIPPITT
James COLVIN = Anne LIPPITT   Thomas BURLINGAME Jr. = Eleanor RALPH
Benjamin COLVIN = Eleanor BURLINGAME
Capt. Oliver POTTER = Mary COLVIN
Capt. Freeborn POTTER = Dolly IRISH
Harvey HYDE = Fidelia Gadcourt POTTER
Benajah Flavel STOCKWELL = Emily Lodiweska (Emma F.) HYDE
George J. HILL = Jessie Fidelia STOCKWELL

_____ (_____) KNOWLES

_____ married **HENRY KNOWLES**, immigrant to New England. They probably married in Rhode Island in about 1644. They had five children. Both parents died in about 1670 (see preceding).

---

[216] Hill, *Fundy to Chesapeake*, 151.
[217] Hill, *Western Pilgrims*, 265.

JOSEPH KNOWLES

JOSEPH KNOWLES,[218] of Trenton, died about 1846, leaving two houses on Green Street. His property was divided *per stirpes* between his five children and their heirs. He is probably from one of the Knowles families of eastern Pennsylvania or southern New Jersey, but his ancestry has thus far been elusive.

Joseph KNOWLES = _____ _____
John Dippolt HESTER = Rhoda "Rhody" KNOWLES
Julien SHOEMAKER = Hannah Ann HESTER
William Toy SHOEMAKER, M.D. = Mabel WARREN

HENRY LAKE

HENRY LAKE[219] was born about 1610 in the parish of Childwell, Lancashire; died at Dartmouth, Plymouth Colony, after 21 February 1672/3. He married in about 1640. In 1650, his wife **ALICE** _____ gave birth to their fifth child, who soon died. In grief and mourning, she claimed that she could still see the baby. She was accused of being a witch, because she saw things that couldn't be seen by others. She was found guilty of witchcraft and executed, probably by hanging on Boston Common in about 1650.

Henry LAKE = Alice _____
Thomas LAKE = Sarah PEET (aka PEAT)
Joseph LAKE = Penelope CASE
Daniel LAKE = Sarah "Sally" _____
Bartholomew TOMPKINS = [unmarried] Martha LAKE (possibly daughter of Daniel Lake)
Reuben John RUNDALL = Martha TOMPKINS
Silas William RUNDALL = Rachel MANLY
William Henry "Will" THOMPSON = Sarah D. "Sadie" RUNDALL

ALICE (_____) LAKE

ALICE _____ was the wife of **HENRY LAKE**. They were married in about 1640 shortly after he arrived in Massachusetts. After the early death of her fifth child, she claimed she could still see the baby. She was accused and convicted of witchcraft and hanged, probably in Boston, in 1650 (see preceding).

WILLIAM LAMBERT

WILLIAM LAMBERT[220] was the father of Sarah Lambert, who married WILLIAM STOCKWELL, Sr. A man named William Lambert came to America from England in May 1635 on the *Susan and Ellen*.

William LAMBERT = _____ _____
William STOCKWELL, Sr. = Sarah LAMBERT
Ebenezer STOCKWELL = Mary SINGLETARY
Ebenezer STOCKWELL [II] = Abi (Holbrook) LEE
Joseph H. STOCKWELL = Anna Maria SAXE
Benajah Flavel STOCKWELL = Emily "Emma F." Lodiweska HYDE
George J. HILL = Jessie Fidelia STOCKWELL
Gerald Leslie HILL = Essie Mae THOMPSON
George James HILL = Helene ZIMMERMANN

EDWARD LARKIN

EDWARD LARKIN,[221] a wheelwright, was probably born in England; he died at Charlestown, Mass., in about 1652. He was in Charlestown on 30 May 1638. He was a member of the Ancient and Honorable Artillery Company of Massachusetts. He married **JOANNA** _____; born about 1616; died in 1686.

---

[218] Hill, *Quakers and Puritans*, 25.
[219] Hill, *Fundy to Chesapeake*, 229; based on the possibility that Martha Lake is the daughter of Daniel Lake.
[220] Hill, *Western Pilgrims*, 174.
[221] Hill, *Quakers and Puritans*, 169.

Edward LARKIN = Joanna _____
John LARKIN = Joanna HALE
Capt. John THORNDIKE = Joanna LARKIN
James THORNDIKE = Anna OBER
Simeon MOORS = Joanna THORNDIKE
Jeduthan WARREN = Joanna MOORS
Jesse WARREN = Betsy JACKSON
Herbert Marshall WARREN = Eliza Caroline COPP
William Toy SHOEMAKER = Mabel WARREN

JOANNA (_____) LARKIN

JOANNA _____ married (1), probably in England, **EDWARD LARKIN**, and came with him to Charlestown, Mass., in about 1638. After bearing six children with him, he died and she married (2) **John PENTECOST**, and died in 1686, aged 70 years (see preceding).

HUGH LASKIN

HUGH LASKIN,[222] born by 1587, died in Massachusetts, probably Salem, by 21 March 1658/9. He first appears in the record of Salem, Mass., on 22 February 1635/6. In the 1636 distribution of Salem land, he held sixty acres in the freemen's section, which was later increased to seventy acres. He married, by about 1612, **ALICE** _____; she died at Salem, 23 July 1658. They had two children, born in England.

Hugh LASKIN = Alice _____
Henry HERRICK = Editha LASKIN
Ephraim "of Beverly" HERRICK = Mary CROSS(E)
Lieutenant Stephen HERRICK = Elizabeth TRASK
Edward HERRICK = Mary DENNISON
Col. Rufus HERRICK = Miss _____ GIBBS, prob. Myra (Mary) GIBBS
Capt. Rufus HERRICK Jr. = Lydia NEWMAN
Rufus HERRICK [III] = Jerusha P. _____ (prob.) PIERCE
William Prince HILL = Sarah P. "Sally" HERRICK
Charles W. HILL = Adelia Catharine "Delia" RILEY
George J. HILL = Jessie Fidelia STOCKWELL

ALICE (_____) LASKIN

ALICE _____, wife of **HUGH LASKIN**, married her husband by about 1612 in England. They came to Salem, Mass., in about 1635/6 with two children. She died in 1658, shortly before he died (see above).

THOMAS LAWRENCE

THOMAS LAWRENCE,[223] son of John and Elizabeth (Bull) Lawrence, died 20 March 1624/5 at St. Albans, co. Hertford. He married, as her first husband, at St. Albans, **Joan ANTROBUS**, daughter of *WALTER ANTROBUS* and his wife JOAN ARNOLD. She was christened at St. Albans, 25 June 1592; died at Carrick Fergus, Ireland, after 30 April 1657. After Thomas Lawrence died, she married (2), in England, between 1626 and 1628, **John TUTTLE**, with whom she came to America in the *Planter* in 1635. She had four or more children by Tuttle, and then returned with him to Ireland, where she died.

Thomas LAWRENCE = Joan ANTROBUS (married [2] John Tuttle)
George GIDDINGS = Jane LAWRENCE (step-daughter of John Tuttle)
John GIDDINGS = Sarah ALCOCK
Thomas GIDDINGS = Sarah ANDREWS
Joseph GIDDINGS = Eunice ANDREWS

---

[222] Hill, *Western Pilgrims*, 47.
[223] Hill, *Western Pilgrims*, 299-300. Also see Richardson, *Royal Ancestry* 3:551-2, for Jane Lawrence = George Giddings, and the **Royal Line** of Jane Lawrence.

Benjamin GIDDINGS = Martha SEELEY
Luther HYDE = Phoebe GIDDINGS
Harvey HYDE = Fidelia Gadcourt POTTER
Benajah Flavel STOCKWELL = Emily Lodiweska (Emma F.) HYDE
George J. HILL = Jessie Fidelia STOCKWELL

ROBERT LAY

ROBERT LAY[224] was born about 1617; died in Essex, Conn., 9 July 1689. He was a large landowner in Essex and Saybrook. He married, in December 1647, as her second husband, **SARAH FENNER**, widow of John Tully; born in co. Surrey, 26 November 1615; died at Saybrook, 25 May 1676.

Robert LAY = Sarah FENNER, widow of John Tully
Capt. John Borodell DENISON = Phebe LAY
Capt. William DENISON = Mary AVERY
Edward HERRICK = Mary DENISON
Col. Rufus HERRICK = Miss _____ GIBBS, prob. Myra "Mary" GIBBS
Capt. Rufus HERRICK Jr. = Lydia NEWMAN
Rufus HERRICK [III] = Jerusha P. _____ (prob.) PIERCE
William Prince HILL = Sarah P. "Sally" HERRICK
Charles W. HILL = Adelia Catharine "Delia" RILEY
George J. HILL = Jessie Fidelia STOCKWELL

[WILLIAM LEARNED]

[**WILLIAM LEARNED**,[225] born about 1581 in Surry; died at Woburn, Mass., 1 March 1645/6. He came to Massachusetts in 1630. He married (2), **Jane _____**, who died at Woburn in 1660/1. Their daughter Sarah married (2) Thomas Lathrop, who was formerly thought to be an ancestor of Jessie Stockwell, but this is probably erroneous (see [ELNATHAN DUNKLEE], above, for details of this complex story)].

TOBY LEECH

TOBY (Tobias) LEECH, Sen., gent.,[226] son of Tobias and Jane (Halinge) Leech of Cheltenham, Gloucestershire, was baptized 1 January 1652; died at Philadelphia, Pa., 13 November 1726. He arrived in Philadelphia in October 1682 on the *Bristol Factor*. Toby Leech was a man of substance at the time of his arrival in America. He married, at Gloucester Meeting, 10 mo. 26, 1679, **ESTHER ASHMEAD**, daughter of Mrs. Mary (___) Ashmead; died at Cheltenham Twp., Pa., 11 August 1726.

Toby (Tobias) LEECH, Sr. = Esther (Hester) ASHMEAD
Bartholomew PENROSE = Hester (Ester) LEECH
Isaac SHOEMAKER Sr. = Dorothy PENROSE
Isaac SHOEMAKER Jr. = Elizabeth POTTS
Jonathan SHOEMAKER Esq. = Hannah LUKENS
Charles SHOEMAKER = Rachel COMLY
Julien SHOEMAKER = Hannah Ann HESTER
William Toy SHOEMAKER = Mabel WARREN

MARY LEVIT

MARY LEVIT[227] married, at Messing, co. Essex, England, 26 December 1622, **JOHN WHITE**. They came to America in 1632, residing first at Cambridge and then at Hartford. They had seven children. She died sometime after their last child was born in 1645. She is an ancestor of Sarah D. Rundall.

---

[224] Hill, *Western Pilgrims*, 71.
[225] Hill, *Western Pilgrims*, 225.
[226] Hill, *Quakers and Puritans*, 110.
[227] Hill, *Fundy to Chesapeake*, 220.

JOHN LIPPITT

JOHN LIPPITT,[228] had a home-lot in Providence, R.I., in 1638. In about 1647, he removed to Warwick. He had five children. Three of his grandchildren were ancestors of Jessie F. Stockwell.

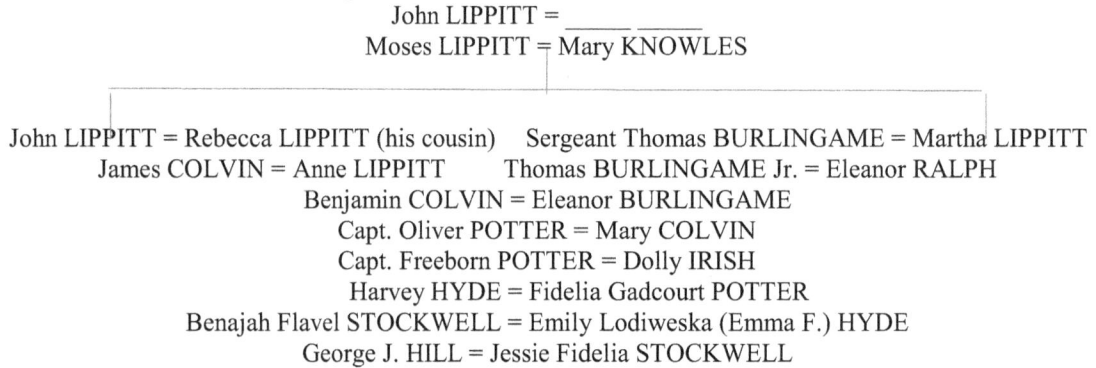

John LIPPITT = ___ ___
Moses LIPPITT = Mary KNOWLES

John LIPPITT = Rebecca LIPPITT (his cousin)   Sergeant Thomas BURLINGAME = Martha LIPPITT
James COLVIN = Anne LIPPITT   Thomas BURLINGAME Jr. = Eleanor RALPH
Benjamin COLVIN = Eleanor BURLINGAME
Capt. Oliver POTTER = Mary COLVIN
Capt. Freeborn POTTER = Dolly IRISH
Harvey HYDE = Fidelia Gadcourt POTTER
Benajah Flavel STOCKWELL = Emily Lodiweska (Emma F.) HYDE
George J. HILL = Jessie Fidelia STOCKWELL

_____ (_____) LIPPITT

_____ _____, wife of **JOHN LIPPITT** of Providence and Warwick, R.I., had five children with him, born in the mid-17th century (see preceding).

JOHN LLOYD

JOHN LLOYD,[229] of Vaynol, St. Asaph, Flintshire, Wales, had two children. His son Edward, later known as **Dr. Edward Jones**, came in the Welcome Fleet, on the *Lyon*, in 1682, and was a member of the Provincial Assembly of Pennsylvania. His daughter *Ann Lloyd*, who married John Thomas "of Llaithgwm," gent. (aka John ap Thomas), was the mother of Thomas ap John (aka THOMAS JONES). He is probably an ancestor of William Toy Shoemaker by his first marriage, to Lowry Jones.

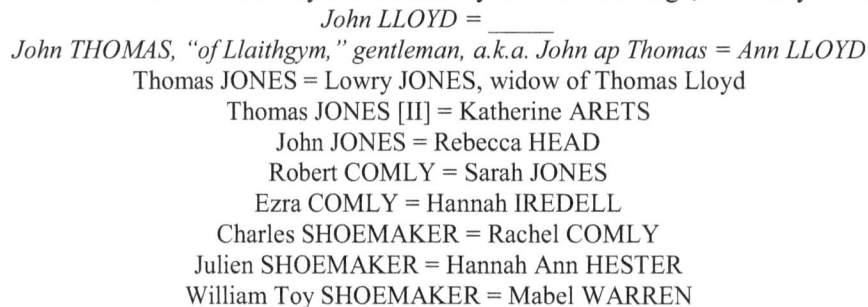

John LLOYD = _____
John THOMAS, "of Llaithgym," gentleman, a.k.a. John ap Thomas = Ann LLOYD
Thomas JONES = Lowry JONES, widow of Thomas Lloyd
Thomas JONES [II] = Katherine ARETS
John JONES = Rebecca HEAD
Robert COMLY = Sarah JONES
Ezra COMLY = Hannah IREDELL
Charles SHOEMAKER = Rachel COMLY
Julien SHOEMAKER = Hannah Ann HESTER
William Toy SHOEMAKER = Mabel WARREN

ROBERT LONG

ROBERT LONG,[230] perhaps a son of John Long, assistant vicar at St. Albans, Herts, was born in England about 1590; died at Charlestown, Mass., 9 January 1663/4. He came from London to Charlestown, Mass., in *Defence* in 1635, bringing with him his second wife, ten children, and a servant. He was a prosperous innkeeper. He married (1), at St. Albans, Herts, 3 October 1614, *Sarah TAYLOR*, who was buried at Dunstable, Bedfordshire, 12 December 1631.

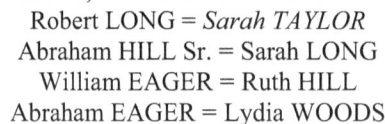

Robert LONG = *Sarah TAYLOR*
Abraham HILL Sr. = Sarah LONG
William EAGER = Ruth HILL
Abraham EAGER = Lydia WOODS

---

[228] Hill, *Western Pilgrims*, 265.
[229] Hill, *Quakers and Puritans*, 103.
[230] Hill, *Western Pilgrims*, 323.

Jabez WARD = Phebe EAGER
Corporal Jabez WARD = Jemima ALLEN
Private Henry HYDE = Thyrina (Therina) WARD
Luther HYDE = Phoebe GIDDINGS
Harvey HYDE = Fidelia Gadcourt POTTER
Benajah Flavel STOCKWELL = Emily Lodiweska (Emma F.) HYDE
George J. HILL = Jessie Fidelia STOCKWELL

[WILLIAM LONGFORD]

[*Sir WILLIAM LONGFORD*[231] was proposed by J. G. Hunt to be an ancestor of WILLIAM BRADFORD of the *Mayflower*. This would make William Bradford of **Royal** descent, in the line given in Douglas Richardson, *Royal Ancestry*, 4:650, 654-7 ("Somerset"). Hunt's note is mentioned as "a speculative piece" by Robert Charles Anderson, *Great Migration Begins*, 1297 ("George Morton"). William Bradford [III], the Pilgrim, was the grandson of William Bradfurth (Bradford) [I], who married Alice _____ . Hunt overreached in suggesting that Anthony Morton, probably grandfather of GEORGE MORTON, had a sister, Alice, who married William Bradfurth (Bradford). There is no record that Anthony Morton had a sister, or that a woman named Alice Morton ever existed.]

WELTHEAN LORING

WELTHEAN LORING,[232] presumed to be the **Welthean _____** who married **THOMAS RICHARDS**, emigrant to Massachusetts in 1633. He wrote his will in December 1650 at the home of Thomas Loring of Hull, Mass., who he called "brother." She was a contentious person who was charged with witchcraft in 1653/4, but the case was not prosecuted and she died in 1679. She is an ancestor of George J. Hill.

[JOHN LOTHROP]

[**The Rev. JOHN LOTHROP**[233] was said in *Western Pilgrims* and *Fundy to Chesapeake* to be an ancestor of both Jessie F. Stockwell and William H. Thompson. This erroneous conclusion was based on a misreading of the many marriages in the first three generations of descendants of Rev. John Lothrop. It appears that the Rev. John Lothrop has connections to the ancestors of Jessie Stockwell and William Thompson, but he is not a direct ancestor of either (see discussion in ELNATHAN DUNKLEE, above).]

JAN LUKENS

JAN LUKENS,[234] a weaver, also known as Johann Lucken, was born say 1650-55, probably in Rheindahlen or Krefeld, Duchy of Jülich; died at Germantown, Philadelphia Co., Pa., in 1744. He came to Pennsylvania on *Concord* in 1683. He married, in about 1683, **MARY TYSON (aka MARIA TEISSEN DOORS)**, daughter of Theiss (Mathias) Doors (Peterschen) and Neesgen (Agnes) Op den Graeff; born about 1660 in Krefeld, Germany; died in Germantown, Philadelphia Co., Pa. in 1742. Two of his grandchildren are ancestors of William Toy Shoemaker.

Johann (Jan) LUKENS = Mary (Maria) TYSON (TEISSEN) (DOORS)
Peter LUKENS = Gaynor EVANS
Joseph LUKENS = Elizabeth SPENCER   Robert IREDELL = Hannah LUKENS
Jonathan SHOEMAKER Esq. = Hannah LUKENS   Ezra COMLY = Hannah IREDELL
Charles SHOEMAKER = Rachel COMLY
Julien SHOEMAKER = Hannah Ann HESTER
William Toy SHOEMAKER = Mabel WARREN

---

[231] Hill, *Western Pilgrims*, 704.
[232] Hill, *Western Pilgrims*, 105-6. The descent to George J. Hill depends on the assumption that Jerusha P., wife of Rufus Herrick (III), was Jerusha Pierce. (See discussion of this question on p.45, Herrick Family.)
[233] Hill, *Fundy to Chesapeake*, 75; and *Western Pilgrims*, 226.
[234] Hill, *Quakers and Puritans*, 52.

SAMUEL LUM

SAMUEL LUM[235] appears in the records of St. Stephen's Parish, Cecil Co., Maryland, where he and his wife Ann are listed as the parents of three children: Samuel, born 1706; Jonas, born 1710; and Sarah, born 1714. Samuel Lum married **ANN _____**. Their son Samuel had a son John, who became a shipbuilder in Philadelphia. John Lum's daughter Mary (1758-1815) married Stephen Girard. Samuel and Ann Lum are probably the parents of a fourth child, Michael Lum, who married Mary Makenne.

Samuel LUM = Ann _____
Michael LUM = Mary MAKENNE
Jacob MANLEY = Rebecca LUM
William MANLY = Rachel JACKSON (prob. daughter of John Jackson, Jr.)
William H. MANLY = Sarah D. WALTER
Silas William RUNDALL = Rachel MANLY
William Henry "Will" THOMPSON = Sarah D. "Sadie" RUNDALL

ANN (_____) LUM

ANN _____, married **SAMUEL LUM** of Cecil Co., Maryland, in about 1705. They had at least three children, and probably four. Her maiden name is unknown, and she disappeared from the public record after her third child was born in 1714 (see preceding).

THOMAS LYON

THOMAS LYON, Sr.,[236] was born about 1621, presumably in Britain, and he died at Byram Neck, Rye, Westchester Co., N.Y., 8 November 1690. He bought property in Fairfield from his father-in-law. He married (1) **Martha Joanna WINTHROP**, daughter of Henry Winthrop and his wife, Elizabeth Fones. Elizabeth (Fones) Wintrop was known as **"that Winthrop Woman."** He married (2) **Mary HOYT**, daughter of **SIMON HOYT** and his wife **SUSANNA**; born about 1646; died after November 1690.

Thomas LYON, Sr. = Mary HOYT
Thomas LYON, Jr. = Abigail OGDEN
Jonathan HOBBY Jr. = Deborah LYON
Reuben RUNDLE Sr. = Amy HOBBY
Shadrack RUNDALL Sr. = Phebe BROWN
Reuben John RUNDALL = Martha TOMPKINS
Silas William RUNDALL = Rachel MANLY
William Henry "Will" THOMPSON = Sarah D. "Sadie" RUNDALL

ALEXANDER MAKENNE

ALEXANDER MAKENNE[237] appeared in Cecil Co., Maryland, in 1718; he was buried there, 3 May 1722. He was probably a young man when he arrived, born say 1690, given the probable year of his marriage in say 1718. He is first recorded when he purchased from Henry Johnson, planter of Cecil County, on 11 March 1718, a messuage and 100 acres of land. He married, in say 1718, **MARY _____**. They had three children, a daughter and two sons.

Alexander MAKENNE = Mary _____, who m. (2) _____ KEMP
Michael LUM = Mary MAKENNE
Jacob MANLEY = Rebecca LUM
William MANLY = Rachel JACKSON (prob. daughter of John Jackson, Jr.)
William H. MANLY = Sarah D. WALTER
Silas William RUNDALL = Rachel MANLY
William Henry "Will" THOMPSON = Sarah D. "Sadie" RUNDALL

---

[235] Hill, *Fundy to Chesapeake*, 257.
[236] Hill, *Fundy to Chesapeake*, 155-6.
[237] Hill, *Fundy to Chesapeake*, 260.

MARY (_____) MAKENNE

MARY _____ first appears in the public record when she gave birth to her first child on 16 August 1720. She married (1) **ALEXANDER MAKENNE**, and they had two more children before he died in 1722. She married (2) **Matthew KEMP**, who died in 1734, without additional issue (see preceding).

PETER MALLORY

PETER MALLORY, Sr.[238] died in New Haven, Conn., between 1697 and 1701. He first appeared in the record when he signed the planters' covenant at New Haven in 1664, and he became a large landowner there. There are strong circumstantial grounds to conclude that his wife Mary was **Mary PRESTON**, daughter of WILLIAM PRESTON and his wife Elizabeth Sale; baptized at Chesham, co. Bucks, 13 December 1629; died, probably in New Haven, in 1690 (see).

Peter MALLORY Sr. = Mary _____ (prob. PRESTON)
Peter MALLORY Jr. = Elizabeth TROWBRIDGE
Stephen MALLORY = Mary _____
Benajah MALLORY = Elizabeth WAKELEE, married (1) _____ Crane
Isaac HILL [Jr.] = Eunice MALLORY
Ephraim HILL = Charlotte PRINCE
William Prince HILL = Sarah P. "Sally" HERRICK
Charles W. HILL = Adelia Catharine "Delia" RILEY
George J. HILL = Jessie Fidelia STOCKWELL

JOHN MANLEY (MANLY)

JOHN MANLEY (MANLY)[239] was in Cecil County, Maryland, in the latter part of the seventeenth century. He is recorded in Cecil County in 1678 and again in 1681-1683. In June 1682, this John Manley was probably also a pirate of the southern Chesapeake. His son, John Manley [II] was born say 1688.

John MANLEY, perhaps John Manly, pirate of the Chesapeake = _____ _____
John MANLEY [II] = Elizabeth PENNINGTON
Private John MANLEY = Elizabeth BARBER
Jacob MANLEY = Rebecca LUM
William MANLY = Rachel JACKSON (prob. daughter of John Jackson, Jr.)
William H. MANLY = Sarah D. WALTER
Silas William RUNDALL = Rachel MANLY
William Henry "Will" THOMPSON = Sarah D. "Sadie" RUNDALL

_____ (_____) MANLEY

_____, whose name is unknown, was the mother of John Manley [II], born about 1688. Her husband, **JOHN MANLEY**, a planter in Cecil Co., Md., was perhaps previously a pirate, who escaped and relocated from Virginia to the northern edge of the Chesapeake Bay (see preceding).

ROBERT MANSFIELD

ROBERT MANSFIELD,[240] a yeoman of Lynn, Essex Co., Mass., was born in about 1594, presumably in England; died at Lynn, 16 December 1666. He first appeared in the records of Lynn in 1644. He acquired a large amount of property in Lynn, and he appears in many town and court records. He married in England, in say 1616, **ELIZABETH** _____; born in England in about 1586; died, probably at Lynn, Mass., 8 September 1673. They had four children.

---

[238] Hill, *Western Pilgrims*, 26-7.
[239] Hill, *Fundy to Chesapeake*, 234-5.
[240] Hill, *Quakers and Puritans*, 266.

Robert MANSFIELD = Elizabeth _____
Andrew MANSFIELD = Bethia _____
John CONANT = Bethiah MANSFIELD
John DARBY Jr. = Deborah CONANT
Andrew "Miller" DARBY = Elizabeth PATCH
Sgt. Josiah JACKSON = Mary DARBY
Oliver JACKSON = Mary PEIRCE
Jesse WARREN = Betsy JACKSON
Herbert Marshall WARREN = Eliza Caroline COPP
William Toy SHOEMAKER = Mabel WARREN

ELIZABETH (_____) MANSFIELD

ELIZABETH _____, wife of **ROBERT MANSFIELD**, was probably born in England in about 1586. She came with her husband to Lynn, Mass., where he was first recorded in 1644 (see preceding).

EULALIA MARCHE

EULALIA MARCHE, [241] born in England in say 1600; died at Springfield, Mass., in 1690. She married, in England, **HENRY BURT**, of co. Devon, with whom she had several children in England. They came to America and were first recorded at Roxbury, Mass., in 1639. The family soon removed to Springfield, Mass., along with others from Roxbury, including Rowland Stebbins, whose son Thomas would later marry her daughter Abigail Burt. She is an ancestor of George J. Hill, the Iowa Pioneer.

ELIZABETH MARSHALL

ELIZABETH MARSHALL, [242] daughter of John and Alice (Bevys) Marshall, was baptized at St. Mary Arches, Exeter, England, 24 March 1602/3; died probably New Haven, Conn., before 1641. Her father was Lord Mayor of Exeter. She married **THOMAS TROWBRIDGE**, son of John and Agnes (Prowse) Trowbridge; born at Taunton, co. Somerset, in March or April 1598; died there, and was buried at St. Mary Magdalen Church, 7 February 1672/3. In 1636, he was the first of his family to come to America. After spending about five years in Massachusetts and Connecticut, he returned to England, where he died 30 years later. She is an ancestor of both George J. Hill, the Iowa Pioneer, and Mabel Warren.

JOHN MASTERS

Mr. JOHN MASTERS, [243] born about 1581, perhaps in co. Essex, England; died at Cambridge, Mass., 21 December 1639. He came to America in the Great Migration of 1630, perhaps with Sir Richard Saltonstall, for whom he was in service. He was later licensed to keep a tavern. His excellent handwriting implies that he had a good education. He married, by about 1606, **JANE _____**, who was probably the mother of all his children, she died at Cambridge, Mass., 26 December 1639.

John MASTERS = Jane _____
Philip TABER = Lydia MASTERS
Rev. Pardon TILLINGHAST = Lydia TABER
Phillip TILLINGHAST, J.P. = Martha HOLMES
William POTTER = Martha TILLINGHAST
Capt. Oliver POTTER = Mary COLVIN
Capt. Freeborn POTTER = Dolly IRISH
Harvey HYDE = Fidelia Gadcourt POTTER
Benajah Flavel STOCKWELL = Emily Lodiweska HYDE
George J. HILL = Jessie Fidelia STOCKWELL

---

[241] Hill, *Western Pilgrims*, 28; *Torrey's New England Marriages*, 256, 661; and *Great Migration* 6:497.
[242] Hill, *Western Pilgrims*, 31.
[243] Hill, *Western Pilgrims*, 273-4.

JANE (_____) MASTERS

JANE _____, wife of **Mr. JOHN MASTERS**, and probably mother of his children, came with her husband and four children to Massachusetts in 1630. She died at Cambridge, Mass., in 1639 (see above).

[MATHER]

[MATHER[244] The family name of Mather appears many times in two of these books in association with the ancestors of George J. Hill, the Iowa Pioneer, and of Mabel Warren. *Western Pilgrims* speaks of the descendants of the immigrant to Massachusetts, Richard Mather. *Quakers and Puritans* tells of connections with the descendants of the immigrant to Pennsylvania, Joseph Mather, who some say is related to Richard. No one named Mather is a direct ancestor in either the Hill family or the Warren family. However, I discovered that the **Rev. Cotton Mather** married, as his first wife, the granddaughter of Mabel Warren's ancestor, **Mary (Miller) Hodges**, by her second husband, John Anderson. Cotton Mather's children by that marriage were thus distant half-cousins of Mabel Warren. However, none of these children of Cotton Mather have living descendants. (See JOHN HODGES and MARY MILLER)]

EDMOND McVAUGH

EDMOND McVAUGH,[245] born say 1664, most likely in Ireland; died in Pennsylvania before his will was proved on 3 November 1739. He emigrated to America as a servant of Captain Thomas Holme, who had been a captain in Cromwell's army. Holme left from London on the *Amity*, and McVaugh probably accompanied him. *Amity* arrived on 3 August 1682. Holme allowed McVaugh to settle on 50 acres in his Well Spring Plantation. By 1702, McVaugh possessed 301 acres of land. He married, in Pennsylvania, between 1699 and 1702, **ALICE DICKINSON**; born say 1669; died before October 1738. She came to America on the ship *Submission*, which arrived in November 1682. Edmond and Alice (Dickinson) McVaugh had at least six children, and perhaps more. They are ancestors of **President Theodore Roosevelt, Jr**.

Edmond McVAUGH = Alice DICKINSON
John POTTS = Elizabeth McVAUGH
Isaac SHOEMAKER Jr. = Elizabeth POTTS
Jonathan SHOEMAKER Esq. = Hannah LUKENS
Charles SHOEMAKER = Rachel COMLY
Julien SHOEMAKER = Hannah Ann HESTER
William Toy SHOEMAKER = Mabel WARREN

WILLIAM MEAD

WILLIAM MEAD,[246] son of Priscilla [sic, a man] and Dorothy (Grey) Mead, was baptized at St. Mary's, Watford, Hertfordshire, 27 December 1592; died at Stamford, Conn., in 1657. He came to New England in about 1635 and settled first at Wethersfield, Conn. He removed to Stamford. His sons John and Joseph were two of the first 27 proprietors of Horseneck (Greenwich), Conn. He married, in England, in 1620, **PHILLIP _____**, [sic, a woman] sometimes called Phillipe; died in Stamford, Conn., 19 July 1657.

William MEAD = Phillip [or Philippa]
John MEAD = Hannah POTTER (originally prob. BROWN)
Ebenezer MEAD, J.P. = Sarah KNAPP
Jonathan HOBBY Sr. = Sarah MEAD
Jonathan HOBBY Jr. = Deborah LYON
Reuben RUNDLE Sr. = Amy HOBBY

---

[244] *Western Pilgrims*, 32, 359. *Quakers and Puritans*, 116.
[245] *Quakers and Puritans*, 86-7. The Welcome Society shows Alice Dickinson as having arrived on the *Submission*.
[246] Hill, *Fundy to Chesapeake*, 147-8.

Shadrack RUNDALL Sr. = Phebe BROWN
Reuben John RUNDALL = Martha TOMPKINS
Silas William RUNDALL = Rachel MANLY
William Henry "Will" THOMPSON = Sarah D. "Sadie" RUNDALL

PHILLIP (_____) MEAD

PHILLIP _____ (aka Phillipe or Phillippa), married, in England, in about 1620, **WILLIAM MEAD**, son of Priscilla and Dorothy (Grey) Mead, born in Hertfordshire in 1592; died at Stamford, Conn., in 1657. They came to New England in about 1635 and she died in Stamford in 1657 (see preceding).

THOMAS MERCER

THOMAS MERCER,[247] of "Ayon-on-the-Hill," co. Northampton, England, was born in about 1660; died at Westtown, Thornbury Twp., Chester Co., Pa., 12 September 1716. He and his wife settled near the Westtown line, where he purchased 238 acres by deed of 1mo. 12, 1699/1700. Thomas Mercer was among the early settlers in Aston Township, near what later became known as Dutton's Mills, with 100 acres on Chester Creek, near the present location of Middletown and Upper Chichester. He married **MARY ____ (perhaps GREENAWAY)**, born in England; died at Westtown, Pa., 3 June 1723.

Thomas MERCER = Mary _____ (perhaps GREENAWAY)
Thomas MERCER Jr. = Hannah TAYLOR
Daniel MERCER = Rebecca TOWNSEND
Solomon MERCER = Abigail SHARPLES
William WALTER = Phebe MERCER
William H. MANLY = Sarah D. WALTER
Silas William RUNDALL = Rachel MANLY
William Henry "Will" THOMPSON = Sarah D. "Sadie" RUNDALL

MARY (_____) MERCER

MARY _____ (perhaps GREENAWAY), born in England, married **THOMAS MERCER**. They came to Pennsylvania in about 1699. She had seven children. She died in Westtown, Pa., in 1723 (see above).

JOSEPH MERRIAM

JOSEPH MERRIAM,[248] son of William Merriam of Hadlow (who died in 1685), was born in co. Kent, England. He arrived with his wife at Charlestown, Mass., in July 1638, and soon moved to Concord, where he was made a freeman and died on 1 January 1640/1. His wife **SARAH _____** survived him.

Joseph MERRIAM = Sarah _____
Sgt. Thomas WHEELER = Sarah MERRIAM
Deacon Joseph WARREN = Ruth WHEELER
Joseph WARREN Jr. = Tabitha PARKER
Capt. Joseph WARREN = Joanna FLETCHER
Jeduthan WARREN = Joanna MOORS
Jesse WARREN = Betsy JACKSON
Herbert Marshall WARREN = Eliza Caroline COPP
William Toy SHOEMAKER = Mabel WARREN

SARAH (_____) MERRIAM

SARAH ____, of co. Kent, England, came to Massachusetts in July 1638 with her husband, **JOSEPH MERRIAM**, who died in 1640/1. They had five children, the last born posthumously. She married (2) **Joseph WHEELER**, of Concord, and died 12 March 1671 (see preceding).

---

[247] Hill, *Fundy to Chesapeake*, 306.
[248] Hill, *Quakers and Puritans*, 164.

JOHN MICHELL

JOHN MICHELL[249] was christened 24 March 1587/8 in Colyton, co. Devon, England; buried there in 1596. He married there, on 26 November 1569, *Emlyn WEEKE.* They had nine children. Their granddaughter emigrated to America. They are ancestors of George J. Hill, the Iowa Pioneer.

John MICHELL = Emlyn WEEKE
Rawkey (Rochee) DOLBERE = Mary MICHELL
Jonathan GILLETT = Mary DOLBERE
(see JONATHAN GILLETT and MARY DOLBERE)

JOHN MILLER

JOHN MILLER,[250] born at Breckenbrough, parish of Kerbywilk, Yorkshire; died in Pennsylvania in 1714. He went to Ireland as a planter in 1657, and was in Armagh, Ireland, when he emigrated to America. He became a member of the Pennsylvania Assembly, and on his death in 1714, Gayen Miller, his son, was elected to fill the vacancy. He married **ANN CLIBBEN**, born 1630, Cowley, co. Durham, England; daughter of William Clibborn. John and Ann (Clibben) Miller had two sons, John and Gayen. Both sons may be ancestors of Sarah D. Rundall.

John MILLER = Ann CLIBBEN
John MILLER = Mary IGNEW   Gayen MILLER = Margaret HENDERSON
Joseph JACKSON = Susanna MILLER   James MILLER = Rachel FRED
John JACKSON Sr. = Sarah MILLER

Susanna JACKSON = John JACKSON Jr.
William MANLY = Rachel JACKSON (prob. daughter of John Jackson, Jr.)
William H. MANLY = Sarah D. WALTER
Silas William RUNDALL = Rachel MANLY
William Henry "Will" THOMPSON = Sarah D. "Sadie" RUNDALL

MARY MILLER

MARY MILLER,[251] probably of co. Middlesex, England, married **JOHN HODGES**, of Wapping, Middlesex; born about 1610; died in Massachusetts, probably Charlestown, after October 1654. He was a mariner and owner of many lots in Charlestown. Their daughter Mary married Robert Taylor and is an ancestor of Jessie Stockwell. After John Hodges died, she married (2), at Charlestown, 3 January 1654/5, **Mr. John ANDERSON**, who owned the ship *John and Sarah.* They had several children and grandchildren, one of whom was "Mrs. Abigail Mather wife to Mr. Cotton Mather."

WILLIAM MILLER

WILLIAM MILLER,[252] a tanner and planter, came from England to Ipswich, Mass., in about 1638; died at Northampton, Mass., 15 July 1690. He served as a soldier against the Indians in 1643 and 1646. He married **PATIENCE ___**, a "skilled physician and surgeon," who died at Northampton, 16 March 1716.

William MILLER = Patience _____
Abraham MILLER = Hannah CLAPP
Samuel ALLEN = Hannah MILLER
Corporal Jabez WARD = Jemima ALLEN
Private Henry HYDE = Thyrina (Therina) WARD

---

[249] Hill, *Western Pilgrims*, 127.
[250] Hill, *Fundy to Chesapeake*, 268. This genealogy is based on the probability that Rachel Jackson is the daughter of John Jackson, Jr.
[251] Hill, *Western Pilgrims*, 359. Although Robert Anderson, in *Great Migration Begins* (962-3) doubts that John Anderson had children, other sources quoted in *Western Pilgrims* name several sons and daughters.
[252] Hill, *Western Pilgrims*, 336.

Luther HYDE = Phoebe GIDDINGS
Harvey HYDE = Fidelia Gadcourt POTTER
Benajah Flavel STOCKWELL = Emily Lodiweska (Emma F.) HYDE
George J. HILL = Jessie Fidelia STOCKWELL

PATIENCE (_____) MILLER

PATIENCE _____, who married **WILLIAM MILLER** and had ten children with him, many in Northampton and perhaps some in England. She was said to be "a skilled physician and surgeon," which was very unusual at that time. She died as a "very aged" woman (see preceding).

GEORGE MILLS

GEORGE MILLS,[253] born in about 1605, probably in Yorkshire, England; died at Jamaica, Long Island, N.Y., 17 October 1694. He probably came by 1632, because his son, Samuel Mills, Sr., is said to have been born in America. He appears in the public records for the first time in the year 1654. He married, probably by 1630, **Rebecca _____**, who died after 17 October 1694, probably at Jamaica, L.I. She was perhaps **Rebecca TANNER**, daughter of NICHOLAS TANNER, of Tolspidle, Dorsetshire.

George MILLS = Rebecca ?TANNER (prob. daughter of Nicholas Tanner)
Samuel MILLS Sr. = Susannah PALMER
William RUNDLE Sr. = Abigail MILLS
Samuel RUNDLE Sr. = Hannah HARDY
Reuben RUNDLE Sr. = Amy HOBBY
Shadrack RUNDALL Sr. = Phebe BROWN
Reuben John RUNDALL = Martha TOMPKINS
Silas William RUNDALL = Rachel MANLY
William Henry "Will" THOMPSON = Sarah D. "Sadie" RUNDALL

MATTHEW MITCHELL

MATTHEW MITCHELL,[254] born at South Owram parish, Halifax, co. York, England, by about 1590-1; died at Stamford, Conn., in about 1646. He came to Boston with his wife and children in the *James* in 1635. He first resided in Charlestown, and removed to Wethersfield in 1637. He was Deputy to the Connecticut Legislature in 1637-8. He married, 16 April 1616, at Halifax, Yorkshire, **Susan (WOOD) BUTTERFIELD**, daughter of Edmund Wood. They had eight children, of whom the eldest, Abigail Mitchell, married the Rev. Abraham Pierson, Sr. (see SUSAN WOOD).

Matthew MITCHELL = Susan (WOOD) BUTTERFIELD
Rev. Abraham PIERSON Sr. = Abigail MITCHELL
Capt. Jonathan BELL = Susannah PIERSON
Ebenezer WEED = Mary BELL
David BROWN = Sarah WEED, prob. daughter of Ebenezer Weed
David BROWN [II] = Deborah JESSUP
Shadrack RUNDALL Sr. = Phebe BROWN
Reuben John RUNDALL = Martha TOMPKINS
Silas William RUNDALL = Rachel MANLY
William Henry "Will" THOMPSON = Sarah D. "Sadie" RUNDALL

THOMAS MITCHELL

THOMAS MITCHELL,[255] of Charlestown, Mass., married, at Malden, November 1655, possibly as his second wife, **Mary MOLTON**, daughter of THOMAS MOULTON and his wife Jane, born at Charlestown, Mass., in about 1635; died at Malden, 7 January 1711/12. He was admitted to the

---

[253] Hill, *Fundy to Chesapeake*, 132-3.
[254] Hill, *Fundy to Chesapeake*, 195-7; *Great Migration* 5:125-31 (Matthew Mitchell) and 7:491-6 (Edmund Wood).
[255] Hill, *Fundy to Chesapeake*, 86.

Charlestown church with "Anne 11 (4) 1636," so he probably married (1) **Anne ____**. He was deputy in 1648. He may have married (3**) Anna _____**.

Thomas MITCHELL = Mary MOLTON
Andrew MITCHELL, poss. son of Thomas Mitchell and Mary Moulton = Abigail ATWOOD
Ebenezer NURSE = Elizabeth MITCHELL, prob. dau. of Andrew Mitchell
Caleb PUTNAM = Elizabeth NURSE
William PUTNAM = Dorothy "Dolly" PRESCOTT
William ARCHIBALD = Susannah "Susan" PUTNAM
Joseph Scott THOMPSON = Ruth E. ARCHIBALD
James Everett THOMPSON = Jane GRANT
William Henry "Will" THOMPSON = Sarah D. "Sadie" RUNDALL

JANE MOOR

JANE MOOR,[256] perhaps a sister of Daniel Moore of Hatherton, Wybunbury, Cheshire, England, was born in 1638 and died at Ridley, near Chester, Pa., 9 mo. 1, 1722. She married, 2 mo. 27, 1662, **JOHN SHARPLES**, son of Geoffrey and Margaret (Ashley) Sharpless; baptized at St. Chad's Church, Wybunbury, 15 August 1624; died at Ridley Township, near Chester, Chester Co., Pa., 4 mo. 11, 1685. A Quaker, he emigrated with his family to Pennsylvania on *Friendship* in 1682. They are ancestors of the **First Lady of the Confederacy, Varina Banks (Howell) Davis**, and of Sarah D. Rundall.

FRANCIS MOORE

Elder **FRANCIS MOORE, Sr.**,[257] son of Enoch and Catherine Moore, was baptized at St. Peter's Church, Malden, co. Essex, England, 2 September 1592; died at Cambridge, Middlesex Co., Mass., 20 August 1671. He became a freeman of Cambridge, Mass., 22 May 1639, where he was "wealthy." He married in 1619, **KATHERINE ____**; born in England about 1599; died at Cambridge, Mass., 5 November 1683.

Elder Francis MOORE Sr. = Katherine _____
Ensign James KIDDER = Anna MOORE
Jonathan HYDE Jr. = Dorothy KIDDER
John WOODWARD = Hannah HYDE James HYDE = Mary UTTER
Henry BACON = Hannah WOODWARD
Hannah BACON = Jabez HYDE
Private Henry HYDE = Thyrina (Therina) WARD
Luther HYDE = Phoebe GIDDINGS
Harvey HYDE = Fidelia Gadcourt POTTER
Benajah Flavel STOCKWELL = Emily Lodiweska (Emma F.) HYDE
George J. HILL = Jessie Fidelia STOCKWELL

KATHERINE (_____) MOORE

KATHERINE _____, probably born in 1599 in co. Essex, England, and married there in about 1619, **FRANCIS MOORE, gent.**, who was born there in 1592. He was of Cambridge, Mass. (see above).

JOSEPH MOORS

Lieutenant **JOSEPH MOORS**,[258] born 4 February 1704; died at Chelmsford, Mass., 5 July 1775. He first appeared in Chelmsford in 1726. He served in Quebec in 1759 and was a lieutenant in 1771. He married, 21 June 1731, **Esther BUTTERFIELD**, daughter of Nathaniel Jr. and Sarah (Fletcher) Butterfield, and great-granddaughter of **BENJAMIN BUTTERFIELD**; born 14 November 1703; died 18 November 1773.

---

[256] Hill, *Fundy to Chesapeake*, 279-83.
[257] Hill, *Western Pilgrims*, 234.
[258] Hill, *Quakers and Puritans*, 132.

Lieut. Joseph MOORS = Esther BUTTERFIELD
Simeon MOORS = Joanna THORNDIKE
Jeduthan WARREN = Joanna MOORS
Jesse WARREN = Betsy JACKSON
Herbert Marshall WARREN = Eliza Caroline COPP
William Toy SHOEMAKER = Mabel WARREN

ROBERT MORGAN

ROBERT MORGAN,[259] a cooper of Salem, was probably born in Wales. He was one of the early settlers of Beverly, Mass., where he was a founder of the church. He married there, in about 1636, **Margaret NORMAN**, daughter of Lieut. RICHARD NORMAN and his wife FLORENCE, with whom he had eight children. He died in about 1673.

Robert MORGAN = Margaret NORMAN
Sgt. Samuel MORGAN = Elizabeth DIXEY
Hezekiah OBER = Ann (Anna) MORGAN
James THORNDIKE = Anna OBER
Simeon MOORS = Joanna THORNDIKE
Jeduthan WARREN = Joanna MOORS
Jesse WARREN = Betsy JACKSON
Herbert Marshall WARREN = Eliza Caroline COPP
William Toy SHOEMAKER = Mabel WARREN

SAMUEL MORSE

SAMUEL MORSE,[260] probably the son of the Rev. Thomas Morse and his first wife, Margaret King, was baptized at Boxted, co. Essex, 12 June 1576; died at Medfield, Mass., 5 December 1654. He embarked for New England on 15 April 1635 on the *Increase*. He was a town officer in Dedham, Mass. He married, in co. Suffolk, 29 June 1602, **ELIZABETH JASPER**, daughter of Lancelot and Rose Jasper; baptized 30 January 1579/80; died at Medfield, Mass., 20 June 1655.

Samuel MORSE = Elizabeth JASPER
Daniel MORSE = Lydia FISHER
Jonathan MORSE = Mary Marie BARBOUR
Jonathan MORSE (Jr.) = Jane WHITNEY
Joseph PARTRIDGE = Eunice MORSE
Lt. Aaron HOLBROOK = Hannah PARTRIDGE
Ebenezer STOCKWELL = Abi HOLBROOK
Joseph H. STOCKWELL = Anna Maria SAXE
Benajah Flavel STOCKWELL = Emily Lodiweska (Emma F.) HYDE
George J. HILL = Jessie Fidelia STOCKWELL

GEORGE MORTON

GEORGE MORTON,[261] whose origin is unknown, first appeared as a "merchant of York" when he was married on 22 July 1612 in Leiden, the Netherlands. He is probably one of the Mortons of Bawtry, who were wealthy Catholic neighbors of WILLIAM BRADFORD and his family. He is said to be the publisher of *Mourt's Relation* (1622). Because of his support for the Pilgrims, he would likely have been disowned by his family. He came to Plymouth Colony soon after the *Mayflower*. He married **JULIANA CARPENTER**, daughter of Alexander and Priscilla (Dillen) Carpenter; born about 1584 in co. Somerset, England; died at Plymouth Colony, 19 February 1664.

George MORTON = Juliana CARPENTER
Hon. John MORTON = Lettice _____

---

[259] Hill, *Quakers and Puritans*, 172.
[260] Hill, *Western Pilgrims*, 207-8.
[261] Hill, *Western Pilgrims*, 162-3.

Dr. John FULLER = Hannah MORTON
Captain John PRINCE = Reliance FULLER
Samuel PRINCE = Abigail HOWELL
Edward Howell PRINCE = Huldah OVIATT
Ephraim HILL = Charlotte PRINCE
William Prince HILL = Sarah P. "Sally" HERRICK
Charles W. HILL = Adelia Catherine RILEY
George J. HILL = Jessie Fidelia STOCKWELL

LETTICE (_____) MORTON

LETTICE ___[262] was born about 1630 and was probably from an immigrant family. She married (1) at Plymouth, in about 1648, **Hon. John MORTON**, son of GEORGE MORTON and his wife JULIANA CARPENTER; born about 1616 in the Netherlands; died at Middleboro, Mass., 3 October 1673. She married (2) or (3) **Andrew RING** and died at Middleboro, Mass., 22 February 1690/1.

THOMAS MOULTON

THOMAS MOULTON,[263] a fisherman, was born about 1609; died at Malden, Mass., in 1657. He probably came to New England in about 1630. He was an inhabitant of Charlestown in 1631, although he was apparently never a church man. He married **JANE ___**; born about 1610; died after 1682/3.

Thomas MOULTON = Jane _____
Thomas MITCHELL = Mary MOLTON
Andrew MITCHELL, poss. son of Thomas Mitchell and Mary Moulton = Abigail ATWOOD
Ebenezer NURSE = Elizabeth MITCHELL, prob. dau. of Andrew Mitchell
Caleb PUTNAM = Elizabeth NURSE
William PUTNAM = Dorothy "Dolly" PRESCOTT
William ARCHIBALD = Susannah "Susan" PUTNAM
Joseph Scott THOMPSON = Ruth E. ARCHIBALD
James Everett THOMPSON = Jane GRANT
William Henry "Will" THOMPSON = Sarah D. "Sadie" RUNDALL

JANE (_____) MOULTON

JANE _____, who married **THOMAS MOULTON**, was probably born in England in about 1610. She came to America with her husband and had seven children before she died in 1682/3. She was admitted to the Charlestown church in 1632/3 (see preceding).

JOSEPH MOYSE

JOSEPH MOYSE[264] was a joiner by profession. He must have been an emigrant to New England, presumably from England, and was a proprietor of Salisbury, N.H., in 1640-1658. He was a legatee in the will of Mr. Nicholas Stanton of Ipswich, England, in 1648, and he made a deposition that was quoted in Old Norfolk County Records. He married **HANNAH _____**, who died at Salisbury in 1658.

Joseph MOYSE = Hannah _____
Andrew GREELEY, Sr. = Mary MOYSE
Andrew GREELEY, Jr. = Sarah BROWN
John SINGLETARY = Mary GREELEY
Ebenezer STOCKWELL = Mary SINGLETARY
Benajah STOCKWELL = Hannah GALE
Ebenezer STOCKWELL = Abi HOLBROOK
Joseph H. STOCKWELL = Anna Maria SAXE

---

[262] Hill, *Western Pilgrims*, 164.
[263] Hill, *Fundy to Chesapeake*, 86.
[264] Hill, *Western Pilgrims*, 189.

Benajah Flavel STOCKWELL = Emily Lodiweska (Emma F.) HYDE
George J. HILL = Jessie Fidelia STOCKWELL

HANNAH (_____) MOYSE

HANNAH _____ married **JOSEPH MOYSE** and had five children with him. She must have been born in England. They first appeared in Salisbury, N.H. in 1640 (see preceding).

WILLIAM MUNROE

WILLIAM MUNROE,[265] son of Robert of Aldie, Commissary of Caithness, was born in Scotland in 1625; died at Lexington, Mass., 27 January 1717. He was in the 18th generation in the line of Clan Munro. He was captured at the Battle of Worcester in 1651 and sent to the New World as a prisoner. He eventually obtained his freedom and settled in Lexington in about 1660. He married (1) in 1665, **Martha GEORGE**, daughter of JOHN GEORGE and his wife ELIZABETH; she died about 1672. They had four children. He married (2) **Elizabeth ___**, who survived him.

William MUNROE = Martha GEORGE
John COMEE = Martha MUNROE
Jonas PEIRCE = Abigail COMEE
John PEIRCE = Abigail BEARD
Oliver JACKSON = Mary PEIRCE
Jesse WARREN = Betsy JACKSON
Herbert Marshall WARREN = Eliza Caroline COPP
William Toy SHOEMAKER = Mabel WARREN

THOMAS NEWBERRY

THOMAS NEWBERRY,[266] merchant, son of Richard Newberry, was baptized at Yarcombe, co. Devon, England, 10 November 1594; died in Dorchester, Mass., in 1635-7. He was shown on the passenger list of *Recovery* in 1634 with his second wife and several children. He was Deputy for Dorchester to the Massachusetts Bay General Court. He married (1), by about 1619, *Joane DABINOTT*, daughter of Christopher Dabinott of Yarcombe; she died before 1632. They had five children.

Thomas NEWBERRY = *Joane DABINOTT*
Capt. Benjamin NEWBERRY = Mary ALLYN
Preserved CLAPP = Sarah NEWBERRY
Abraham MILLER = Hannah CLAPP
Samuel ALLEN = Hannah MILLER
Corporal Jabez WARD = Jemima ALLEN
Private Henry HYDE = Thyrina (Therina) WARD
Luther HYDE = Phoebe GIDDINGS
Harvey HYDE = Fidelia Gadcourt POTTER
Benajah Flavel STOCKWELL = Emily Lodiweska (Emma F.) HYDE
George J. HILL = Jessie Fidelia STOCKWELL

NICHOLAS NEWLIN

NICHOLAS NEWLIN[267] was the head of a prominent Quaker family of Mountmellick, Ireland. He came with his wife **ELIZABETH _____** and at least two of their children to Pennsylvania in the 1690s. Their son Nathaniel built the Newlin Mill in 1704 on Chester Creek. Their daughter Rachel married EPHRAIM JACKSON, who represented Chester County in the Provincial Assembly.

---

[265] Hill, *Quakers and Puritans*, 233.
[266] Hill, *Western Pilgrims*, 341-2.
[267] Hill, *Fundy to Chesapeake*, 276. This genealogy is based on the probability that Rachel Jackson is the daughter of John Jackson, Jr.

Nicholas NEWLIN = Elizabeth ____
Ephraim JACKSON = Rachel NEWLIN
Joseph JACKSON = Susanna MILLER
John JACKSON Jr. = Susanna JACKSON [not a relative]
William MANLY = Rachel JACKSON (prob. daughter of John Jackson, Jr.)
William H. MANLY = Sarah D. WALTER
Silas William RUNDALL = Rachel MANLY
William Henry "Will" THOMPSON = Sarah D. "Sadie" RUNDALL

ELIZABETH (_____) NEWLIN

ELIZABETH ____, who married **Nicholas NEWLIN**, came with her husband and children to
Pennsylvania in the 1690s (see preceding).

LYDIA NEWMAN

LYDIA NEWMAN,[268] of unknown origin, was married in Dutchess Co., N.Y., 2 June 1775, by Roswell
Hopkins, J.P., to **Capt. Rufus HERRICK, Jr.**, son of Lt. Col. Rufus Herrick and his first wife, Miss ___
Gibbs, and a descendant of HENRY HERRICK. Rufus Herrick, Jr., was born in Preston, Conn., in about
1755; died in Shoreham, Addison Co., Vt., probably before 7 October 1788, but surely before 29
November 1788. She is an ancestor of George J. Hill, the Iowa Pioneer.

ESTHER NORMAN

ESTHER NORMAN,[269] who was born in 1690 and died 22 March 1741, married in Aston by Sutton,
Cheshire, England, 25 July 1710, **JOSEPH JACKSON**, said to have been born in Ireland and died in
Connecticut in 1738. They are presumed to be ancestors of George J. Hill.

RICHARD NORMAN

Lieut. RICHARD NORMAN,[270] was born in England in about 1587; died at Beverly, Mass., in 1683.
He was in Salem in 1626. He married, by 1612, **FLORENCE** ____, who bore at least six children.

Lt. Richard "Old Goodman" NORMAN = Florence _____
Robert MORGAN = Margaret NORMAN
Sgt. Samuel MORGAN = Elizabeth DIXEY
Hezekiah OBER = Ann (Anna) MORGAN
James THORNDIKE = Anna OBER
Simeon MOORS = Joanna THORNDIKE
Jeduthan WARREN = Joanna MOORS
Jesse WARREN = Betsy JACKSON
Herbert Marshall WARREN = Eliza Caroline COPP
William Toy SHOEMAKER = Mabel WARREN

FLORENCE (_____) NORMAN

FLORENCE ____, wife of **RICHARD NORMAN**, who was an "old planter" of Salem and Beverly, but
"not of the Puritan persuasion." She gave testimony in 1645 and then vanished (see preceding).

FRANCIS NURSE

FRANCIS NURSE,[271] born in England in about 1617; died in Salem Village, Mass., 22 November 1695.
He was an indentured servant when he came to New England and he became a successful farmer after he

---

[268] Hill, *Western Pilgrims*, 51.
[269] Hill, *Western Pilgrims*, 10.
[270] Hill, *Quakers and Puritans*, 171.
[271] Hill, *Fundy to Chesapeake*, 84.

obtained his freedom. He married, in the part of Salem then known as Marblehead, 24 August 1644, **Rebecca TOWNE**, daughter of WILLIAM TOWNE and his wife, JOANNA BLESSING; born at Great Yarmouth, co. Norfolk, 21 February 1620/21; hanged as a witch at Salem, Mass., 19 July 1692.

Francis NURSE = Rebecca "Goody Nurse" TOWNE
Samuel NURSE = Mary SMITH
Ebenezer NURSE = Elizabeth MITCHELL, prob. dau. of Andrew Mitchell
Caleb PUTNAM = Elizabeth NURSE
William PUTNAM = Dorothy "Dolly" PRESCOTT
William ARCHIBALD = Susannah "Susan" PUTNAM
Joseph Scott THOMPSON = Ruth E. ARCHIBALD
James Everett THOMPSON = Jane GRANT
William Henry "Will" THOMPSON = Sarah D. "Sadie" RUNDALL

MILES OAKLEY

MILES OAKLEY[272] is said to have been born in Saffron Walden, co. Essex, England, on 10 August 1612; he is said to have died at Boston, Mass., 19 October 1672. He perhaps married at Saffron Walden, **MARY BROWNE**, who died in New York in December 1682. They had one child.

Miles OAKLEY = Mary BROWNE
Miles OAKLEY [II] = Mary WILMOT
Thomas OAKLEY = Abigail FARRINGTON
Elisha OAKLEY = Elizabeth YEOMAN
Nathaniel TOMPKINS [IV] = Elizabeth "Polly" OAKLEY
Bartholomew TOMPKINS = [unmarried] Martha LAKE (possibly daughter of Daniel Lake)
Reuben John RUNDALL = Martha TOMPKINS
Silas William RUNDALL = Rachel MANLY
William Henry "Will" THOMPSON = Sarah D. "Sadie" RUNDALL

RICHARD OBER

RICHARD OBER,[273] son of John and Elizabeth (Butcher) Ober, was born at Abbotsbury, co. Dorset, England; baptized there, 21 November 1641; died intestate at Beverly, Essex Co., Mass., 4 March 1715/6. His was first recorded in America when he was married in December 1671, in Beverly. On 3 December 1677, he took the Oath of Fidelity. He later became a wealthy man. He married, at Beverly, 26 December 1671, **Abigail WOODBURY**, daughter of Nicholas Woodbury and his wife ANN PALGRAVE; born at Beverly in say 1653 to 1655; died there, in 1741-2.

Richard OBER = Abigail WOODBURY
Hezekiah OBER = Ann (Anna) MORGAN
James THORNDIKE = Anna OBER
Simeon MOORS = Joanna THORNDIKE
Jeduthan WARREN = Joanna MOORS
Jesse WARREN = Betsy JACKSON
Herbert Marshall WARREN = Eliza Caroline COPP
William Toy SHOEMAKER = Mabel WARREN

JOHN OGDEN

JOHN OGDEN,[274] whose origin is unknown, was probably born in England and came to New England in about 1638; he died, probably in Fairfield Co., Conn., in about 1682. He is known as "John Ogden of Rye." He married, in New Haven, in perhaps April 1638, probably soon after he arrived in America, **Judith BUDD**, daughter of Lieut. JOHN BUDD, an early planter of New Haven.

---

[272] Hill, *Fundy to Chesapeake*, 227.
[273] Hill, *Quakers and Puritans*, 159-60.
[274] Hill, *Fundy to Chesapeake*, 163-4.

John OGDEN = Judith BUDD
Thomas LYON, Jr. = Abigail OGDEN
Jonathan HOBBY Jr. = Deborah LYON
Reuben RUNDLE Sr. = Amy HOBBY
Shadrack RUNDALL Sr. = Phebe BROWN
Reuben John RUNDALL = Martha TOMPKINS
Silas William RUNDALL = Rachel MANLY
William Henry "Will" THOMPSON = Sarah D. "Sadie" RUNDALL

MARY OP den GRAEFF

MARY OP den GRAEFF[275] is probably the daughter of Isaac Herman Op den Graeff, and granddaughter of Hermann Isaac Op Den Graeff. He was probably the son of Johann Wilhelm de la Marck, Graff (Duke) of Jülich-Cleves-Berg, and Anna Van Aldekerk, who was born at Aldekerk, Duchy of Jülich (now in the state of Westphalia-North Rhineland, Germany), 26 November 1585; died at Krefeld, Jülich, 27 December 1642. He is said to be the ancestor of all the Op de Graeffs of America. Hermann Isaac Op Den Graeff married, probably in Kempen, Duchy of Jülich, 16 August 1605, Grietjen Gobels Pletjes. Their son, Isaac Hermann Op Den Graeff, was born about 1616 at Krefeld, Duchy of Julich; died at Krefeld, 17 January 1679. His sister Neesgen married Theiss (aka Mathias) Doors. Neesgen and Theiss were parents of several founders of Germantown, including Mary Tyson (aka Theiss), who married Jan Lukens. Isaac Hermann Op den Graeff married Margaret Peters Doors, born say 1620; died about 1683. They were parents of the three "Op den Graeff brothers" and probably also a daughter, Mary, who married Johannes Peter Cassell. I believe Hermann Isaac Op Den Graeff is an ancestor of William T. Shoemaker through descent from both his granddaughter, Mary, and from his daughter Neesgen.

Hermann Isaac OP den GRAEFF = Grietjen Gobels PLETJES
Isaac Herman OP den GRAEFF = Margaret Peters DOORS
Johannes Peter CASSEL = Mary OP den GRAEFF (prob. dau. of Isaac Hermann Op den Graeff)
Rev. John CADWALADER = Mary CASSELL (aka CASTLE)
Robert COMLY = Jane CADWALADER
Robert COMLY = Sarah JONES
Ezra COMLY = Hannah IREDELL
Charles SHOEMAKER = Rachel COMLY
Julien SHOEMAKER = Hannah Ann HESTER
William Toy SHOEMAKER = Mabel WARREN

Hermann Isaac OP den GRAEFF = Grietjen Gobels PLETJES
Theiss (aka Mathias) DOORS = Neesgen OP den GRAEFF
Jan LUKENS = Mary TYSON (aka THEISS)
Peter LUKENS = Gaynor EVANS
Joseph LUKENS = Elizabeth SPENCER
Jonathan SHOEMAKER Esq. = Hannah LUKENS
Charles SHOEMAKER = Rachel COMLY
Julien SHOEMAKER = Hannah Ann HESTER
William Toy SHOEMAKER = Mabel WARREN

THOMAS OVIATT

THOMAS OVIATT,[276] said to be a son of Thomas and Alice (Bryan) Oviatt, was born at Tring, co. Herts, England, 16 July 1626; died at Milford, Conn., 28 May 1691. He appeared in Milford in about

---

[275] Hill, *Quakers and Puritans*, 58-63 (Tyson), 64-6 (Op den Graeff).
[276] Hill, *Western Pilgrims*, 138-9.

1664/5 with his wife Frances. He was town clerk in Milford, where he was a soap maker and tallow chandler. He married **FRANCES ___ (probably BRYAN)**, who died sometime after 1680.

Thomas OVIATT = Frances _____ (maybe BRYAN)

Samuel OVIATT = Mary _____ (maybe BALDWIN)

John OVIATT = Susanna HINE

John OVIATT = Abigail SMITH

Edward Howell PRINCE = Huldah OVIATT

Ephraim HILL = Charlotte PRINCE

William Prince HILL = Sarah P. "Sally" HERRICK

Charles W. HILL = Adelia Catherine RILEY

George J. HILL = Jessie Fidelia STOCKWELL

FRANCES (_____) OVIATT

FRANCES _____, whose name may be **FRANCES BRYAN**, married **THOMAS OVIATT**, born in co. Herts, England, 16 July 1626; died at Milford, Conn., 28 May 1691. She died after 1680. He was a soap maker and she was the mother of eight children. Their third child married Richard Baldwin, son of John and Mary (Bruen) Baldwin, who has **Royal ancestry**. Their fifth child married Mary ____, who is believed to be Richard Baldwin's sister (see preceding).

ANN PALGRAVE

ANN PALGRAVE,[277] daughter of Richard and Joan (Harris) Palgrave, was baptized at Great Yarmouth, co. Norfolk, 29 October 1626; died at Beverly, Mass., 10 June 1701. She was the step-daughter of the Rev. John Young, of Southold, co. Norfolk, who died at Beverly, Mass., in 1701. He was also of Southold, L.I., in America. After her father died, her mother remarried, and then died. Ann, now an orphan, came to Salem with her step-father, who had married again. She married, by about 1652, at Salem, Mass., **Nicholas WOODBURY**, son of WILLIAM WOODBURY and his wife, ELIZABETH PATCH; born in 1618 in South Petherton, co. Somerset; died at Beverly, Mass., 16 May 1686. She is an ancestor of Mabel Warren.

[JERUSHA PALMER]

[**JERUSHA PALMER**[278] is believed by some to be the wife of Rufus Herrick [III] of Caton, Steuben Co., N.Y. The gravestone of Jerusha P., wife of Rufus Herrick, says that she died on 25 June 1827, and Steuben County records show her as Jerusha Palmer. The Herrick family of Steuben Co., who descend from Rufus Herrick [III], believes that his wife was Jerusha Pierce, not Palmer. The argument for this conclusion is given in *Western Pilgrims* (see THOMAS PIERCE).]

WILLIAM PALMER

Lieut. **WILLIAM PALMER**,[279] was surely born in England, probably near London in about 1610-1615; died in Newtown, Long Island, in 1661. He probably came to America in about 1638. He was commissioned as an ensign in 1638 in Plymouth Colony. He married, in about 1638, as her first husband, **JUDITH FEAKE**, daughter of James Feake, Jr., goldsmith of London, and his wife Awdrey Crompton; born at London, in 1621; died at Greenwich, Conn., in 1667-8. She was the niece of Robert Feake, second husband of Elizabeth (Fones) Winthrop, known as "that Winthrop woman."

Lieut. William PALMER = Judith FEAKE

Samuel MILLS Sr. = Susannah PALMER

William RUNDLE Sr. = Abigail MILLS

Samuel RUNDLE Sr. = Hannah HARDY

---

[277] Hill, *Quakers and Puritans*, 179-80.
[278] Hill, *Western Pilgrims*, 83-6.
[279] Hill, *Fundy to Chesapeake*, 139-40.

Reuben RUNDLE Sr. = Amy HOBBY
Shadrack RUNDALL Sr. = Phebe BROWN
Reuben John RUNDALL = Martha TOMPKINS
Silas William RUNDALL = Rachel MANLY
William Henry "Will" THOMPSON = Sarah D. "Sadie" RUNDALL

MARY PANTON

MARY PANTON,[280] born in Flushing, N.Y., in about 1648, married, in 1670, **VAN THOMAS FARRINGTON.** They had a child, Abigail Farrington, who is an ancestor of Sarah D. Rundall.

JACOB PARKER

JACOB PARKER,[281] was of Woburn, Mass., in 1644. In 1653, he became one of the founders of Chelmsford, Mass., where he was the first town clerk. He died before 6 April 1669. He married, as her first husband, **SARAH _____**, born about 1626; died at Malden, Mass., 13 January 1707/8. They are ancestors of **President Franklin Pierce.**

Jacob PARKER = Sarah _____
Benjamin PARKER = Sarah HOWARD
Joseph WARREN Jr. = Tabitha PARKER
Capt. Joseph WARREN = Joanna FLETCHER
Jeduthan WARREN = Joanna MOORS
Jesse WARREN = Betsy JACKSON
Herbert Marshall WARREN = Eliza Caroline COPP
William Toy SHOEMAKER = Mabel WARREN

SARAH (_____) PARKER

SARAH _____, born in England in about 1620, married (1) **JACOB PARKER**, town clerk of Chelmsford, Mass., who died there before 1669. They had nine children, born in Massachusetts. She married (2) **Captain John WAYTE** (see preceding).

JOHN PARTIDGE

JOHN PARTRIDGE,[282] probably son of Captain John Partridge of Navestock, co. Essex, England, was probably born there in about 1620 and died in Medfield, Mass., 28 May 1706. He came to Dedham, Mass., in about 1652, where he was clerk. He married, in Medfield, 18 December 1655, **Magdalen BULLARD**, daughter of JOHN BULLARD and his wife MAGDALEN; died 27 December 1677.

John PARTRIDGE = Magdalen BULLARD
Eleazer PARTRIDGE = Elizabeth ALLEN
Joseph PARTRIDGE = Eunice MORSE
Lt. Aaron HOLBROOK = Hannah PARTRIDGE
Ebenezer STOCKWELL = Abi HOLBROOK
Joseph H. STOCKWELL = Anna Maria SAXE
Benajah Flavel STOCKWELL = Emily Lodiweska (Emma F.) HYDE
George J. HILL = Jessie Fidelia STOCKWELL

ELIZABETH PATCH

ELIZABETH PATCH,[283] daughter of Nicholas and Jane Patch, was baptized at South Petherton, co. Somerset, England, 16 April 1594; died in Massachusetts after 5 (4) 1663. She married, at South

---

[280] Hill, *Fundy to Chesapeake*, 227-8.
[281] Hill, *Quakers and Puritans*, 150.
[282] Hill, *Western Pilgrims*, 199.
[283] Hill, *Quakers and Puritans*, 179.

Petherton, **WILLIAM WOODBURY**, born in 1589 in England, probably in South Petherton, co. Somerset; died at Beverly, Mass., 29 January 1677. They had six children when they came to America. She is an ancestor of Mabel Warren.

[SUSANNA PEABODY]

[The Ahnentafel for Stephen Jordan[284] erroneously shows his wife as Susannah Peabody. Susanna (Peabody) Merrill, a widow, was his second wife, and not the mother of Anna Jordan, who married Robert Cross. Her maiden name was not shown in the text (see STEPHEN JORDAN, above).]

SARAH PEET

SARAH PEET,[285] whose ancestry is unknown, married, possibly in Dartmouth, Mass., in about 1676, **THOMAS LAKE**, son of Henry and Alice Lake. Her mother-in-law was hanged as a witch in Boston. Thomas and Sarah (Peet) Lake had six children. Her brother-in-law, David Lake, married Sarah (Earle) Cornell, widow of Thomas Cornell, Jr., who was falsely accused and executed for killing his mother. By her son Daniel Lake, she may be an ancestor of Sarah D. Rundall.

JOHN PEIRCE

JOHN PEIRCE,[286] weaver, was born in England in about 1583, probably Norwich, co. Norfolk; died at Watertown, Mass., 19 August 1661. His last record in Norwich was on 8 April 1637, when he applied for permission, as "John Pers," to pass to Boston in New England, at age 49, with his wife, Elizabeth, 36; four children, John, Barbre, Elizabeth, and Judeth; and a servant. Later in 1637, John Peirce became one of the earliest settlers in Watertown, Mass. He was made freeman in March 1638/9. He married, in England, **ELIZABETH _____**; born in England in about 1588; died at Watertown, Mass., 12 Mar 1666/7. The family name has been spelled many ways, and it has shifted from Peirce to Pierce.

John PEIRCE = Elizabeth _____
Anthony PEIRCE = Ann _____
Daniel PEIRCE = Elizabeth _____
John PEIRCE = Elizabeth SMITH
Jonas PEIRCE = Abigail COMEE
John PEIRCE = Abigail BEARD
Oliver JACKSON = Mary PEIRCE
Jesse WARREN = Betsy JACKSON
Herbert Marshall WARREN = Eliza Caroline COPP
William Toy SHOEMAKER = Mabel WARREN

ELIZABETH (_____) PEIRCE

ELIZABETH _____, who was probably born in co. Norfolk, England, in about 1588, married **JOHN PEIRCE**, a weaver. She came with him and four of their eight children to America in 1637. They were wealthy enough to come with a servant (see preceding).

THOMAS PELLET

THOMAS PELLET, Sr.,[287] was born in England and probably died there. He married, as her first husband, **SARAH _____**, who had one son, born in about 1639. She married (2) in England, as his first

---

[284] Hill, *Western Pilgrims*, xx, 302.

[285] Hill, *Fundy to Chesapeake*, 231.

[286] Hill, *Quakers and Puritans*, 211. The Ahnentafel for this book shows Joseph Peirce as the father of John Peirce in the 4th generation. This reiterates what I believe is an error in the primary text by Davis, *Warren, Jackson*, which I noted on p.213. I failed to correct the Ahnetafel in *Quakers and Puritans*.

[287] Hill, *Western Pilgrims*, 92. The descent to George J. Hill, the Iowa Pioneer, depends on the assumption that Jerusha P., wife of Rufus Herrick (III), was Jerusha Pierce. (See discussion on p.45, Herrick Family.)

wife, William Underwood, Esq. Sarah came to America with him and Thomas Pellet, Jr. She and Underwood had six children, born in Massachusetts between 1640 and 1656. Sarah (___) (Pellet) Underwood died in 1684. William Underwood married (2), as her second husband, Anna (Moore) Kidder, who died in 1691. These marriages unite the families of George J. Hill, Jessie Stockwell, and Mabel Warren (see also WILLIAM UNDERWOOD, JAMES KIDDER, and FRANCIS MOORE). The probable lines of descent from Sarah (___) Pellet to George J. Hill, the Iowa Pioneer, and Mabel Warren, is shown below.

Thomas PELLET Sr. = Sarah _____ = William UNDERWOOD
Thomas PELLET Jr. = Mary DANE   Josiah RICHARDSON = Remembrance U.   Nathan. BUTTERFIELD = Deborah U.
Richard PELLET = Ann BROOKS   Wm. FLETCHER = S. RICHARDSON   N. BUTT. Jr. = Sarah FLETCHER
Jonathan PELLET = Jerusha BRADFORD   Josiah FLETCHER = Joanna SPAL.   Joseph MOORS = Esther BUTT.
Willard PIERCE = Jerusha PELLET   Joseph WARREN = J. FLETCHER   Simeon MOORS = J. THORNDIKE
Rufus HERRICK [III] = Jerusha prob..PIERCE   Jeduthan WARREN = Joanna MOORS
William Prince HILL = Sarah HERRICK   Jesse WARREN = Betsy JACKSON
Charles W. HILL = Adelia RILEY   Herbert Marshall WARREN = Eliza Caroline COPP
George J. HILL = Jessie STOCKWELL   William Toy SHOEMAKER = Mabel WARREN

SARAH (_____) PELLET

SARAH _____ married, in England, ***Thomas PELLET, Sr.,*** and had a son, born in about 1639. Thomas Sr. soon died and she married (2) **WILLIAM UNDERWOOD, Esq**. She came to America with her second husband and her son, Thomas Pellet, Jr. She had six more children in Massachusetts and died in Concord, 5 November 1684. Her second husband, William Underwood, married (2) a widow, **Anna (MOORE) KIDDER**. The many children of these several marriages produce a complicated family tree. The possible line from Sarah (___) Pellet to George J. Hill, the Iowa Pioneer, and two lines of descent from Sarah (___) (Pellet) Underwood to Mabel Warren, are shown immediately above. The line of descent from William Underwood and Anna (Moore) (Kidder) Underwood to Jessie Stockwell is outlined in FRANCIS MOORE, JAMES KIDDER and WILLIAM UNDERWOOD.

ROBERT PENNELL

ROBERT PENNELL, Jr.,[288] son of Robert and Isabel Pennell, of Balderton, Notts, was baptized at Balderton, 25 October 1640; died early in 1728/9 (O.S.), probably in Chester Co., Pa. He married in England and had three children there, two of whom survived to come to America. After his first wife died he married again, in England, and had five more children with his second wife. He was an early colonial settler in Middletown Twp., Delaware Co., Pa., where he resided from 1684 to 1686. He is an ancestor of Sarah D. Rundall by each of his wives. He married (1), in England, ***Isobel (Elizabeth) ____ (possibly HYANDSON)***, in say 1664. By this marriage, he is an ancestor of **President Richard Milhous Nixon**. He married (2), in England, **HANNAH** _____, who probably came with him to America.

*Isobel (Elizabeth)*_____ = Robert PENNELL Jr. = Hannah _____
Josiah TAYLOR = Elizabeth PENNELL   John SHARPLES = Hannah PENNELL
Bartholomew COPPOCK Jr. = Phoebe TAYLOR
Sarah COPPOCK = Daniel SHARPLES
Solomon MERCER = Abigail SHARPLES
William WALTER = Phebe MERCER
William H. MANLY = Sarah D. WALTER
Silas William RUNDALL = Rachel MANLY
William Henry "Will" THOMPSON = Sarah D. "Sadie" RUNDALL

Hill, *Quakers and Puritans*, 152-9: Descent to Mabel Warren in Spalding, Butterfield, and Undewood Families.
Hill, *Western Pilgrims*, 234-6: Descent to Jessie Stockwell in Moore and Kidder Families.
[288] Hill, *Fundy to Chesapeake*, 297.

HANNAH (_____) PENNELL

HANNAH _____[289] married, in England, as his second wife, **ROBERT PENNELL, Jr.**, son of Robert and Isabel Pennell. He was baptized at Balderton, Notts, in 1640 and died in Pennsylvania in 1728/9. She raised the surviving children of his first wife and had five more. She probably came to America in 1684 when her youngest child was about three years old, but her death is unrecorded (see preceding).

HENRY PENNINGTON

HENRY PENNNINGTON[290] was probably born in England in 1630. He "was transported by 1650/1." He claimed land for service in Maryland in 1670, and in August 1671 he purchased 400 acres, known as *Happy Harbour*, on the Sassafras River. He married **RACHEL ___**, who immigrated by 1677.

Henry PENNINGTON = Rachel _____

John MANLEY [II] = Elizabeth PENNINGTON

Private John MANLEY = Elizabeth BARBER

Jacob MANLEY = Rebecca LUM

William MANLY = Rachel JACKSON (prob. daughter of John Jackson, Jr.)

William H. MANLY = Sarah D. WALTER

Silas William RUNDALL = Rachel MANLY

William Henry "Will" THOMPSON = Sarah D. "Sadie" RUNDALL

RACHEL (_____) PENNINGTON

RACHEL _____, immigrant to Maryland in about 1677, whose family name is unknown, married **HENRY PENNINGTON**, who emigrated in about 1650/1. They had many children (see preceding).

CICELY PENNY

CICELY PENNY[291] was probably the daughter of Henry and Jane (Dabinott) Penny who was christened 21 February 1601 in Paington, Devonshire. She died at Springfield, Mass., 3 February 1682/3. Her parents were probably French Huguenots. She married in Devonshire, probably 9 February 1628, **SAMUEL CHAPIN**. They came to America in 1638 and are ancestors of Jessie Stockwell.

BARTHOLOMEW PENROSE

BARTHOLOMEW PENROSE[292] was baptized at Bristol, England, 21 January 1674, according to one account; died at Philadelphia, Pa., 17 November 1711. He was in the ship building business with William Penn Sr., and built the ship *Diligence*. He married, at Philadelphia, in 1703, **Esther LEECH**, daughter of TOBY LEECH and his wife ESTHER ASHMEAD; born at Philadelphia, in 1685; died 1 April 1713.

Bartholemew PENROSE = Hester (Ester) LEECH

Isaac SHOEMAKER Sr. = Dorothy PENROSE

Isaac SHOEMAKER Jr. = Elizabeth POTTS

Jonathan SHOEMAKER Esq. = Hannah LUKENS

Charles SHOEMAKER = Rachel COMLY

Julien SHOEMAKER = Hannah Ann HESTER

William Toy SHOEMAKER = Mabel WARREN

WILLIAM PHELPS

WILLIAM PHELPS,[293] born about 1593; died at Windsor, Conn., 14 July 1672. He was of Crewkerne, co. Somerset, when he left England on the *Mary and John* in 1630 and landed at Nantasket (now Hull),

---

[289] Hill, *Fundy to Chesapeake*, 297.

[290] Hill, *Fundy to Chesapeake*, 254.

[291] Hill, *Western Pilgrims*, 203-5.

[292] Hill, *Quakers and Puritans*, 50-1.

[293] Hill, *Western Pilgrims*, 21.

Mass. He relocated to Windsor, Conn., in 1635, where he held many offices. He married (1) **Mary** _____, who was buried at Crewkerne, co. Somerset, 13 August 1626. He married (2) at Crewkerne, 14 November 1626, **ANNE DOVER**; born there in 1610; died at Windsor, Conn., 30 August 1689.

William PHELPS = Anne DOVER
Joseph PHELPS Sr. = Hannah NEWTON
John HILL = Sarah PHELPS
Ephriam WILCOX = Hannah HILL
Michael JACKSON = Susannah WILCOX
Sergeant Isaiah J. HENDRYX = Esther JACKSON
Josiah (Isaiah) RILEY = Susannah HENDRYX
Simeon RILEY = Katharine "Catherine" GILLETT
Charles W. HILL = Adelia Catharine "Delia" RILEY
George J. HILL = Jessie Fidelia STOCKWELL

JAMES PHILLIPS

JAMES PHILLIPS,[294] who was perhaps born in Wales in 1676; died at New Castle, Del., in 1772. He emigrated to Philadelphia in 1700 and resided at Springfield, Delaware Co., (then Chester Co.) Pa. He married, in Philadelphia, in 1707, **HANNAH TAYLOR**, born in England in about 1690; died in 1745.

James PHILLIPS = Hannah TAYLOR
Jacob DIXON = Esther PHILLIPS
James WALTER = Sarah DIXON (prob. daughter of Jacob Dixon)
William WALTER = Phebe MERCER
William H. MANLY = Sarah D. WALTER
Silas William RUNDALL = Rachel MANLY
William Henry "Will" THOMPSON = Sarah D. "Sadie" RUNDALL

WALTER PHILLIPS

WALTER PHILLIPS[295] was probably born in about 1619. He was at Salem, Mass., in 1689, said "perhaps driven by the Indians from Wiscasset, Maine." He was made freeman in 1690 at Salem Village, now known as Danvers. He apparently had at least two children, by a wife whose name is unknown.

Walter PHILLIPS = _____ _____
Jacob PHILLIPS = Sarah RAY (aka REA)
Caleb PUTNAM = Silence PHILLIPS (m. [1] _____ Dunklee)
Caleb PUTNAM [II] = Elizabeth NURSE
William PUTNAM = Dorothy "Dolly" PRESCOTT
William ARCHIBALD = Susannah "Susan" PUTNAM
Joseph Scott THOMPSON = Ruth E. ARCHIBALD
James Everett THOMPSON = Jane GRANT
William Henry "Will" THOMPSON = Sarah D. "Sadie" RUNDALL

_____ (_____) PHILLIPS

_____ _____[296] married **WALTER PHILLIPS**, of Wiscasset, Maine, and Salem, Mass. They had two children. Her granddaughter married (1) _____ Dunklee; and (2) Caleb Putnam (see preceding).

DAVID PHIPPEN

DAVID PHIPPEN,[297] son of Robert Fitzpen als Fippen and his wife, Cecily Jordan, was born in co. Dorset, probably at Weymouth, in say 1584; died at Boston, Mass., before October 1650. He came with

---

[294] Hill, *Fundy to Chesapeake*, 342.
[295] Hill, *Fundy to Chesapeake*, 75. See ELNATHAN DUNKLEE for discussion of Silence Phillips.
[296] Hill, *Fundy to Chesapeake*, 75.
[297] Hill, *Western Pilgrims*, 134-5; 310-11.

his wife and children in 1633 in *Recovery* and was in Hingham in 1635. He was constable in Boston in 1646/7. He married **SARAH ___**, who died in 1659 after marrying again. He is an ancestor of both George J. Hill, the Iowa Pioneer, and his wife Jessie F. Stockwell.

<pre>
                        David PHIPPEN = Sarah _____
   Joseph PHIPPEN = Dorcas (probably aka Dorothy) WOOD George VICKERY = Rebecca PHIPPEN
   John WALLIS = Mary PHIPPEN   John PRINCE = Rebecca VICKERY
   James WALLIS = Martha STANDFORD   Captain John PRINCE = Reliance FULLER
   John ANDREWS = Elizabeth WALLIS   Samuel PRINCE = Abigail HOWELL
   Capt. Joseph GIDDINGS = Eunice ANDREWS   Edward Howell PRINCE = Huldah OVIATT
   Benjamin GIDDINGS = Martha SEELEY   Ephraim HILL = Charlotte PRINCE
   Luther HYDE = Phoebe GIDDINGS   William Prince HILL = Sarah P. "Sally" HERRICK
   Harvey HYDE = Fidelia Gadcourt POTTER   Charles W. HILL = Adelia Catherine RILEY
   Benajah F. STOCKWELL = Emily L. HYDE

            Jessie Fidelia STOCKWELL = George J. HILL
</pre>

SARAH (_____) PHIPPEN

SARAH _____ was born in England, perhaps Weymouth or Melcom Regis, co. Dorset; died in Massachusetts in August 1659. She came to America in 1633 with her first husband and many children. She married (1) **DAVID PHIPPEN**, with whom she had ten children. After 1654, she married (2) **George HULL**, without further issue (see preceding).

THOMAS PIERCE

THOMAS PIERCE[298] (also spelled **PERS**), was born about 1583; died in Woburn, Mass., 7 October 1666. He may have come to America in 1633-4 with his wife Elizabeth and settled in Charlestown, Mass. He was admitted to the church in Charlestown on 21, 12mo. 1634, and he was later a Commissioner appointed by the General Court. His will included a bequest to Harvard College. He had three children in England by a wife whose name is unknown. He married (2) **Elizabeth WORTHINGTON**; born about 1596; died after 1666/7; with whom he had five children, born at Charlestown.

<pre>
                Thomas PIERCE (PERS) = _____ _____
            Sgt. Thomas PIERCE Jr. = Elizabeth COLE
                   Thomas PIERCE = Eliza ____
            Judge Timothy PIERCE = Lydia SPAULDING
            Nathaniel PIERCE = Elizabeth STEVENS
               Willard PIERCE = Jerusha PELLET
   Rufus HERRICK [III] = Jerusha P._____ (prob. PIERCE)
      William Prince HILL = Sarah P. "Sally" HERRICK
      Charles W. HILL = Adelia Catharine "Delia" RILEY
         George J. HILL = Jessie Fidelia STOCKWELL
</pre>

ABRAHAM PIERSON

Rev. ABRAHAM PIERSON, Sr.,[299] baptized at Guiseley Chapel, Yorkshire, 22 September 1611; died at Newark, N.J., 9 August 1678. He graduated B.A. from Trinity College, Cambridge, in 1632. He emigrated to Massachusetts in 1640 and became pastor at Lynn. Abraham Pierson soon moved with his congregation to Long Island. He returned to the mainland in 1647 to organize a new church at Branford, which was then in the New Haven Colony. Most of his congregation at Branford then relocated, along with others from New Haven, to found the city that became Newark, New Jersey. He married, by about 1640, **Abigail MITCHELL**, daughter of MATTHEW MITCHELL and his wife Susan (Wood)

---

[298] Hill, *Western Pilgrims*, 83-4. The descent to George J. Hill, the Iowa Pioneer, depends on the assumption that Jerusha P., wife of Rufus Herrick (III), was Jerusha Pierce. See discussion on p.45, Herrick Family.
[299] Hill, *Fundy to Chesapeake*, 192-3.

(Butterfield) Mitchell; baptized at Halifax, Yorkshire, England, 26 April 1618; died in America, at a time and place that was not recorded. Their son, the Rev. Abraham Pierson, Jr., was the first head of the institution that is now called Yale University.

Rev. Abraham PIERSON Sr. = Abigail MITCHELL
Capt. Jonathan BELL = Susannah PIERSON
Ebenezer WEED = Mary BELL
David BROWN = Sarah WEED, prob. daughter of Ebenezer Weed
David BROWN [II] = Deborah JESSUP
Shadrack RUNDALL Sr. = Phebe BROWN
Reuben John RUNDALL = Martha TOMPKINS
Silas William RUNDALL = Rachel MANLY
William Henry "Will" THOMPSON = Sarah D. "Sadie" RUNDALL

GYLES PLOMER

GYLES PLOMER[300] was born say 1515 and lived in Hertfordshire. He had several children, including a daughter Margaret. Her granddaughter came to New England in 1636 and married Capt. Isaac Johnson, son of JOHN JOHNSON. He is an ancestor of Jessie F. Stockwell.

Gyles Plomer = _____ _____
Rev. Robert PORTER = Margaret PLOMER
Adrian PORTER = Elizabeth ALLOTT
Capt. Isaac JOHNSON = Elizabeth PORTER
(see JOHN JOHNSON)

ELIZABETH PORTER

ELIZABETH PORTER,[301] daughter of Adrian and Elizabeth (Allott) Porter, was baptized at Ware, co. Herts, 10 February 1610/11; died at Roxbury, Mass., 15 August 1683/4. She came to New England probably with her brother Edward and his wife and children. She married, at Roxbury, Mass., 20 January 1636/7, **Capt. Isaac JOHNSON**, son of Capt. JOHN JOHNSON and Mary Heath; baptized at Great Amwell, Herts, 11 February 1615/6; died in the Great Swamp Battle, 19 December 1675.

ROBERT POTTER

ROBERT POTTER[302] came to America in 1634; died in Rhode Island, probably at Warwick, in 1656. He came on the same ship with the Rev. Nathaniel Ward. He settled at Lynn, Mass., and then Roxbury. Potter soon became a follower of Samuel Gorton. He was excommunicated in 1643. He married (1) **ISABEL ANTHONY**, daughter of John and Susannah Anthony. She died of exposure in 1643, when her husband was arrested by Massachusetts authorities and taken to prison. They had four children.

Robert POTTER = Isabel ANTHONY
John POTTER = Ruth FISHER
John POTTER = Jane BURLINGAME
William POTTER = Martha TILLINGHAST
Capt. Oliver POTTER = Mary COLVIN
Capt. Freeborn POTTER = Dolly IRISH
Harvey HYDE = Fidelia Gadcourt POTTER
Benajah Flavel STOCKWELL = Emily Lodiweska HYDE
George J. HILL = Jessie Fidelia STOCKWELL

---

[300] Hill, *Western Pilgrims*, 245.
[301] Hill, *Western Pilgrims*, 246.
[302] Hill, *Western Pilgrims*, 254. See *Fundy to Chesapeake*, 536-8, for discussion of the claim that Robert Potter's daughter Elizabeth[2] Potter, who married Richard Harcourt, was the mother of Susannah[3] Harcourt, long said to have married John[2] Townsend 2d. However, I believe that she married his cousin, James[3] Townsend.

DAVID POTTS

DAVID POTTS,[303] probably the son of Thomas and Elizabeth Potts, of Llangirrig, Wales, was born about 1670 in Wales, probably Llangirgg; died in or near Philadelphia, Pa., 16 November 1730. He became bondsman for his mother on 24, 7mo. 1692, and he represented Philadelphia in the Provincial Assembly in 1728-30. He married, at Middletown Meeting, Bucks Co., Pa., 1 mo. 22, 1694, **Alice CROASDALE**, daughter of THOMAS CROSDALE and AGNES HATHORNTHWAITE; born in Yorkshire, England, in 1673; died at Germantown, Pa., before 1729. He is an ancestor of **President Theodore Roosevelt**.

David POTTS = Alice CROASDALE
John POTTS = Elizabeth McVAUGH
Isaac SHOEMAKER, Jr. = Elizabeth POTTS
Jonathan SHOEMAKER, Esq. = Hannah LUKENS
Charles SHOEMAKER = Rachel COMLY
Julien SHOEMAKER = Hannah Ann HESTER
William Toy SHOEMAKER = Mabel WARREN

JANE POWYS

JANE POWYS[304] married **THOMAS HOLBROOK** at St. Johns, Glastonbury, co. Somerset, England, 12 September 1616. He was possibly the son of William Holbrook; born about 1589, probably at Glastonbury; died in Massachusetts between 1673 and 1676. He was enrolled as a passenger on the *Marygould* in March 1634/5, with his wife and children. They had six children; the last one or two were born in America. They are ancestors of Jessie F. Stockwell, and through their eldest son, Capt. John Holbrook, they are also ancestors of **President James A. Garfield**.

PHINEAS PRATT

PHINEAS PRATT, Senr.,[305] a joiner, was born about 1593 in England; died at Charlestown, Mass., 19 April 1680. Phineas (aka Phinehas) Pratt was one of ten men who came to New England on behalf of Thomas Weston in 1622 on the *Sparrow*. He married, by 1633, **Mary PRIEST**, daughter of DEGORY PRIEST and SARAH ALLERTON, and step-daughter of Gilbert Godbertson; born at Leiden, the Netherlands, in say 1612; died at Charlestown, Mass., in July 1689.

Phineas PRATT = Mary PRIEST
Joseph PRATT = Dorcas FOLGER
Joseph EDMANDS = Mary PRATT
Lieut. Joseph SCOTT = Mary EDMANDS
Sheriff Joseph SCOTT = Sarah CUTTING
James THOMPSON Sr. = Hannah _____, prob. Hannah SCOTT
Joseph Scott THOMPSON = Ruth E. ARCHIBALD
James Everett THOMPSON = Jane GRANT
William Henry "Will" THOMPSON = Sarah D. "Sadie" RUNDALL

JAMES PRESCOTT

JAMES PRESCOTT,[306] the emigrant, was born in about 1643; died at Hampton Falls (now Kingston), Rockingham Co., N.H., 25 November 1728. In 1665, he appeared in Hampton, N.H., which was then

---

[303] Hill, *Quakers and Puritans*, 78-80.
[304] Hill, *Western Pilgrims*, 194.
[305] Hill, *Fundy to Chesapeake*, 34-5. The line of descent for Phineas Pratt depends on the assumption that Hannah ___, who married James Thompson, Sr., is Hannah Scott, daughter of Joseph Scott, as discussed on pp.3-4.
[306] Hill, *Fundy to Chesapeake*, 90-9; and note, 602-3. George J. Hill, "Was James Prescott of Hampton, New Hampshire (in 1665), the son of Sir William and Margaret (Babington) Prescott (bp. 1637/8), for whom an arrest warrant was issued in 1659/60?" *Mayflower Quarterly* 74 (No. 3, September 2008), 245-68; and Hill and Richard Fallquist, "James Prescott: A Continuing Mystery, and a Correction" *Mayflower Quarterly* (No. 3, September 2012):

part of Old Norfolk Co., Mass. After he was married, he removed to the wilderness west of Hampton, now known as Hampton Falls, where his fortified house was known as "Fort Prescott." He was known as "Venturesome James" and his farm, "Applecrest," persists to this day. He married, in 1668, **Mary BOULTER**, daughter of NATHANIEL BOULTER and his wife Grace Swaine, daughter of RICHARD SWAINE; born at Exeter, N.H., 15 May 1648; died at Kingston, N.H., 4 October 1735. They had ten children. His origin has been subject to much speculation. I suggest that the James Prescott, who was a fugitive from Parliament in London in 1659/60, could be the James Prescott who appeared five years later in New Hampshire; and that he might be an unrecorded son of Sir William Prescott and his wife, Margaret Babington.

James PRESCOTT Sr. = Mary BOULTER
Joshua PRESCOTT = Sarah CLIFFORD, prob. dau. of Israel Clifford
Joshua PRESCOTT (Jr.) = Abigail AMBROSE
William PUTNAM = Dorothy "Dolly" PRESCOTT
William ARCHIBALD = Susannah "Susan" PUTNAM
Joseph Scott THOMPSON = Ruth E. ARCHIBALD
James Everett THOMPSON = Jane GRANT
William Henry "Will" THOMPSON = Sarah D. "Sadie" RUNDALL

WILLIAM PRESTON

WILLIAM PRESTON,[307] born in England; died in New Haven, Conn., in say 1647. He married, in Chesham, co. Bucks, (1) 11 October 1613, *Elizabeth SALE*, baptized 8 June 1590; buried 22 February 1633/4. They had eight children, including a daughter, Mary. She is probably the Mary ___ who married Peter Mallory, Sr. In 1639, shortly before emigrating, he married (2) **Mary _____**, perhaps daughter of Robert Seabrook, with whom he had four children, born in America. He was a founder of the New Haven Colony. His widow married (2) Thomas Kimberly.

William PRESTON = *Elizabeth SALE*
Peter MALLORY Sr. = Mary _____ (prob. PRESTON)
Peter MALLORY Jr. = Elizabeth TROWBRIDGE
Stephen MALLORY = Mary _____
Benajah MALLORY = Elizabeth WAKELEE, married (1) _____ Crane
Isaac HILL [Jr.] = Eunice MALLORY
Ephraim HILL = Charlotte PRINCE
William Prince HILL = Sarah P. "Sally" HERRICK
Charles W. HILL = Adelia Catharine "Delia" RILEY
George J. HILL = Jessie Fidelia STOCKWELL

DEGORY PRIEST

DEGORY PRIEST[308] was born about 1579; died at Plymouth Colony, New England, 1 January 1620/1. He came from London to Leiden, the Netherlands, and from thence to New England on the *Mayflower* in November 1620. He died two months after arrival in the "general sickness" that afflicted many of the passengers. He married, in Leiden, 4 November 1611, as her second husband, **SARAH ALLERTON**, widow of John Vincent, of London, sister of Isaac Allerton of the *Mayflower*; she died at Plymouth Colony, in about 1633 "within a short time of her [third] husband." They had two daughters. She stayed

256-7. In the first paper (*MQ* 2008), I reported finding six children of William and Margaret (Babingon) Prescott, including a son James. In the second paper (*MQ* 2012), I reported the discovery that James Prescott died a year later. I now propose that William and Margaret (Babington) Prescott may have had a seventh child, born after their first son James died, and that he could have been given the name of his deceased brother. Because of chaos in the war between Cromwell and King Charles I, the baptismal records of that period are incomplete. Margaret Babington's two brothers were also fugitives from Parliament at that time, which lends credibility to the hypothesis.
[307] Hill, *Western Pilgrims*, 26.
[308] Hill, *Fundy to Chesapeake*, 37. This line of descent depends on the assumption that Hannah ___, who married James Thompson, Sr., is Hannah Scott, daughter of Joseph Scott, as discussed in *Fundy to Chesapeake*, 3-4.

behind with her daughters, and planned to come later, but after her husband died, she married (3), as his second wife, Godbert Godbertson, by whom she had a son. The Godbertson family, including Godbert, his wife, and their children – his son and his two step-daughters – came on the *Anne* in 1623.

Degory PRIEST = Sarah ALLERTON (widow of John VINCENT)
Phineas PRATT = Mary PRIEST
Joseph PRATT = Dorcas FOLGER
Joseph EDMANDS = Mary PRATT
Lieut. Joseph SCOTT = Mary EDMANDS
Sheriff Joseph SCOTT = Sarah CUTTING
James THOMPSON Sr. = Hannah _____, prob. Hannah SCOTT
Joseph Scott THOMPSON = Ruth E. ARCHIBALD
James Everett THOMPSON = Jane GRANT
William Henry "Will" THOMPSON = Sarah D. "Sadie" RUNDALL

JOHN PRINCE

Elder JOHN PRINCE,[309] eldest child of the Rev. John and Elizabeth (Toldervey) Prince, was born at Oxford, England, in 1610; died at Hull, Mass., 16 August 1676. He studied at Oxford University but because of his dissenting principles he did not receive his degree. In 1633, he emigrated to Massachusetts and was first recorded in Cambridge on 4 August 1634. He married (1) at Watertown, Mass., in May 1637, **ALICE HONOR**, daughter of Ambrose Honor of Blewberry, Berks, England; died at Hull, Mass., in 1668. They had ten children. He married (2), as her second husband, **Anne (HUBBARD) BARSTOW**.

Elder John PRINCE = Alice HONOR
John PRINCE = Rebecca VICKERY
Captain John PRINCE = Reliance FULLER
Samuel PRINCE = Abigail HOWELL
Edward Howell PRINCE = Huldah OVIATT
Ephraim HILL = Charlotte PRINCE
William Prince HILL = Sarah P. "Sally" HERRICK
Charles W. HILL = Adelia Catherine RILEY
George J. HILL = Jessie Fidelia STOCKWELL

REBECCA PRINCE

REBECCA PRINCE,[310] whose origin is unknown, married, at Salem, Mass., 3 September 1652, **Captain John PUTNAM**, son of the Emigrant, JOHN PUTNAM and his wife PRISCILLA GOULD. They had ten children, and by their son John Putnam 3d, they are ancestors of Sarah D. Rundall.

AGNES PROWSE

AGNES PROWSE,[311] daughter of John Prowse II, Gent., and his wife, Elizabeth Collack, was christened in Tiverton, co. Devon, 15 April 1576, and buried at Taunton, co. Somerset, 6 June 1622. Through her father, she descends from Richard de Clare; Hugh Capet, King of France; and **Charlemagne**. She married, as his first wife, *John TROWBRIDGE*, merchant and mayor of Taunton; son of Thomas and Joan (Lawrence) Trowbridge; christened at Taunton, 25 March 1570; died there in July 1649. Her son THOMAS TROWBRIDGE is an ancestor of both George J. Hill, the Iowa Pioneer, and Mabel Warren.

John TROWBRIDGE = Agnes PROWSE
Thomas TROWBRIDGE = Elizabeth MARSHAL
(see THOMAS TROWBRIDGE)

---

[309] Hill, *Western Pilgrims*, 130-1.
[310] Hill, *Fundy to Chesapeake*, 59.
[311] Hill, *Quakers and Puritans*, 237; and *Western Pilgrims*, 30.

JOHN PUTNAM

JOHN PUTNAM,[312] founder of the Putnam Family of Salem, Mass., was the son of Nicholas and Margaret (Goodspeed) Putnam; baptized at Wingrave, co. Bucks, 17 January 1580; died at Salem Village, Mass., 30 December 1662. He came to America in about 1640 with his wife and children and settled at Salem, Mass., in the part that is now Danvers. He married, in Buckinghamshire, England, in 1611, **PRISCILLA GOULD**, daughter of Richard Gould of Bovingdon, Herts; died at Salem, 30 December 1662. Their descendants were some of the most prominent accusers in the witchcraft delusion of 1692.

John PUTNAM Sr. = Priscilla GOULD
Captain John PUTNAM = Rebecca PRINCE
John PUTNAM 3rd = Hannah _____
Caleb PUTNAM = Silence PHILLIPS (m. [1] _____ Dunklee)
Caleb PUTNAM [II] = Elizabeth NURSE
William PUTNAM = Dorothy "Dolly" PRESCOTT
William ARCHIBALD = Susannah "Susan" PUTNAM
Joseph Scott THOMPSON = Ruth E. ARCHIBALD
James Everett THOMPSON = Jane GRANT
William Henry "Will" THOMPSON = Sarah D. "Sadie" RUNDALL

GRACE RAVENS

GRACE RAVENS,[313] daughter of Richard and Elizabeth (Hedge) Ravens, was probably born at East Bergholt, co. Suffolk, in about 1591; died at Watertown, Mass., 3 June 1662. She married (1) at Wattisfield, **John SHERMAN**; baptized at Dedham, co. Essex, 17 August 1585. Their son John Jr. is an ancestor of **Roger Sherman, Signer of the Declaration of Independence**. She married (2) **THOMAS ROGERS**, with whom she emigrated to Watertown, Mass., sometime before 1636. They had a daughter, Elizabeth Rogers. Grace (Ravens) (Sherman) (Rogers) married (3) **Roger PORTER**, and died without further issue. Her daughter Elizabeth took the name of her step-father and was known as Elizabeth Porter at the time of her marriage. She is an ancestor of Mabel Warren (see THOMAS ROGERS).

DANIEL RAY

DANIEL RAY,[314] a seaman and later a farmer, was born by 1597; died at Salem, Mass., by 24 June 1662. He first appeared in Plymouth Colony in 1630. He was in Salem by 1631, and was constable there in 1639. By 1627, he married **BETHIA** _____; died after 1662. The family name was later spelled Rea.

Daniel RAY = Bethia _____
Joshua REA = Mary WALTERS
Jacob PHILLIPS = Sarah RAY (aka REA)
Caleb PUTNAM = Silence PHILLIPS (m. [1] _____ Dunklee)
Caleb PUTNAM [II] = Elizabeth NURSE
William PUTNAM = Dorothy "Dolly" PRESCOTT
William ARCHIBALD = Susannah "Susan" PUTNAM
Joseph Scott THOMPSON = Ruth E. ARCHIBALD
James Everett THOMPSON = Jane GRANT
William Henry "Will" THOMPSON = Sarah D. "Sadie" RUNDALL

BETHIA (_____) RAY

BETHIA _____, wife of **DANIEL RAY**, immigrant to Massachusetts in 1630, died after 1662. She had two children, Joshua and Bethia. After her husband died, she was cared for by her son-in-law, Capt. Thomas Lothrop, who was killed at the Battle of Bloody Brook in 1675 (see preceding).

---

[312] Hill, *Fundy to Chesapeake*, 57-8.
[313] Hill, *Quakers and Puritans*, 256.
[314] Hill, *Fundy to Chesapeake*, 76-7.

RICHARD RAYMENT

RICHARD RAYMENT,[315] a fisherman and coastal trader, was born in about 1602; died in Saybrook, Conn., in 1692. He is believed to have been in Salem, Mass., in 1631, and he became a freeman of Salem in 1634. He relocated to Norwalk, Conn., after 1662, and then to Saybrook. He married, by about 1635, **JUDITH _____**. They had ten children. The family name was spelled Raymond in later generations.

Richard RAYMENT = Judith _____
Deacon Joshua RAYMOND = Elizabeth SMITH
Lieut. Thomas BRADFORD = Ann RAYMOND
James BRADFORD = Edith ADAMS
Jonathan PELLET = Jerusha BRADFORD
Willard PIERCE = Jerusha PELLET
Rufus HERRICK [III] = Jerusha P. _____ (prob.) PIERCE
William Prince HILL = Sarah P. "Sally" HERRICK
Charles W. HILL = Adelia Catherine RILEY
George J. HILL = Jessie Fidelia STOCKWELL

JUDITH (_____) RAYMENT

JUDITH _____, wife of **RICHARD RAYMENT**, of Salem, Mass., had nine children with him. She died at a time and place unknown. Her son was a successful entrepreneur in New London, and his daughter married the grandson of Governor **WILLIAM BRADFORD** of Plymouth Colony (see above).

RICHARD RICE

RICHARD RICE,[316] cowherd of Concord, was born about 1610; died at Concord, 9 June 1709, an aged man. He probably came to America from England in about 1635. He was recorded in Cambridge, Mass., on 1 March 1636. He removed to Concord later that year and was granted land for 100 cows. He later was sergeant of the Concord Train Band. He married, by 1641 (1) **ELIZABETH _____**, who was living in 1693/4. They had nine children. He may have married (2) **Mary _____**, who died in 1698, without issue (unless her name was mis-transcribed and was Elizabeth). His daughter Hannah, born in 1646, married Samuel Wilcockson, son of WILLIAM WILCOCKSON and his wife MARGARET HARVEY.

Richard RICE = Elizabeth _____
Sergeant Samuel WILCOCKSON = Hannah RICE
Samuel WILCOX [Jr.] = _____ _____
Ephriam WILCOX = Hannah HILL
Michael JACKSON = Susannah WILCOX
Sergeant Isaiah J. HENDRYX = Esther JACKSON
Josiah (Isaiah) RILEY = Susannah HENDRYX
Simeon RILEY = Katharine "Catherine" GILLETT
Charles W. HILL = Adelia Catharine "Delia" RILEY
George J. HILL = Jessie Fidelia STOCKWELL

ELIZABETH (_____) RICE

ELIZABETH _____ married, by 1641, **RICHARD RICE**, cowherd, who was born in about 1610 and died at Concord, Mass., 9 June 1709. They probably came separately to America, for she had the first of her nine children several years after he arrived. She was living in 1693/4, but perhaps died in 1698.

---

[315] Hill, *Western Pilgrims*, 110. The descent to George J. Hill depends on the assumption that Jerusha P., wife of Rufus Herrick (III), was Jerusha Pierce. See *Western Pilgrims*, 45, Herrick Family.

[316] Anderson, *Great Migration* 6:49-52 (RICHARD RICE). Also see: Hill, *Western Pilgrims*, 24. The account of William Wilcockson and his wife Margaret Harvey is taken from *Great Migration* 7:396-401 (WILLIAM WILCOCKSON). He was called Wilcox in *Western Pilgrims*, as the family name has become normalized, but in his lifetime, the documents quoted in *Great Migration* show that it was spelled Wilcockson.

THOMAS RICHARDS

THOMAS RICHARDS, Jr.,[317] merchant, son of Thomas Richards of Pitminster, co. Somerset, England, was baptized there, 15 April 1596; died in 1650/1 in Massachusetts. He emigrated in 1633, settling at Dorchester, and was selectman on 8 October 1633. He relocated to Weymouth and signed his will at the home of Thomas Loring in Hull, Mass. He married, by 1620, **WELTHEAN LORING** (if she was the sister of Thomas Loring); she died in 1679. They had nine children.

Thomas RICHARDS = Welthean LORING (her presumed name)
Major William BRADFORD, Jr. = Alice RICHARDS
Lieut. Thomas BRADFORD = Ann RAYMOND
James BRADFORD = Edith ADAMS
Jonathan PELLET = Jerusha BRADFORD
Willard PIERCE = Jerusha PELLET
Rufus HERRICK [III] = Jerusha P. _____ (prob.) PIERCE
William Prince HILL = Sarah P. "Sally" HERRICK
Charles W. HILL = Adelia Catherine RILEY
George J. HILL = Jessie Fidelia STOCKWELL

EZEKIEL RICHARDSON

EZEKIEL RICHARDSON, Esq.,[318] son of Thomas and Katherine (Duxford) Richardson, was probably born at West Mill, Herts, England, in about 1604; died at Woburn, Mass., 21 October 1647. He came in the Great Migration with the Winthrop Fleet in 1630, although the name of his ship and his arrival date are unknown. He is first mentioned when he and his wife became members of the church in Boston, in the winter of 1630/1. In September 1634, was elected a deputy to the General Court. He married, in about 1630, perhaps in England or soon after he arrived in Massachusetts, **SUSANNA _____**, whose origin is unknown. Their first known child, presumably the eldest, was baptized at Boston.

Ezekiel RICHARDSON Esq. = Susanna _____
Capt. Josiah RICHARDSON = Remembrance UNDERWOOD
Lieut. William FLETCHER = Sarah RICHARDSON
Josiah FLETCHER = Joanna SPALDING
Capt. Joseph WARREN = Joanna FLETCHER
Jeduthan WARREN = Joanna MOORS
Jesse WARREN = Betsy JACKSON
Herbert Marshall WARREN = Eliza Caroline COPP
William Toy SHOEMAKER = Mabel WARREN

SUSANNA (_____) RICHARDSON

SUSANNA _____, who married in England or shortly after they arrived in in Massachusetts in 1630, **EZEKIEL RICHARDSON,** born in about 1604; died at Woburn, Mass., in 1647. They became members of the church in Boston in 1630/1. He was said to be a "follower of Ann Hutchinson," but repented and was granted a reprieve. He then became one of the founders of Woburn. They had seven children. She survived him and married (2) **Henry BROOKS** of Concord and they moved to Woburn, where she died 15 September 1681 (see preceding).

JOHN RILEY

JOHN RILEY,[319] known as "the Settler," died at Wethersfield, Conn., in May or June 1674. He is said to have come from Stepney, a village near London, England, to Wethersfield, where he became a landholder in 1645. His cattle ear-mark is shown in Wethersfield's early records. He made his will on 13

---

[317] Hill, *Western Pilgrims*, 105-6. The descent to George J. Hill depends on the assumption that Jerusha P., wife of Rufus Herrick (III), was Jerusha Pierce. See *Western Pilgrims*, 45, Herrick Family.

[318] Hill, *Quakers and Puritans*, 166-7.

[319] Hill, *Western Pilgrims*, 38.

May 1674. He married **GRACE _____**; born about 1624; died in 1703. They had at least eight children. The line of descent to Josiah (Isaiah) Riley is based on the best available evidence, but it is still speculative.

John "the Settler" RILEY = Grace _____
Lieut. Isaac RILEY =Ann BUTLER
Samuel RILEY (poss. son of Isaac) = Martha SMITH
Simeon RILEY (poss. son of Samuel) = Simon [sic, a woman] ?RILEY [not related]
Josiah (Isaiah) RILEY = Susannah HENDRYX
Simeon RILEY = Katharine "Catherine" GILLETT
Charles W. HILL = Adelia Catharine "Delia" RILEY
George J. HILL = Jessie Fidelia STOCKWELL

GRACE (_____) RILEY

GRACE _____, born in England, probably Stepney, near London, in 1624; died in Wethersfield, Conn. in 1703, married **JOHN RILEY**, who died in Wethersfield in 1674. They came to New England in 1645 (see preceding).

DANIEL RINDGE

DANIEL RINDGE[320] appeared in Roxbury, Mass., as early as 1639, and he was of Ipswich, Mass., in 1648; died in 1661-2. He married **Mary KINSMAN**, daughter of ROBERT KINSMAN of Ipswich, with whom he had three sons and three daughters.

Daniel RINDGE = Mary KINSMAN
Joseph ANDREWS = Sarah RINDGE
John ANDREWS = Elizabeth WALLIS   Thomas GIDDINGS = Sarah ANDREWS
Capt. Joseph GIDDINGS = Eunice ANDREWS
Benjamin GIDDINGS = Martha SEELEY
Luther HYDE = Phoebe GIDDINGS
Harvey HYDE = Fidelia Gadcourt POTTER
Benajah Flavel STOCKWELL = Emily Lodiweska (Emma F.) HYDE
George J. HILL = Jessie Fidelia STOCKWELL

RICHARD ROBBINS

RICHARD ROBBINS[321] came to America from England in 1639 with his wife Rebecca. He was admitted to the church at Charlestown in 1640 and removed to Cambridge. He married (1) **REBECCA _____**, with whom he had four children. He married (2) **Mrs. Elizabeth CRACKBONE**, without issue.

Richard ROBBINS = Rebecca _____
John WOODWARD = Rebecca ROBBINS
John WOODWARD = Hannah HYDE
Henry BACON = Hannah WOODWARD
Jabez HYDE = Hannah BACON
Private Henry HYDE = Thyrina (Therina) WARD
Luther HYDE = Phoebe GIDDINGS
Harvey HYDE = Fidelia Gadcourt POTTER
Benajah Flavel STOCKWELL = Emily Lodiweska (Emma F.) HYDE
George J. HILL = Jessie Fidelia STOCKWELL

REBECCA (_____) ROBBINS

REBECCA _____ married, as his first wife, and mother of his four children, **RICHARD ROBBINS**. She came with him to Massachusetts in 1639 and probably died, unrecorded, in Cambridge (see above).

---

[320] Hill, *Western Pilgrims*, 305.
[321] Hill, *Western Pilgrims*, 238.

SARAH ROBERTS

SARAH ROBERTS[322] married in Wales, in 1667 or 1670, **JOHN CADWALADER**; she died in October 1737 in Goshen Twp., Pa. In Wales, Sarah was known as "verch Robert" (daughter of Robert). In English, this would be "Robert's daughter," or Roberts. John and Sarah (Roberts) Cadwalader had two children: John, who is an ancestor of William Toy Shoemaker; and Gwen, who married Robert Williams and whose daughter, Ann Williams, married Griffith John, a large freeholder in Chester County, Pa. The house of Sarah Roberts and John Cadwalader has been preserved in Lionville, Pa.

John CADWALADER = Sarah ROBERTS
Rev. John CADWALADER = Mary CASSELL (aka CASTLE)
Robert COMLY = Jane CADWALADER
Robert COMLY = Sarah JONES
Ezra COMLY = Hannah IREDELL
Charles SHOEMAKER = Rachel COMLY
Julien SHOEMAKER = Hannah Ann HESTER
William Toy SHOEMAKER = Mabel WARREN

GAIN ROBINSON

GAIN ROBINSON,[323] son of the Rev. Munster Robinson and probably Catherine Mary Fitzgerald, was born in Scotland in about 1682; died at East Bridgewater, Plymouth Co., Mass., 7 July 1736. The Robinsons were Covenanters and were persecuted in Scotland. They emigrated to Ireland and then to New England. He probably came to America by 1719. He had two children by his first wife, and married (2), in about 1719, **MARGARET WATSON**, born in Scotland in 1682; died in Massachusetts in 1777.

Gain ROBINSON = Margaret WATSON
Archibald THOMPSON = Martha ROBINSON
James THOMPSON Sr. = Hannah ____, prob. Hannah SCOTT
Joseph Scott THOMPSON = Ruth E. ARCHIBALD
James Everett THOMPSON = Jane GRANT
William Henry "Will" THOMPSON = Sarah D. "Sadie" RUNDALL

THOMAS ROGERS

THOMAS ROGERS,[324] probably of Dedham, co. Essex, was born about 1588; died at Watertown, Mass., 12 November 1638. He was a proprietor of Watertown in 1636-7, and died soon after that. He married, in England, by 1617, as her second husband, **Grace (RAVENS) SHERMAN**; daughter of Richard and Elizabeth (Hedge) Ravens; born probably at East Bergholt, co. Suffolk, in about 1591; died at Watertown, Mass., 3 June 1662. She had two children by her first marriage to John Sherman; these sons emigrated to Watertown. She had one child, Elizabeth, by her marriage to Thomas Rogers. After Thomas Rogers died, she married (3) Roger Porter, without issue. Thomas Rogers' daughter Elizabeth took the name of her stepfather, and became known as Elizabeth Porter (see GRACE RAVENS).

Thomas ROGERS = Grace RAVENS (who m. [1] John Sherman and [3] Roger Porter]
Daniel SMITH, Sr. = Elizabeth ROGERS [known as Elizabeth Porter]
Daniel SMITH Jr. = Mary GRANT
John PEIRCE = Elizabeth SMITH
Jonas PEIRCE = Abigail COMEE
John PEIRCE = Abigail BEARD
Oliver JACKSON = Mary PEIRCE
Jesse WARREN = Betsy JACKSON
Herbert Marshall WARREN = Eliza Caroline COPP
William Toy SHOEMAKER = Mabel WARREN

---

[322] Hill, *Quakers and Puritans*, 37-43.
[323] Hill, *Fundy to Chesapeake*, 12-13.
[324] Hill, *Quakers and Puritans*, 256.

WILLIAM RUNDLE

WILLIAM RUNDLE, Sr.,[325] son of John and Ann (Goldstone) Randall, was born at Tonbridge, co. Kent, England, in about December 1646. He is probably the man of the same name who died at Greenwich, Conn., in October or November 1714. He is also presumed to be the same person as the William Rundle who appeared in Easthampton, Long Island, in 1667. William Rundle of Greenwich was one of the twenty-seven proprietors of Greenwich, also in 1667. Many of the descendants of the twenty-seven proprietors were later related to each other, including 23 of the original 27 who have a cognate or in-law relationship to William Rundle. He married three times and left a good estate. He appears to have been a thrifty, hard-working man who had a privileged childhood and then married well, and who also inherited an estate in Easthampton from his father-in-law. His grandson Jonathan purchased an island in the harbor of New York, now known as Randall's Island. William Rundle, Sr., married (1) in 1670, **Hannah EDWARDS;** (2) in about 1675, **Abigail MILLS**, daughter of Samuel and Susanna (Palmer) Mills; born at Jamaica, L.I.; and (3) in about 1689, **Abigail TYLER**. He had issue by all three wives. (See GEORGE MILLS and WILLIAM PALMER for the ancestors of William Rundle's second wife.)

William RUNDLE, Sr. = Abigail MILLS
Samuel RUNDLE Sr. = Hannah HARDY
Reuben RUNDLE Sr. = Amy HOBBY
Shadrack RUNDALL Sr. = Phebe BROWN
Reuben John RUNDALL = Martha TOMPKINS
Silas William RUNDALL = Rachel MANLY
William Henry "Will" THOMPSON = Sarah D. "Sadie" RUNDALL
Gerald Leslie HILL = Essie Mae THOMPSON
George James HILL = Helene ZIMMERMANN

[JOHN RUSSELL]

[JOHN¹ RUSSELL[326] is said to have come from Lewes in Sussex, England, with his wife **Mary** and his only child Elizabeth. He came on the *Submission* in 1632 and worked off his indenture, which ended on 9mo. 2, 1697. His daughter **Elizabeth² RUSSELL** married **Joseph¹ MATHER**, born at Radcliffe Bridge, Lancashire, England; died at Cheltenham Twp., Philadelphia Co., Pa., in 1724. Joseph Mather may be related to the New England Mathers, who descend from the Rev. Richard Mather, who came from Lancashire in 1632. Connections between the Mathers of Pennsylvania and the ancestors of William Toy Shoemaker are described in *Quakers and Puritans*. However, he is not a descendant of Joseph Mather.]

ISRAEL RUST

ISRAEL RUST[327] was doubtless born in England and came to Northampton, Mass., where he died 11 November 1712. He married, at Northampton, 9 December 1669, **Rebecca CLARK**, daughter of Lieut. WILLIAM CLARK and his wife Sarah. They had nine children.

Israel RUST = Rebecca CLARK
Deacon Samuel ALLEN = Sarah RUST
Samuel ALLEN = Hannah MILLER
Corporal Jabez WARD = Jemima ALLEN
Private Henry HYDE = Thyrina (Therina) WARD
Luther HYDE = Phoebe GIDDINGS
Harvey HYDE = Fidelia Gadcourt POTTER
Benajah Flavel STOCKWELL = Emily Lodiweska (Emma F.) HYDE
George J. HILL = Jessie Fidelia STOCKWELL

---

[325] Hill, *Fundy to Chesapeake*, 113-121.
[326] Hill, *Quakers and Puritans*, 116-8.
[327] Hill, *Western Pilgrims*, 335-6.

EZEKIEL SANFORD

EZEKIEL SANFORD[328] was of Sag Harbor, Long Island, then part of Southampton, now New York, and was married to **Hannah MITCHELL**, whose ancestry is unknown. They had a daughter, Abigail, known as "The Hackleberry Picker of Poxabogue," who married, 13 June 1712, Edward Howell, great-grandson of Mr. EDWARD HOWELL.

Ezekiel SANFORD = Hannah MITCHELL
Edward HOWELL = Abigail SANFORD
Samuel PRINCE = Abigail HOWELL
Edward Howell PRINCE = Huldah OVIATT
Ephraim HILL = Charlotte PRINCE
William Prince HILL = Sarah P. "Sally" HERRICK
Charles W. HILL = Adelia Catherine RILEY
George J. HILL = Jessie Fidelia STOCKWELL

ELIZABETH SANGHURST

ELIZABETH SANGHURST[329] was the wife of **GODWIN WALTER**, who was probably baptized at Froxfield, Wiltshire and died in Chester Co., Pa., in 1735. She was born in say 1679, probably in England, and died in about 1732. They were married at Concord Quaker Meeting in Chester Co., Pa., 9 November 1696. They had many children. She is an ancestor of Sarah D. Rundall.

JOHN SAXE

JOHN SAXE,[330] son of Godfrey Saxe, was born at Langensalza, Kingdom of Hanover, 10 November 1732; died at Highgate, Vermont, 12 March 1808. He came to Philadelphia in 1750 as an indentured servant, and he learned the trade of a miller. He was in Rhinebeck, N.Y., when the Revolutionary War broke out and he refused to violate his oath of allegiance to the King. As a Tory, and perhaps also a spy for the British, he and his family were expelled to Canada after the war. His farm near Lake Champlain extended across the border into Vermont. He married, in Rhinebeck, **Catherine WEAVER**, daughter of WILLIAM WEAVER; born in 1744; died in 1791. They had nine children.

John SAXE = Catherine WEAVER
Godfrey SAXE = _____
Joseph H. STOCKWELL = Anna Maria SAXE
Benajah Flavel STOCKWELL = Emily Lodiweska (Emma F.) HYDE
George J. HILL = Jessie Fidelia STOCKWELL

BENJAMIN SCOTT

BENJAMIN SCOTT[331] was born in England in about 1612; died at Rowley, Essex Co., Mass., in 1671. He had two children by his first wife, **Mary _____**. He married (2), at Rowley, Mass., sometime after 1645, **MARGARET STEPEHNSON**, born at Cambridge, Mass., in 1616; died at Salem, Mass., 22 September 1692. They had five children. She was hanged as a witch on the last day of the hangings.

Benjamin SCOTT = Margaret STEPHENSON
John SCOTT (prob. son of Benjamin Scott) = Hannah DUNCAN
Joseph SCOTT = Hannah PRIOR
Lieut. Joseph SCOTT = Mary EDMANDS
Sheriff Joseph SCOTT = Sarah CUTTING
James THOMPSON Sr. = Hannah _____, prob. Hannah SCOTT

---

[328] Hill, *Western Pilgrims*, 152.
[329] Hill, *Fundy to Chesapeake*, 320-1.
[330] Hill, *Western Pilgrims*, 217-21; Hill, *John Saxe, Loyalist (1732-1808) and his Descendants for Five Generations.*
[331] Hill, *Fundy to Chesapeake*, 14. The line of descent for Benjamin Scott depends on the assumption that Hannah _____, who married James Thompson, Sr., is Hannah Scott, daughter of Joseph Scott. See *Fundy to Chesapeake*, .3-4.

Joseph Scott THOMPSON = Ruth E. ARCHIBALD
James Everett THOMPSON = Jane GRANT
William Henry "Will" THOMPSON = Sarah D. "Sadie" RUNDALL

SARAH SCOTT

SARAH SCOTT,[332] who may have been previously married, is the Sarah ____ who married **Richard HOWELL**, cooper and Trustee of Southampton. He was born probably at Southampton, Long Island, in about 1659; died there about 1737. He was the son and namesake of Richard Howell and his wife Elizabeth Halsey, and grandson of the emigrant, **EDWARD HOWELL**.

SARAH SEELEY

SARAH SEELEY[333] married **Mr. OBADIAH BRUEN**, draper, and Deputy for New London to the Connecticut Legislature. They came to America in 1640 and settled originally at Marshfield, Mass. Her ancestry is unknown, but he is known to be a descendant of English Royalty. Through her daughter Mary Bruen, who married John Baldwin, she may be an ancestor of George J. Hill, the Iowa Pioneer.

SUSANNAH SELBEE

SUSANNAH SELBEE,[334] probably born at Harrod, co. Bedford, England; died at Boston, Mass., 20 January 1659/60. She married, at Harrod, 31 August 1609, **ROBERT BLOTT**, perhaps son of Robert Blott of Harrod; probably born at Puddington, co. Bedford, in say 1584; died in Boston in 1665. They had ten children. Her daughter Mary is an ancestor of Jessie F. Stockwell.

MARY SHARP

MARY SHARP,[335] daughter of Henry and Jane (Ffeylde) Sharpe, was christened 10 October 1614 in co. Kent; died at Concord, Mass., before 1653. She married, as his first wife, at Marden, co. Kent, 13 October 1628, **SIMON WILLARD**, son of Richard and Margery (Humphrey) Willard; baptized 7 April 1605 at Horsmandon, co. Kent; died at Charlestown, Mass., in April 1677. They came in the Great Migration to America in 1634. Her daughter Sarah Willard is an ancestor of Mabel Warren.

JOHN SHARPLES

JOHN SHARPLES,[336] son of Geoffrey and Margaret (Ashley) Sharpless, was baptized at St. Chad's Church, Wybunbury, 15 August 1624; died at Ridley Township, near Chester, Chester Co., Pa., 4 mo. 11, 1685. John Sharples came to America with his family on the *Friendship* in 1682. He and his family settled along the bank of Ridley Creek about three miles west of the Delaware River. He married, in England, 2 mo. 27, 1662, **JANE MOOR**, who was born in 1638 and died at Ridley, near Chester, Pa., 9 mo. 1, 1722. She was probably a sister of Daniel Moore of Hatherton, Wybunbury, Cheshire. John and Jane (Moor) Sharples had eight children, all of whom were born in England.

John SHARPLES "The Emigrant" = Jane MOOR
John SHARPLES = Hannah PENNELL
Daniel SHARPLES = Sarah COPPOCK
Solomon MERCER = Abigail SHARPLES
William WALTER = Phebe MERCER
William H. MANLY = Sarah D. WALTER
Silas William RUNDALL = Rachel MANLY
William Henry "Will" THOMPSON = Sarah D. "Sadie" RUNDALL

---

[332] Hill, *Western Pilgrims* 151.
[333] Hill, *Western Pilgrims*, 139. Richardson, *Royal Ancestry*, 1:587-8.
[334] Hill, *Western Pilgrims*, 332-3. Anderson, *Great Migration* 1:334-8 (ROBERT BLOTT).
[335] Hill, *Quakers and Puritans*, 174-5.
[336] Hill, *Fundy to Chesapeake*, 279-83.

[EDMOND SHEFFIELD]

[EDMOND[1] SHEFFIELD,[337] father of Ichabod[2] and grandfather of Capt. Amos[3] Sheffield, who was the first husband of Sarah Davis, is profiled in *Western Pilgrims*. This is done to explain the complicated relationships that exist with the three husbands of Sarah (Davis) (Sheffield) (Alleby) Camp. She is the mother of Mary Albee, who is an ancestor of Jessie Stockwell, but the Sheffields and Stockwells are not related by blood (See AARON DAVIS and BENJAMIN ALBEE)]

[JOHN SHERMAN]

[JOHN SHERMAN,[338] son of Henry and Susan (Lawrence) Sherman; baptized at Dedham, co. Essex, 17 August 1585; was buried at Great Horkesley, co. Essex, 24 January 1615/6. He married, as her first husband, at Wattisfield, co. Suffolk, England, 26 September 1611, **Grace RAVENS**, daughter of Richard and Elizabeth (Hedge) Ravens, probably born at East Bergholt, co. Suffolk, in about 1591; died at Watertown, Mass., 3 June 1662. They had two sons, baptized at Great Horkesley, co. Essex; one was Capt. John Sherman [II], ancestor of **Roger Sherman, Signer of the Declaration of Independence**. Grace (Ravens) Sherman married (2), by 1617, in England, Thomas Rogers; born about 1588; died at Watertown, Mass., 12 November 1638. By her second marriage, but not by John Sherman, GRACE RAVENS is an ancestor of Mabel Warren.]

GEORGE SHOEMAKER

GEORGE SHOEMAKER, Sr.[339] was born at Kriegsheim, Lower Palitante (now Germany) in say 1635. As a Mennonite, he refused to bear arms, and he accepted membership in the Society of Friends after a visit by Quaker missionaries. He married in 1662 **SARAH _____ (perhaps SARAH HENDRICHS)** who died in Cheltenham Twp. after 1708. George Shoemaker, Sr., left Kriegsheim and emigrated to America with his wife and seven of their eight children. They sailed from London the ship *Jeffries* in the fall of 1685, and arrived at Philadelphia on 20 March 1686. He died of smallpox on the passage, and was buried at sea. His widow settled with their children in Cheltenham Township, north of Germantown.

George SHOEMAKER, Sr. = Sarah _____ (perhaps Hendrichs)
George SHOEMAKER, Jr. = Sarah WALL
Isaac SHOEMAKER, Sr. = Dorothy PENROSE
Isaac SHOEMAKER, Jr. = Elizabeth POTTS
Jonathan SHOEMAKER, Esq. = Hannah LUKENS
Charles SHOEMAKER = Rachel COMLY
Julien SHOEMAKER = Hannah Ann HESTER
William Toy SHOEMAKER = Mabel WARREN
Albert Walter ZIMMERMANN = Barbara SHOEMAKER
George James HILL = Helene ZIMMERMANN

RICHARD SINGLETARY

RICHARD SINGLETARY[340] was born somewhere in the British Isles, in say 1599; died at Haverhill, Mass., 25 October 1687. He came from England as a youth, under circumstances that are unknown but are interesting and mysterious, and he became the founder of the Singletary family in America. He is also the founder of one branch of the Dunham family, which changed its surname from Singletary. He received a grant of land in Salem, Mass., in 1637. He resided in Haverhill where he became a proprietor. He married, probably in Newbury, Mass., in about 1638-9, **SUSANNAH COOK**, born say 1616, probably in England; died at Haverhill, 11 April 1682. One of their descendants was Stanley Dunham, mother of **President Barack Obama**.

[337] Hill, *Western Pilgrims*, 356-7.
[338] Hill, *Quakes and Puritans*, 255.
[339] Hill, *Quakers and Puritans*, 5-22.
[340] Hill, *Western Pilgrims*, 183-4.

Richard SINGLETARY = Susannah M. COOK(E)
Nathaniel SINGLETARY = Sarah BELKNAP
John SINGLETARY = Mary GREELEY
Ebenezer STOCKWELL = Mary SINGLETARY
Benajah STOCKWELL = Hannah GALE
Ebenezer STOCKWELL = Abi HOLBROOK
Joseph H. STOCKWELL = Anna Maria SAXE
Benajah Flavel STOCKWELL = Emily Lodiweska (Emma F.) HYDE
George J. HILL = Jessie Fidelia STOCKWELL

[WILLIAM SKIPWITH]

[*Sir WILLIAM SKIPWITH, Knt.,*[341] was the father of Alice Skipwith. She married Sir John Markham, Knt., who was proposed by J. G. Hunt to be an ancestor of GEORGE MORTON. Hunt's suggestion is mentioned here for the sake of completeness, but it is believed to be fanciful. See also *CONSTABLE of HALSHAM* and *WILLOUGHBY D'ERESBY*.]

SMITH

_____ SMITH[342] was an emigrant to Massachusetts who died before 1663. His widow, **Alice (?BAYLEY) SMITH**, died in 1663, in Boston, Mass. Administration of her estate was granted on 14, 8 mo. 1663 to her kinsman, Joseph Bayley, and two of her sons, Samuel and Abraham Smith. Daniel Smith, of Watertown, calls Abraham his "brother," so Daniel can be added to the list of Alice's children. Daniel married Elizabeth Rogers, daughter of THOMAS ROGERS and GRACE RAVENS.

_____ SMITH = Alice _____, perhaps Alice BAYLEY
Daniel SMITH, Sr. = Elizabeth ROGERS (known as Elizabeth Porter)
Daniel SMITH Jr. = Mary GRANT
John PEIRCE = Elizabeth SMITH
Jonas PEIRCE = Abigail COMEE
John PEIRCE = Abigail BEARD
Oliver JACKSON = Mary PEIRCE
Jesse WARREN = Betsy JACKSON
Herbert Marshall WARREN = Eliza Caroline COPP
William Toy SHOEMAKER = Mabel WARREN

JOHN SMITH

Sergeant JOHN SMITH[343] was an early settler of Milford, New Haven Co., Conn; he died there between 21 June and 9 December 1684. He married **GRACE _____**, perhaps **HAWLEY**; she died at Milford in 1689. His will was dated 21 June 1684 and his estate was inventoried on 9 December 1684.

Sergeant John SMITH = Grace _____, perhaps Grace HAWLEY
John SMITH = Phebe CANFIELD
John SMITH = Ruth BRISCOE
Caleb SMITH = Abigail CLARK
John OVIATT = Abigail SMITH
Edward Howell PRINCE = Huldah OVIATT
Ephraim HILL = Charlotte PRINCE
William Prince HILL = Sarah P. "Sally" HERRICK
Charles W. HILL = Adelia Catharine "Delia" RILEY
George J. HILL = Jessie Fidelia STOCKWELL

---

[341] Hill, *Western Pilgrims*, 704.
[342] Hill, *Quakers and Puritans*, 252. This is the only male immigrant in this Synopsis whose given name is unknown.
[343] Hill, *Western Pilgrims*, 141.

GRACE (_____) SMITH

GRACE _____, perhaps **GRACE HAWLEY**, married **Sergeant JOHN SMITH**, an early settler of Milford, Conn. He died in 1684 and she died in 1689. They had six children (see preceding).

JOHN SMITH

JOHN SMITH[344] married **MARGARET THOMPSON** in about 1644. They had three daughters, born at Salem, Mass., all of whom married sons of Francis and Rebecca (Towne) Nurse.

John SMITH = Margaret THOMPSON
Samuel NURSE = Mary SMITH
Ebenezer NURSE = Elizabeth MITCHELL, prob. dau. of Andrew Mitchell
Caleb PUTNAM = Elizabeth NURSE
William PUTNAM = Dorothy "Dolly" PRESCOTT
William ARCHIBALD = Susannah "Susan" PUTNAM
Joseph Scott THOMPSON = Ruth E. ARCHIBALD
James Everett THOMPSON = Jane GRANT
William Henry "Will" THOMPSON = Sarah D. "Sadie" RUNDALL

NEHEMIAH SMITH

Mr. NEHEMIAH SMITH[345] was born in England in about 1605; died at New London, Conn., about 1686. He came to the New World at the age of about 33 with his brother John, and was followed to America in 1652 by his nephew Edward. He lived in many places in Massachusetts, Connecticut, and Long Island, receiving and purchasing much land, but he was not above controversy. He married in 1639/40, **Ann BOURNE**, daughter of **THOMAS BOURNE** and his wife Elizabeth; born in England in about 1615; died at New London, Conn., after 12 January 1684.

Mr. Nehemiah SMITH = Anne BOURNE
Deacon Joshua RAYMOND = Elizabeth SMITH
Lieut. Thomas BRADFORD = Ann RAYMOND
James BRADFORD = Edith ADAMS
Jonathan PELLET = Jerusha BRADFORD
Willard PIERCE = Jerusha PELLET
Rufus HERRICK [III] = Jerusha P. _____ (prob.) PIERCE
William Prince HILL = Sarah P. "Sally" HERRICK
Charles W. HILL = Adelia Catherine RILEY
George J. HILL = Jessie Fidelia STOCKWELL

EDWARD SPALDING

EDWARD SPALDING[346] probably came from England and is first recorded in America when he became a freeman in Braintree, Mass., 13 May 1640; died in Chelmsford, Mass., 26 February 1670. He was mentioned in a petition to the General Court in 1645, with thirty-two others, to set off land which eventually became the town of Chelmsford. He married (1) **Margaret _____**; she died in Braintree, Mass., in August 1640. They had three children. He married, (2) **RACHEL _____**, sometime after August 1640; she died, probably at Chelmsford, Mass., shortly after February 1670. They had four children.

Edward SPALDING = Rachel _____
Joseph SPALDING = Mercy JEWELL
Judge Timothy PIERCE = Lydia SPAULDING
Nathaniel PIERCE = Elizabeth STEVENS

---

[344] Hill, *Fundy to Chesapeake*, 79.
[345] Hill, *Western Pilgrims*, 108. The descent to George J. Hill depends on the assumption that Jerusha P., wife of Rufus Herrick (III), was Jerusha Pierce. (See discussion of this question in *Western Pilgrims*, 45, Herrick Family.)
[346] Hill, *Western Pilgrims*, 88-9. The descent to George J. Hill depends on the assumption that Jerusha P., wife of Rufus Herrick (III), was Jerusha Pierce. (See discussion of this question in *Western Pilgrims*, 45, Herrick Family.)

Willard PIERCE = Jerusha PELLET
Rufus HERRICK [III] = Jerusha P._____ (prob. PIERCE)
William Prince HILL = Sarah P. "Sally" HERRICK
Charles W. HILL = Adelia Catharine "Delia" RILEY
George J. HILL = Jessie Fidelia STOCKWELL

RACHEL (_____) SPALDING

RACHEL ____,[347] second wife of **EDWARD SPALDING**, married him in 1640 after his first wife died. She raised three children by his first marriage, born between 1631 and 1641. She had four of his children; the first was born in April 1643. She died shortly after he died in February 1970 (see preceding).

JOHN SPENCER

JOHN SPENCER,[348] tailor of London, in 1681, made a land lease assignment with William Penn in Philadelphia. It appears that he came to Pennsylvania within the first year or two – say 1682 or 1683 – after the first of Penn's settlers arrived. He died, along with his wife, in a flood of the Neshaminy Creek, in Bucks County, Pa., 22, 10mo. 1683, leaving two children: James and Samuel. In about 1668, John Spencer married **MARGARET ____**; perhaps from co. York; died with her husband in a flood in 1683.

John SPENCER = Margaret ____
Samuel SPENCER Sr. = Elizabeth WHITTON
Samuel SPENCER, Jr. = Mary DAWES
Joseph LUKENS = Elizabeth SPENCER
Jonathan SHOEMAKER Esq. = Hannah LUKENS
Charles SHOEMAKER = Rachel COMLY
Julien SHOEMAKER = Hannah Ann HESTER
William Toy SHOEMAKER = Mabel WARREN

MARGARET (_____) SPENCER

MARGARET ____, wife of **JOHN SPENCER**, was perhaps from co. York, where the Spencer family originally came from. They were married in England in about 1668. She died with her husband on their farm in Bucks Co., Pa., in a flood on the Neshaminy Creek in 1683 (see preceding).

EDITH SQUIRE

EDITH SQUIRE,[349] eldest of the five children of Henry Squire, blacksmith, and granddaughter of the Rev. William Squire, of Charlton Mackrell, co. Somerset, was baptized, 29 May 1587; died at Medfield, Mass., 21 January 1672/3. She married (1) at Charlton Mackrell, 19 October 1609, **HENRY ADAMS**, son of John and Agnes (Stone) Adams; born about 1583 and died in Braintree, Mass., 8 October 1646. She migrated with him and their nine children to New England. She married (2), about 1651, as his second wife, **John FUSSELL** of Weymouth and Medfield, Mass.; born in England about 1578; died at Medfield, Mass., 21 February 1676/7, at the time his house was burned by the Indians, without issue.

CATHERINE STARKEY

CATHERINE STARKEY,[350] of co. Cavan, Ireland, was married at Belturbet, co. Cavan, 11 mo. 6, 1685, to **JOHN FRED(D)**, born in Ireland. They came to America with their children and settled in Chester Co., Pa., where she died in 1723. Their daughter Rachel is an ancestor of Sarah D. Rundall.

---

[347] Hill, *Western Pilgrims*, 88-9.
[348] Hill, *Quakers and Puritans*, 72-3.
[349] Hill, *Western Pilgrims*, 112-7. The descent to George J. Hill depends on the assumption that Jerusha P., wife of Rufus Herrick (III), was Jerusha Pierce. (See discussion of this question in *Western Pilgrims*, 45, Herrick Family.)
[350] Hill, *Fundy to Chesapeake*, 274. This line assumes that Rachel Jackson is the daughter of John Jackson, Jr.

MARGARET STEPHENSON

MARGARET STEPHENSON,[351] daughter of Andrew and Joane Stephenson, was born at Cambridge, Mass., in 1616; died at Salem, Mass., 22 September 1692. She was hanged on the last day that witches were hanged in Salem. She married, as his second wife, **BENJAMIN SCOTT**, born in England in about 1612; died at Rowley, Essex Co., Mass., in 1671. Benjamin and Margaret (Stephenson) Scott had four children, one of whom was a son, John. He may have been the John Scott who married Hannah Duncan and is probably an ancestor of William Henry Thompson.

JOHN STEVENS

JOHN STEVENS,[352] son of Michaell and Catherine Stevens, was born near Uffington, Berkshire, and was baptized there, 2 December 1621. He is probably the same John Stevens who was buried at Ore, near Uffington, 23 June 1695. "John Stevens of Uffington, a professed Quaker," held Meetings at his house, and in June 1670 was confined in "his Majesty's Goal at Reading," Berks, so that "no Rebellion might be contrived in his House." He is believed to be the same John Stevens, master of the *Bristol Merchant*, when that ship sailed from Bristol to Virginia in 1678 and 1679 with a group of indentured servants. He married **Ann ____**, who was buried at Oar (probably Ore) in October 1699. Their daughter Jeane, born in 1642, came to America with her husband RICHARD THATCHER to Bucks Co.

John STEVENS = *Ann _____*
Richard THATCHER = Jeane (Jane) STEVENS
William BRINTON the Younger = Jane (or Jean) THATCHER
William BRINTON = Hannah BULLER
Joseph WALTER Sr. = Jane BRINTON
James WALTER = Sarah DIXON
William WALTER = Phebe MERCER
William H. MANLY = Sarah D. WALTER
Silas William RUNDALL = Rachel MANLY
William Henry "Will" THOMPSON = Sarah D. "Sadie" RUNDALL

ANN STEVENSON

ANN STEVENSON,[353] daughter of Peter Stephenson, was born about 1598; died at Stonington, Conn., 9 June 1667. She married, 15 December 1620, **WILLIAM CHESEBROUGH**, blacksmith, of Boston, co. Lincoln; born about 1595; died at Stonington, 9 June 1667. She had eight children before they emigrated to America in 1630, and two more were baptized in Boston, Mass. He held the office of Deputy to the General Court in Massachusetts and Connecticut. They are ancestors of George J. Hill, the Iowa Pioneer.

WILLIAM STOCKWELL

WILLIAM STOCKWELL, Sr.,[354] who was perhaps born in Scotland, died in Sutton, Mass., in 1727/28. His ancestry is unknown and it is also unknown how and when he came to America. Legend has it that he may have been a sea-faring man, who came ashore as an indentured servant. He first appears in the records of Ipswich, Mass., when he married there, 14 April 1685, **Sarah LAMBERT**, daughter of WILLIAM LAMBERT, one of several who bore that name in New England at that time; she was born at Ipswich, 4 July 1661; died at Sutton, Mass., after 1738. In 1717, at age 67, he moved with his wife and their eight children to central Massachusetts as founders of the town of Sutton.

William STOCKWELL, Sr. = Sarah LAMBERT
Ebenezer STOCKWELL = Mary SINGLETARY

---

[351] Hill, *Fundy to Chesapeake*, 14. The line of descent for Benjamin Scott depends on the assumption that Hannah ___, who married James Thompson, Sr., is Hannah Scott, daughter of Joseph Scott, as discussed on pp.3-4.
[352] Hill, *Fundy to Chesapeake*, 332. A typographical error in the baptismal date is corrected here (1621 vs. 1521).
[353] Hill, *Western Pilgrims*, 77-8.
[354] Hill, *Western Pilgrims*, 172-6.

Ebenezer STOCKWELL [II] = Abi (Holbrook) LEE
Joseph H. STOCKWELL = Anna Maria SAXE
Benajah Flavel STOCKWELL = Emily "Emma F." Lodiweska HYDE
George J. HILL = Jessie Fidelia STOCKWELL
Gerald Leslie HILL = Essie Mae THOMPSON
George James HILL = Helene ZIMMERMANN

ELIZABETH STRATTON

ELIZABETH STRATTON,[355] daughter of John and Anne (Dearhaugh) Stratton, was born in 1614 in Shotley, Suffolk, England. She probably died before 1668. She married **Mr. JOHN THORNDIKE**, son of Francis and Alice (Coleman) Thorndike; born about 1603 at Great Carlton, Lincs, England; buried at Westminster Abbey, 3 November 1668. He was a planter of Ipswich, Mass. Their daughter Elizabeth married John Proctor, whose second wife, Elizabeth Basset, was sentenced to death at Salem; her execution was delayed because she was pregnant, and she was released after the hangings were stopped. Her husband, John Proctor, the former son-in-law of John and Elizabeth (Stratton) Thorndike, was hanged in August 1692. He was portrayed in *The Crucible*. Elizabeth Stratton is an ancestor of Mabel Warren.

RICHARD SWAINE

RICHARD SWAINE,[356] planter and husbandman, son of William Swaine the younger, was baptized at Binfield, Berkshire, England, 26 September 1595; died at Nantucket Island, Mass., 14 April 1682. He probably came on the *Truelove*, embarked 20 September 1635, enrolled as "Richard Srayne." He first resided at Newbury from 1635 until 1639, and he was one of nine purchasers of the property of Nantucket on 2 July 1659. He married (1), perhaps before 1619, if she was his first wife, **BASILL ____**, who died at Hampton, N.H., 15 June 1657. He married (2 or 3), at Hampton, N.H., 15 September 1658, **Jane (GODFREY) BUNKER**; she died at Nantucket, 31 October 1662, without further issue. His daughter, Grace Swaine, and her daughter, Mary Boulter, were accused of witchcraft in Hampton, N.H.

Richard SWAINE = Basill ____
Nathaniel BOULTER = Grace SWAINE
James PRESCOTT Sr. = Mary BOULTER
Joshua PRESCOTT = Sarah CLIFFORD, prob. dau. of Israel Clifford
Joshua PRESCOTT (Jr.) = Abigail AMBROSE
William PUTNAM = Dorothy "Dolly" PRESCOTT
William ARCHIBALD = Susannah "Susan" PUTNAM
Joseph Scott THOMPSON = Ruth E. ARCHIBALD
James Everett THOMPSON = Jane GRANT
William Henry "Will" THOMPSON = Sarah D. "Sadie" RUNDALL

BASILL (_____) SWAINE

BASILL ____, who married, probably as his first wife, and probably before 1619, **RICHARD SWAINE**, son of William Swaine, the younger; baptized in Berkshire, England, 26 September 1595; died at Nantucket Island, Mass., 14 April 1682. He and Basill probably came on the *Truelove* in 1635 and they resided at Newbury, Mass., until 1639. He then purchased a share of Nantucket Island, and they lived there and at Hampton, N.H., where she died in 1657 (see preceding).

PHILIP TABER

PHILIP TABER,[357] a sawyer and carpenter, was born in England in 1605; died, probably at Providence, R.I., between 3 June 1671 and 27 April 1682. He came to America in 1633, and on 1 April 1634, at

---

[355] Hill, *Quakers and Puritans*, 149.
[356] Hill, *Fundy to Chesapeake*, 102-3.
[357] Hill, *Western Pilgrims*, 274-5.

Watertown, Mass., he pledged to provide 200 feet of four-inch planks for the building of the sea fort. He settled at Portsmouth, R.I., in 1656. He married, by 1669, **Lydia MASTERS**, daughter of JOHN MASTERS and his wife Jane of Cambridge, Mass.; born in England, about 1615; died before 1669. They had five children. After Lydia died he married (2) **Jane _____**, without issue.

Philip TABER = Lydia MASTERS
Rev. Pardon TILLINGHAST = Lydia TABER
Phillip TILLINGHAST, J.P. = Martha HOLMES
William POTTER = Martha TILLINGHAST
Capt. Oliver POTTER = Mary COLVIN
Capt. Freeborn POTTER = Dolly IRISH
Harvey HYDE =Fidelia Gadcourt POTTER
Benajah Flavel STOCKWELL = Emily Lodiweska HYDE
George J. HILL = Jessie Fidelia STOCKWELL

NICHOLAS TANNER

NICHOLAS TANNER,[358] originally of Tolspidle, Dorsetshire, of New Haven in 1639-1641, and an emigrant to Hempstead and Jamaica, L.I., where he probably died 23 June 1666. He was one of 66 men who were proprietors of early Hempstead, L.I. He was the father of Rebecca Tanner, who was probably the Rebecca _____ who married GEORGE MILLS.

Nicholas TANNER = _____ _____
George MILLS = Rebecca _____, prob. TANNER
Samuel MILLS Sr. = Susannah PALMER
William RUNDLE Sr. = Abigail MILLS
Samuel RUNDLE Sr. = Hannah HARDY
Reuben RUNDLE Sr. = Amy HOBBY
Shadrack RUNDALL Sr. = Phebe BROWN
Reuben John RUNDALL = Martha TOMPKINS
Silas William RUNDALL = Rachel MANLY
William Henry "Will" THOMPSON = Sarah D. "Sadie" RUNDALL

_____ (_____) TANNER

_____ _____, whose name is unknown, married **NICHOLAS TANNER**, who came to America from Dorsetshire, England, as a servant, in 1639. He traveled between New Haven and Long Island. He eventually became a proprietor of Hempstead, L.I., where he died in 1666. The accounts of his life are fragmentary (see preceding).

HANNAH TAYLOR

HANNAH TAYLOR,[359] born in England in about 1690; died in 1745 in Delaware Co. Pa.; married **JAMES PHILLIPS**, born in Wales in 1676; died at New Castle, Del., in 1772. She had five children and is an ancestor of Sarah D. Rundall.

MATTHEW TAYLOR

MATTHEW TAYLOR, Sr.,[360] farmer, was born in Northern Ireland in 1690; died at Beaver Lake, N.H., 22 Jan 1770/[1]; buried in East Derry, N.H. He married, in 1720, possibly in the Parish of Templemore, Ireland, **Janet WILSON**, daughter of ALEXANDER WILSON; born at Londonderry, Ireland, 1705; died after 1800 in Beaver Lake, N.H.

Matthew TAYLOR Sr. = Janet WILSON
Samuel ARCHIBALD = Eleanor TAYLOR
Lt. Col. John ARCHIBALD 2nd = Margaret FISHER

---

[358] Hill, *Fundy to Chesapeake*, 134.
[359] Hill, *Fundy to Chesapeake*, 342.
[360] Hill, *Fundy to Chesapeake*, 51.

William ARCHIBALD = Susannah "Susan" PUTNAM
Joseph Scott THOMPSON = Ruth E. ARCHIBALD
James Everett THOMPSON = Jane GRANT
William Henry "Will" THOMPSON = Sarah D. "Sadie" RUNDALL

ROBERT TAYLOR

ROBERT TAYLOR,[361] yeoman, of Clatterwick, Cheshire, England, son of Thomas and Mary (Barrow) Taylor, was born at Great Budworth, co. Cheshire; baptized there, 12-15-1633; died at Springfield, Chester Co., Pa., in about 1695. He is shown in Besse's *Sufferings* for being at an unlawful Quaker meeting in Coddington. He came to Pennsylvania in about 1682, in a ship whose name is not recorded, preceding his wife and some of their children. He married, probably at Great Budworth, in about 1663, as her first husband, **MARY HAYES**, sister of Assemblyman Jonathan Hayes of Pennsylvania; she died 4-11-1728. Robert and Mary (Hayes) Taylor had nine children who were born at Great Budworth between 1665 and 1681; a tenth child was born in Pennsylvania. Two are ancestors of Sarah D. Rundall.

Robert TAYLOR = Mary HAYES
Josiah TAYLOR = Elizabeth PENNELL   Bartholomew COPPOCK Jr. = Phoebe TAYLOR
Thomas MERCER Jr. = Hannah TAYLOR   Daniel SHARPLES = Sarah COPPOCK
Daniel MERCER = Rebecca TOWNSEND
Solomon MERCER = Abigail SHARPLES
William WALTER = Phebe MERCER
William H. MANLY = Sarah D. WALTER
Silas William RUNDALL = Rachel MANLY
William Henry "Will" THOMPSON = Sarah D. "Sadie" RUNDALL

ROBERT TAYLOR

ROBERT TAYLOR[362] probably came to America from co. Kent, England; died in Rhode Island, probably Newport, R.I., 13 January 1688. He was of Scituate, Mass., and Newport, R.I., where he was a ropemaker. He became a freeman in 1655, and was appointed prison-keeper by the Assembly in 1673. He married (1), in 1646, **Mary HODGES**, probably the daughter of Capt. JOHN HODGES and his wife MARY MILLER. They had six children. Their son John is an ancestor of Jessie F. Stockwell.

Robert TAYLOR = Mary HODGES
John TAYLOR = Abigail _____
Jonathan IRISH = Mary TAYLOR
Jesse IRISH = Mary ALLEBEE
William IRISH = Dolly _____
Capt. Freeborn POTTER = Dolly IRISH
Harvey HYDE = Fidelia Gadcourt POTTER
Benajah Flavel STOCKWELL = Emily Lodiweska (Emma F.) HYDE
George J. HILL = Jessie Fidelia STOCKWELL

SARAH TAYLOR

SARAH TAYLOR,[363] daughter of John and Margaret (Willmote) Taylor, was baptized at St. Albans Abbey, St. Albans, Hertfordshire, 29 May 1595; buried at Dunstable, Bedfordshire, 12 December 1631. She married, as his first wife, **ROBERT LONG**, perhaps a son of John Long; born in England in about 1590; died at Charlestown, Mass., 9 January 1663/4. They had ten children; their daughter Sarah Long is an ancestor of Jessie F. Stockwell. He came to America with his second wife, ten children, and a servant. He married (2), by 1634, in England, Elizabeth _____, who died at Charlestown, Mass., in 1687.

---

[361] Hill, *Fundy to Chesapeake*, 302-3.
[362] Hill, *Western Pilgrims*, 359. Also see correction in footnote for JOHN HODGES.
[363] Hill, *Western Pilgrims*, 323.

RICHARD THATCHER

RICHARD THATCHER,[364] born at Uffington, Berkshire, England, in about 1620; perhaps died at Philadelphia or Bucks Co., Pa., in 1697. He was an original landowner in Bucks Co., with 1000 acres straddling the Nashaminy Creek near its entrance into the Delaware River. He is said to have had eight children, with a wife who died before he emigrated. A Richard Thatcher who died in Chester Co., Pa., in 1722, presumed to be his son and namesake, married Jeane Stevens, daughter of **JOHN STEVENS**. Many named Thatcher later changed their name to Hatcher.

Richard THATCHER = _____ _____
Richard THATCHER [II] = Jeane (Jane) STEVENS
William BRINTON the Younger = Jane (or Jean) THATCHER
William BRINTON = Hannah BULLER
Joseph WALTER Sr. = Jane BRINTON
James WALTER = Sarah DIXON
William WALTER = Phebe MERCER
William H. MANLY = Sarah D. WALTER
Silas William RUNDALL = Rachel MANLY
William Henry "Will" THOMPSON = Sarah D. "Sadie" RUNDALL

ARCHIBALD THOMPSON

ARCHIBALD THOMPSON[365] was born in Ulster Province, Ireland, in about 1691 and died at South Bridgewater, Mass., in 1776. He is said to have made the first spinning foot-wheel in New England. He is said to have arrived with his wife and a son in 1724. His second child was born at Bridgewater, Mass. in about 1729. The name of his wife is unknown, but she has been called **ELIZABETH or Betty.** His son and namesake went to Canada as a soldier in 1758. He went north again after he was married in 1761 and settled in Nova Scotia. After three generations in Nova Scotia, some descendants of Archibald Thompson returned to Massachusetts, and later to Iowa, where William H. Thompson was born.

Archibald THOMPSON = perhaps Elizabeth or Betty _____
Archibald THOMPSON [II] = Martha ROBINSON
James THOMPSON Sr. = Hannah _____, prob. Hannah SCOTT
Joseph Scott THOMPSON = Ruth E. ARCHIBALD
James Everett THOMPSON = Jane GRANT
William Henry "Will" THOMPSON = Sarah D. "Sadie" RUNDALL

ELIZABETH (_____) THOMPSON

ELIZABETH _____, or Betty, was the wife of **ARCHIBALD THOMPSON**. They came from Ulster, Ireland, to America, with their first child in 1724. Their second child was born at Bridgewater, Mass.

MARGARET THOMPSON

MARGARET THOMPSON[366] married **JOHN SMITH** in about 1644, probably in Salem, Mass. They had three daughters who married sons of Francis and Rebecca (Towne) Nurse. All three were convicted as witches in 1692, and two were hanged. She is an ancestor of William H. Thompson.

JOHN THORNDIKE

Mr. JOHN THORNDIKE,[367] son of Francis and Alice (Coleman) Thorndike, was baptized, 23 July 1603 at Great Carlton, co. Lincs, England; buried in Westminster Abbey, 3 November 1668. He came to America in 1632. In 1633, he was one of the men who, with Governor Winthrop's son, John Winthrop,

---

[364] Hill, *Fundy to Chesapeake*, 330.
[365] Hill, *Fundy to Chesapeake*, 1-11. For Hannah _____, prob. Hannah SCOTT, see *Fundy to Chesapeake*, 3-4.
[366] Hill, *Fundy to Chesapeake*, 79.
[367] Hill, *Quakers and Puritans*, 138-9.

Jr., settled Ipswich, Mass. He returned to England to visit his brother, the Rev. Herbert Thorndike, prebendery of Westminster Abbey. He married, at Salem, Mass., 1640, **ELIZABETH STRATTON**, daughter of John Stratton and Anne Bearhaugh; born 1614; she is of **Royal descent**.

Mr. John THORNDIKE = Elizabeth STRATTON
Capt. Paul THORNDIKE = Mary PATCH
Capt. John THORNDIKE = Joanna LARKIN
James THORNDIKE = Anna OBER
Simeon MOORS = Joanna THORNDIKE
Jeduthan WARREN = Joanna MOORS
Jesse WARREN = Betsy JACKSON
Herbert Marshall WARREN = Eliza Caroline COPP
William Toy SHOEMAKER = Mabel WARREN

JOHN THORNE

JOHN THORNE,[368] born about 1739, probably in co. Devon, England; buried at Littleham by Exmouth, 20 November 1807. He married, at Littleham, 3 March 1767, ***Mary HOW***, daughter of John and Mary (Dido) How; baptized at Littleham by Exmouth, 2 October 1744; buried there, 27 October 1832.

John THORN(E) = Mary HOW
Josiah COPP, Sr. = Elizabeth (Betty or Bettey) THORN
James John COPP = Caroline BIGWOOD
Herbert Marshall WARREN = Eliza Caroline COPP
William Toy SHOEMAKER = Mabel WARREN

PARDON TILLINGHAST

Rev. PARDON TILLINGHAST,[369] son of Pardon and Sarah (Browne) Tillinghast, was born at Severn Cliffs, co. Sussex, England, in about 1622; died at Providence, R.I., 29 January 1717/18. He was trained as a cooper, as was his father. He received 25 acres of land in Providence, R.I., on 19 January 1645/6. He became a wealthy trader, and a Six Principle Baptist minister. He married (1) by about 1654, _____ **BUTERWORTH**. He married (2), 16 April 1664, **Lydia TABER**, daughter of **PHILIP TABER** and Lydia Masters, daughter of **JOHN MASTERS**; born at Barnstable, Mass 8 Nov 1640; died at Providence, 27 January 1718.

Rev. Pardon TILLINGHAST = Lydia TABER
Phillip TILLINGHAST, J.P. = Martha HOLMES
William POTTER = Martha TILLINGHAST
Capt. Oliver POTTER = Mary COLVIN
Capt. Freeborn POTTER = Dolly IRISH
Harvey HYDE =Fidelia Gadcourt POTTER
Benajah Flavel STOCKWELL = Emily Lodiweska HYDE
George J. HILL = Jessie Fidelia STOCKWELL

JOHN TOMPKINS

JOHN TOMPKINS,[370] was of Concord, Mass., in 1640, where he had two children, by a wife whose name is unknown; he died at Fairfield, Conn., in about 1660. In 1644, he and his wife and two children joined the Rev. John Jones, pastor of Concord, who took a group of families to Fairfield.

John TOMPKINS = _____ _____
Nathaniel TOMPKINS = Elizabeth WHITE
Nathaniel TOMPKINS [II] = Elizabeth CORNELL
Nathaniel TOMPKINS [III] = Mary FORSHAY

---

[368] Hill, *Quakers and Puritans*, 195.
[369] Hill, *Western Pilgrims*, 267-70.
[370] Hill, *Fundy to Chesapeake*, 208.

Nathaniel TOMPKINS [IV] = Elizabeth "Polly" OAKLEY
Bartholomew TOMPKINS = [unmarried] Martha LAKE
Reuben John RUNDALL = Martha TOMPKINS
Silas William RUNDALL = Rachel MANLY
William Henry "Will" THOMPSON = Sarah D. "Sadie" RUNDALL

_____ (_____) TOMPKINS

_____ _____ is the unnamed wife of **JOHN TOMPKINS**, of Concord, Mass., in 1640, who went with him and their two sons to Fairfield, Conn. in about 1660. She and John are the ancestors of the Tompkins family of America, which includes **Daniel Tompkins**, Governor of New York and 6th **Vice President of the United States** (see preceding).

WILLIAM TOWNE

WILLIAM TOWNE,[371] son of John and Elizabeth (Clarke) Towne, was baptized at Great Yarmouth, co. Norfolk, 18 March 1598/9; died at Topsfield, Essex Co., Mass., 24 Jun 1673. He married, at Great Yarmouth, at St. Nicholas Church, 25 April 1620, **JOANNA BLESSING**, daughter of John and Joane (Preaste) Blyssyng; born at Caister, co. Norfolk; died at Topsfield, Mass., in 1682. They had three daughters who were accused of witchcraft in Salem in 1692. The daughters were known by their married names: Rebecca (Towne) Nurse; Mary (Towne) Easty; and Sarah (Towne) (Bridges) Cloyse. All three were convicted, and the first two were hanged (see also FRANCIS NURSE and JOHN SMITH).

William TOWNE = Joanna "Joan" BLESSING
Francis NURSE = Rebecca "Goody Nurse" TOWNE
Samuel NURSE = Mary SMITH
Ebenezer NURSE = Elizabeth MITCHELL, prob. dau. of Andrew Mitchell
Caleb PUTNAM = Elizabeth NURSE
William PUTNAM = Dorothy "Dolly" PRESCOTT
William ARCHIBALD = Susannah "Susan" PUTNAM
Joseph Scott THOMPSON = Ruth E. ARCHIBALD
James Everett THOMPSON = Jane GRANT
William Henry "Will" THOMPSON = Sarah D. "Sadie" RUNDALL

JOHN TOWNSEND
RICHARD TOWNSEND

JOHN TOWNSEND, RICHARD TOWNSEND and their brother Henry Townsend,[372] probably came to America in about 1641. John came to Massachusetts, and soon removed to Manhattan, where he was joined by his brothers. They removed to Flushing, Long Island, in 1645. They relocated to Warwick, R.I., and then returned to Long Island, where they signed the Flushing Remonstrance, and in 1661, founded Oyster Bay. Several other unrelated Townsend families also appeared in America.

_____ *TOWNSEND* [father of John, Henry & Richard of Long Island] = _____
John TOWNSEND Sr. = Elizabeth ?MONTGOMERY   Richard TOWNSEND = Deliverance COLES
John TOWNSEND 2d [later called Sr.] = Hannah ____   Thomas WILLETS Sr. = Dinah TOWNSEND
John TOWNSEND [III], Jr. = Catherine (?)WILLITS
Daniel MERCER = Rebecca TOWNSEND
Solomon MERCER = Abigail SHARPLES
William WALTER = Phebe MERCER
William H. MANLY = Sarah D. WALTER
Silas William RUNDALL = Rachel MANLY
William Henry "Will" THOMPSON = Sarah D. "Sadie" RUNDALL

---

371 Hill, *Fundy to Chesapeake*, 84-5.
372 Hill, *Fundy to Chesapeake*, 309-12. The two lines of descent to Sarah Rundall depend on the possibility that Catherine (?)Willets, who m. John Townsend [III], is a daughter of Thomas Willets and his wife Dinah Townsend.

OSMOND TRASK

OSMOND TRASK,[373] perhaps the son of Nicholas Trask of East Coker, co. Somerset, England, was born about 1627; died at Beverly, Essex Co., Mass., in about 1675/6. He first appeared in Massachusetts in the record of his marriage in Salem in 1649. In 1664, Osmond was fined for "rescuing hogs and cattle as they were being driven to the pound." However, he reformed and was elected constable in 1665. He married (1), in Salem, Mass., 1 January 1649/50[?], **Mary _____**; she died at Salem, 2 January 1661/2[?]; they had five children. He married (2), in Salem, 22 May 1663, **Elizabeth GALLEY**, daughter of JOHN GALLEY and his wife Florence; born say 1624; died in Beverly, Mass., 5 May 1679. They had seven children. She married (2), John Giles, without issue.

Osmond TRASK = Elizabeth GALLEY
Lieutenant Stephen HERRICK = Elizabeth TRASK
Edward HERRICK = Mary DENNISON
Col. Rufus HERRICK = Miss _____ GIBBS, prob. Myra (Mary) GIBBS
Capt. Rufus HERRICK Jr. = Lydia NEWMAN
Rufus HERRICK [III] = Jerusha P. _____ (prob.) PIERCE
William Prince HILL = Sarah P. "Sally" HERRICK
Charles W. HILL = Adelia Catharine "Delia" RILEY
George J. HILL = Jessie Fidelia STOCKWELL

THOMAS TROWBRIDGE

THOMAS TROWBRIDGE,[374] eldest child of John and Agnes (Prowse) Trowbridge, was probably born at Taunton, co. Somerset, England, in March or April 1598; died there, and was buried at St. Mary Magdalen Church, 7 February 1672/3. His father and grandfather were wealthy merchants in the wool business of Taunton. In about 1636, he was the first of his family to come to America. After spending about five years in Massachusetts and Connecticut, he returned to England, where he died some 30 years later. He married, at St. Mary Arches Church, Exeter, 26 March 1627, **ELIZABETH MARSHALL**, daughter of the late John Marshall and his wife, Alice (Bevys) Marshall; baptized at St. Mary Arches, Exeter, 24 March 1602/3; died in New England, probably New Haven, Conn., before 1641. He is an ancestor of both George J. Hill, the Iowa Pioneer, and Mabel Warren.

Thomas TROWBRIDGE = Elizabeth MARSHALL
Lieut. James TROWBRIDGE = Margaret ATHERTON   William TROWBRIDGE = Elizabeth LAMBERTON
John GREENWOOD, Esq. = Hannah TROWBRIDGE   Peter MALLORY Jr. = Elizabeth TROWBRIDGE
Isaac JACKSON = Ruth GREENWOOD   Stephen MALLORY = Mary _____
Sgt. Josiah JACKSON = Mary DARBY   Benajah MALLORY = Elizabeth WAKELEE
Oliver JACKSON = Mary PEIRCE   Isaac HILL [Jr.] = Eunice MALLORY
Jesse WARREN = Betsy JACKSON   Ephraim HILL = Charlotte PRINCE
Herbert Marshall WARREN = Eliza Caroline COPP   William Prince HILL = Sarah P. "Sally" HERRICK
William Toy SHOEMAKER = Mabel WARREN   Charles W. HILL = Adelia Catharine "Delia" RILEY
George J. HILL = Jessie Fidelia STOCKWELL

JOHN TURNER

JOHN TURNER,[375] who died sometime after 1654, first appeared as a workman employed at the iron forge that began operations in Lynn, Mass., in 1643. Many of the workers came from Hammersmith, near London, England. He was last mentioned in the record in Lynn in 1654. His wife, whose name is unknown, probably died in England. He had two sons, who came with him to America.

John TURNER = _____ _____
John TURNER [II] = Jane _____

[373] Hill, *Western Pilgrims*, 62-3.
[374] Hill, *Quakers and Puritans*, 238; and *Western Pilgrims*, 30.
[375] Hill, *Western Pilgrims*, 196-7.

Richard GODFREY = Jane TURNER
Deacon Peter HOLBROOK = Alice GODFREY
Cornet John HOLBROOK = Hannah CHAPIN
Lt. Aaron HOLBROOK =Hannah PARTRIDGE
Ebenezer STOCKWELL = Abi HOLBROOK
Joseph H. STOCKWELL = Anna Maria SAXE
Benajah Flavel STOCKWELL = Emily Lodiweska (Emma F.) HYDE
George J. HILL = Jessie Fidelia STOCKWELL

JOAN TYLER

JOAN TYLER,[376] born in Wilton, near Bristol, England, in 1630, and was buried at Middletown, Bucks Co., Pa., on 20 December 1689. She married, as his second wife, at Bristol Quaker Meeting, **HENRY COMLY**; born in 1674 in Bedminster, near Bristol, England; died at Moreland, Philadelphia Co., Pa., 16 March 1726/7. He had four children with his first wife. His son with Joan Tyler, Henry Comly, Jr., came to America with his parents at the age of seven in November 1683 in *The Samuel and Mary*. He is an ancestor of William T. Shoemaker. She married (2), 26 February 1685, **Joseph ENGLISH**.

MARY TYSON

MARY TYSON, aka MARIA TEISSEN DOORS,[377] probably a daughter and one of the youngest of the 14 children of Theiss Doors and Neesgen Op Den Graeff, was born about 1660, probably in Kaldenkirchen, Duchy of Jülich; died at Germantown, Philadelphia Co., Pa., in 1742. She was probably the sister of Reiner Theissen (later known as Tyson), one of the Thirteen Founders of Germantown, who came on the *Concord* in 1683. The early immigrants to Germantown soon anglicized their names, and the family name in America is Tyson, so she is usually called Mary Tyson. She married, probably at Kaldenkirchen, Duchy of Jülich (now part of Germany), in about 1683, **JAN LUKENS**, also known as Johann Luken; born perhaps at Dahlen or Krefeld, Duchy of Jülich, say 1650-55; died at Germantown, Pa., in January 1743/44/45. Her son Peter Lukens is an ancestor of Dr. William T. Shoemaker.

WILLIAM UNDERWOOD

WILLIAM UNDERWOOD, Esq.[378] was presumably born in England; he died, probably at Chelmsford, Mass., soon after 14 March 1693. The birth of his first child was recorded at Concord, Mass., 25 February 1639/40. He was admitted freeman at Concord in 1650, and he removed from Concord in 1652 to Chelmsford, where he served as a town officer. He married (1), in about 1640, as her second husband, **SARAH (___) PELLET**; she died 5 November 1684. William and Sarah (___) (Pellet) Underwood had five children born at Concord and two born at Chelmsford, Mass. They had two daughters who are ancestors of Mabel Warren: Remembrance and Deborah. Remembrance Underwood is an ancestor of **President Franklin Pierce**. William Underwood married (2), 17 Mar 1684/5, **Mrs. Anna (MOORE) KIDDER**, daughter of FRANCIS MOORE and widow of James Kidder, without issue.

William UNDERWOOD Esq. = Sarah (___) PELLET, widow of *THOMAS PELLET*.

Josiah RICHARDSON= Remembrance UNDERWOOD · Nathaniel BUTTERFIELD = Deborah UNDERWOOD
Lieut. William FLETCHER = Sarah RICHARDSON · Nathaniel BUTTERFIELD Jr. = Sarah FLETCHER
Josiah FLETCHER = Joanna SPALDING · Lieut. Joseph MOORS = Esther BUTTERFIELD
Capt. Joseph WARREN = Joanna FLETCHER · Simeon MOORS = Joanna THORNDIKE
Jeduthan WARREN = Joanna MOORS
Jesse WARREN = Betsy JACKSON
Herbert Marshall WARREN = Eliza Caroline COPP
William Toy SHOEMAKER = Mabel WARREN

---

[376] Hill, *Quakers and Puritans*, 30.

[377] Hill, *Quakers and Puritans*, 58-63 (Tyson), 64-6 (Op den Graeff).

[378] Hill, *Western Pilgrims*, 235: William Underwood = Anna (Moore) Kidder; *Quakers and Pilgrims*, 157: William Underwood = Sarah (___) Pellet.

NICHOLAS UTTER

NICHOLAS UTTER[379] was probably born as early as 1630, and surely by 1640, somewhere in Northern Europe. He appeared in Westerly, R.I., and he died in Stonington, Conn., in 1722. His name, "utter," means otter in Swedish, and it is usually taken by a family of high rank, or by a soldier. He first appeared in the public record when he was fined in 1678 for opening Indian graves. He married twice in America, and had children by both wives. By his first wife, who he married in say 1659, he had two children, including Jabez. By his second wife, **Mrs. Eleanor ____**, he had five children, all of whom had issue.

Nicholas UTTER = _____ _____
Jabez UTTER = Mary ___
James HYDE = Mary UTTER
Jabez HYDE = Hannah BACON
Private Henry HYDE = Thyrina (Therina) WARD
Luther HYDE = Phoebe GIDDINGS
Harvey HYDE = Fidelia Gadcourt POTTER
Benajah Flavel STOCKWELL = Emily Lodiweska (Emma F.) HYDE
George J. HILL = Jessie Fidelia STOCKWELL

_____ (_____) UTTER

_____ _____, who married **NICHOLAS UTTER**, a soldier of fortune who came to Rhode Island, perhaps from Sweden, in the mid-seventeenth century. He was fined in Newport in 1678, but he was probably in America long before that appearance in court. They had at least two children; the eldest was born in about 1660. He remarried in say 1672. We can presume that his first wife was born in about 1640 and died in about 1670 (see preceding).

GEORGE VICKERY

GEORGE VICKERY[380] was born about 1615; died 12 July 1679. He was at Salem on 1 January 1637 when he was one of 24 inhabitants assessed for £24. He then lived in Marblehead, where deeds and court records name him as a fisherman and seaman. He removed to Hull, where he was recorded as a proprietor in 1657. He married, in 1647, **Rebecca PHIPPEN**, probably daughter of DAVID PHIPPEN and his wife Sarah, died in Hull, Plymouth Co., Mass., in 1687.

George VICKERY = Rebecca PHIPPEN
John PRINCE = Rebecca VICKERY
Captain John PRINCE = Reliance FULLER
Samuel PRINCE = Abigail HOWELL
Edward Howell PRINCE = Huldah OVIATT
Ephraim HILL = Charlotte PRINCE
William Prince HILL = Sarah P. "Sally" HERRICK
Charles W. HILL = Adelia Catherine RILEY
George J. HILL = Jessie Fidelia STOCKWELL

HARRY VYE

HARRY VYE[381] was of Cadhayne, Colyton parish, co. Devon, England. His daughter Agnes was the mother of John Michell, christened at Colyton, 24 March 1587/8. John's daughter Mary Michell was the mother of MARY DOLBERE, who married JONATHAN GILLETT in 1634, and emigrated to America.

Harry VYE = _____ _____
_____ MICHELL = Agnes VYE
John MICHELL = Emlyn WEEKE

---

[379] Hill, *Western Pilgrims*, 248-50.
[380] Hill, *Western Pilgrims*, 135-6.
[381] Hill, *Western Pilgrims*, 127.

Rawkey DOLBERE = Mary MICHELL
Jonathan GILLETT = Mary DOLBERE
(see JONATHAN GILLETT and MARY DOLBERE)

JAMES WAKELEE

JAMES WAKELEE,[382] probably born by 1610, had lands recorded in Hartford, Conn., in February 1639/40. For several years thereafter his name appeared in lawsuits. He married (1), a wife whose name is **unknown**, and had two children, Henry and Richard. He married (2) **Alice (_____) BOOSEY**, widow of James Boosey of Wethersfield, and he removed there. He was constable of Wethersfield in 1656/7, but before January 1663, he fled from his wife and family to Rhode Island. He had been accused of a capital crime, presumably witchcraft. His wife Alice died at Wethersfield in 1683, and he was living in Providence as late as 1690. (See HENRY BURT for the father-in-law of his son Henry Wakelee).

James WAKELEE (aka WAKELY) = _____ _____ [He later married Alice (___) Boosey]
Henry WAKELEE (prob. son of James, by an unknown wife) = Sarah BURT, widow of Judah GREGORY
Jacob WAKELEE = _____ (_____) WALLIS
Henry WAKELEE = Sarah FROST
Benajah MALLORY = Elizabeth WAKELEE, married (1) _____ CRANE
Isaac HILL [Jr.] = Eunice MALLORY
Ephraim HILL = Charlotte PRINCE
William Prince HILL = Sarah P. "Sally" HERRICK
Charles W. HILL = Adelia Catharine "Delia" RILEY
George J. HILL = Jessie Fidelia STOCKWELL

MARY WALES

MARY WALES[383] was the daughter of John and Margaret Wales, and sister of NATHANIEL WALES who was baptized at St. Wilfred's, Calverly, West Riding, Yorkshire. She married, in England, **HUMPHREY ATHERTON**, probably the son of Edmund Atherton of co. Lancaster; born before 1615; died as a major-general in Boston, Mass., 17 September 1661. She died at Dorchester, Mass., in 1672. Her husband was first mentioned in the records of New England on 18 March 1637/[?8]. They had many children, perhaps thirteen or more; the first was baptized in England, 28 September 1628. She is an ancestor of Mabel Warren, and she may also be an ancestor of William H. Thompson.

NATHANIEL WALES

NATHANIEL WALES, Sr.,[384] weaver, son of John and Margaret Wales, was baptized at St. Wilfred's, Calverly, West Riding, Yorkshire, 26 February 1586/7; died at Boston, Mass., 4 December 1661. He was an emigrant on the *James* of Bristol in 1635 with his second wife and children. He first resided in Dorchester, Mass., and removed to Boston in 1654. He made his will on 20 June 1661, naming his wife, several children, two maids, and others. His wife was named executor and his "loving brother-in-law Humphrey Atherton" was named overseer. He married (1) _____ _____, who was the mother of all his children. She died in England. He married (2) **Susannah GREENAWAY**, who survived him.

---

[382] Hill, *Western Pilgrims*, 28. This account of James Wakelee and his descendants is summarized from *Families of Old Fairfield*, v.1 (627-30) and v.2 (981-8). Many additional but questionable lineages for the spouses of James[1], Henry[2], Jacob[3], and Henry[4] Wakelee can be seen in Public Trees of Ancestry.com. Sarah Frost is often said to be the daughter of Joseph and Elizabeth (Hubbell) Frost. However, I reject this, for it is not shown in *Families of Old Fairfield*; or Torrey, *New England Marriages Prior to 1700*; or in the *Barbour Collection.*

[383] Hill, *Quakers and Puritans*, 263-5, for her descent to Mabel Warren. For the descent to William Thompson, see Hill, *Fundy to Chesapeake*, 3-4, and 46-7. This genealogy depends on the presumption that Hannah _____, wife of James Thompson, Sr., is Hannah Scott, daughter of Sheriff Joseph Scott.

[384] Hill, *Fundy to Chesapeake*, 3-4, 42. This genealogy depends on the presumption that Hannah _____, wife of James Thompson, Sr., is Hannah Scott, daughter of Sheriff Joseph Scott.

Nathaniel WALES Sr. = _____ _____
Nathaniel WALES Jr. = Isabel ATHERTON
Jonathan WALES = Sarah BAKER
David CUTTING = Elizabeth WALES
Sarah EDMUNDS = David CUTTING (Jr.)
Sheriff Joseph SCOTT = Sarah CUTTING
James THOMPSON Sr. = Hannah ____, prob. Hannah SCOTT
Joseph Scott THOMPSON = Ruth E. ARCHIBALD
James Everett THOMPSON = Jane GRANT
William Henry "Will" THOMPSON = Sarah D. "Sadie" RUNDALL

RICHARD WALL

RICHARD WALL, Sr.,[385] born perhaps at Blackmore, Wedmore, Somersetshire, 1 Nov 1635; died at Cheltenham Twp., Pa., 26 Jan 1698. He was granted a certificate of removal of his family from the Monthly Meeting in Gloucestershire, on 26 April 1682. The family sailed on the the *Bristol Factor*, which arrived in October 1682. The family included Richard Jr.'s daughter Sarah, who later married George Shoemaker. On his arrival, he bought six hundred acres of land in Cheltenham Twp., Philadelphia Co. The "Richard Wall House" was the original meeting place for the Quakers of Cheltenham Township. He married, at Gloucester Monthly Meeting of Friends, England, 1 Aug 1658, **JOANE WHEEL**, born in Gloucestershire, 1640; died at Cheltenham, Pa., 2 Feb 1701/2. They had one child, born in England.

Richard WALL, Sr. = Joanne WHEEL
Richard WALL Jr. = Rachel _____
George SHOEMAKER Jr. = Sarah WALL
Isaac SHOEMAKER Sr. = Dorothy PENROSE
Isaac SHOEMAKER Jr. = Elizabeth POTTS
Jonathan SHOEMAKER Esq. = Hannah LUKENS
Charles SHOEMAKER = Rachel COMLY
Julien SHOEMAKER = Hannah Ann HESTER
William Toy SHOEMAKER = Mabel WARREN

GODWIN WALTER

GODWIN WALTER,[386] of Wiltshire, England, arrived in Pennsylvania on 16 December 1685. He may be Godwin Walter, son of William and Ann Walter, who was baptized at Froxfield, Wiltshire, 17 October 1661. He reportedly died at Chester, Chester Co., Pa., 6 November 1735. "Goodwin Walter" was on the list of "taxables" in Concord Twp., Chester Co., Pa., in 1715. He married, at Concord Meeting, Chester Co., Pa., 9 November 1696, **ELIZABETH SANGHURST**; born perhaps 1679; died say 1732. They may have had as many as ten children.

Godwin WALTER = Elizabeth SANGHURST
Joseph WALTER Sr. = Jane BRINTON
James WALTER = Sarah DIXON
William WALTER = Phebe MERCER
William H. MANLY = Sarah D. WALTER
Silas William RUNDALL = Rachel MANLY
William Henry "Will" THOMPSON = Sarah D. "Sadie" RUNDALL

WILLIAM WALTON

Rev. WILLIAM WALTON[387] was born in England in about 1602; died, intestate, at Marblehead, Mass., 9 November 1668. He was admitted as a scholarship student at Emmanuel College, Cambridge

[385] Hill, *Quakers and Puritans*, 8.
[386] Hill, *Fundy to Chesapeake*, 320-1.
[387] Hill, *Quakers and Puritans*, 250.

University, in 1618; B.A., 1621-2; M.A., 1625. He came to New England in 1635 from Seaton, co. Devon. He was the pastor at Marblehead from 1638 until his death in October 1668. He married, at Dorchester, co. Dorset, 10 April 1627, **ELIZABETH COOKE**, daughter of William and Martha (White) Cooke; she came with him to New England and died in 1682. They had seven children.

Rev. William WALTON = Elizabeth COOKE
Lot CONANT = Elizabeth WALTON
John CONANT = Bethiah MANSFIELD
John DARBY Jr. = Deborah CONANT
Andrew "Miller" DARBY = Elizabeth PATCH
Sgt. Josiah JACKSON = Mary DARBY
Oliver JACKSON = Mary PEIRCE
Jesse WARREN = Betsy JACKSON
Herbert Marshall WARREN = Eliza Caroline COPP
William Toy SHOEMAKER = Mabel WARREN

WILLIAM WARD

Deacon **WILLIAM WARD**,[388] born about 1603, presumably in England; died in Marlborough, Massachusetts, 10 August 1687. His origin is unknown, though it has been speculated that he came from Durham. He came to America in about 1639, and he was granted land at Sudbury, Mass., 18 November 1640. He was chairman of the board of selectmen of Sudbury. In 1660 the town of Marlborough was incorporated, with William Ward as one of the first selectmen. He married (1), in England, ____ _____, with whom he had two children. He married (2) in England, **ELIZABETH** _____, born about 1613; died at Marlborough, Mass., 9 December 1700. By his first wife, William Ward is an ancestor of Mabel Warren, and by his second wife, he is an ancestor of George J. Hill, the Iowa Pioneer. He is an ancestor of the author of this book, George J. Hill, M.D., and also of his wife, Helene Zimmermann, Ph.D.

_____ _____ = Deacon William WARD = Elizabeth _____

Ens. John WARD = Hannah JACKSON	Lt. Obadiah WARD = Mary _____
Thomas GREENWOOD, Esq. = Hannah WARD	Obadiah WARD = Elizabeth _____
John GREENWOOD, Esq. = Hannah TROWBRIDGE	Jabez WARD = Phebe EAGER
Isaac JACKSON = Ruth GREENWOOD	Corporal Jabez WARD = Jemima ALLEN
Sgt. Josiah JACKSON = Mary DARBY	Private Henry HYDE = Thyrina (Therina) WARD
Oliver JACKSON = Mary PEIRCE	Luther HYDE = Phoebe GIDDINGS
Jesse WARREN = Betsy JACKSON	Harvey HYDE = Fidelia Gadcourt POTTER
Herbert Marshall WARREN = Eliza Caroline COPP	Benajah F. STOCKWELL = Emily L. HYDE
William Toy SHOEMAKER = Mabel WARREN	George J. HILL = Jessie Fidelia STOCKWELL

ELIZABETH (_____) WARD

ELIZABETH _____, who married, as his second wife, **WILLIAM WARD**, came with him to America in about 1639. She was born about 1613 and died at Marlborough, Mass., 9 December 1700. He had two children with his first wife, and she raised them along with twelve of her own. She was said to have had "great fortitude, and possessed of physical powers in an eminent degree" when she was 74 years old.

ARTHUR WARREN

ARTHUR WARREN,[389] presumably born in England, died at Weymouth, Norfolk Co., Mass., 6 July 1658. He may have come to New England in about 1635 and was in Weymouth by 1638. He married, at Weymouth, in 1638, **MARY** _____; born in 1617; died after 1663. In March 1638/9, he was charged with "keeping company with the wife of Clement Briggs." His first child was born in November 1639, so it was conceived at about the same time he was enjoined for having a wandering eye. He nevertheless

---

[388] Hill, *Western Pilgrims*, 315-6; Hill, *Quakers and Puritans*, 259-60.
[389] Hill, *Quakers and Puritans*, 120-32.

became a proprietor of the plantation of Weymouth, and he was a member of the church in Braintree.   He founded one line of the Warren family in Massachusetts.

Arthur WARREN = Mary _____
Jacob WARREN = Mary HILDRETH
Deacon Joseph WARREN = Ruth WHEELER
Joseph WARREN Jr. = Tabitha PARKER
Capt. Joseph WARREN = Joanna FLETCHER
Jeduthan WARREN = Joanna MOORS
Jesse WARREN = Betsy JACKSON
Herbert Marshall WARREN = Eliza Caroline COPP
Dr. William Toy SHOEMAKER = Mabel WARREN

MARY (_____) WARREN

MARY _____, born in England in 1617; died in Massachusetts after 1663; married, at Weymouth, Mass., in 1638, **ARTHUR WARREN**, who died at Weymouth, 6 July 1658. He came to America in about 1635 and was in Weymouth by 1638. Nothing is known of her ancestry. She seven children and is the founding mother of the Warren family which is featured in Part II of the book *Quakers and Puritans*.

WILLIAM WASHBURN

WILLIAM WASHBURN,[390] is probably William Washborune, son of John and Martha (Timbrell) (Stevens) Washbourne, who was baptized at Bengeworth, Evesham, Worcestershire, in 1601; died at Hempstead, L.I., New Netherlands, in October 1657. He was in Stratford, Conn., before 1647, when he was one of 35 men from Stratford who relocated to Hempstead, L.I. He and his son John acquired more land in Oyster Bay in 1653. William Washburn made his will on 29 September 1657, and he died shortly before 11 June 1659. Assuming our William Washburn is of Bengeworth, Worcestershire, he married, at Bengeworth, **JANE** _____, and had eight children.

William WASHBURN = Jane _____
Richard WILLET = Mary WASHBURN
Thomas WILLETS Sr. = Dinah TOWNSEND
John TOWNSEND [III], Jr. = Catherine (?) WILLITS (poss. dau. of Thomas Willets and Dinah Townsend)
Daniel MERCER = Rebecca TOWNSEND
Solomon MERCER = Abigail SHARPLES
William WALTER = Phebe MERCER
William H. MANLY = Sarah D. WALTER
Silas William RUNDALL = Rachel MANLY
William Henry "Will" THOMPSON = Sarah D. "Sadie" RUNDALL

JANE (_____) WASHBURN

JANE _____ married, at Bengeworth, Evesham, Worcestershire, **WILLIAM WASHBURN**, son of John and Martha (Timbrell) Washbourne, who was baptized there in 1601; died at Hempstead, L.I., New Netherlands, in October 1657. She was probably his only wife and mother of all his children. They came to America in 1647, settling first at Stratford, Conn., and then to Hempstead, L.I., where he also became a landowner in Oyster Bay. She presented his will to the authorities after he died (see preceding).

BRIDGET WATERS

BRIDGET WATERS[391] was born at Oakely Grove, Oakley Parish, co. Cumberland, England, in 1627; died in 1698 in Westchester Co., N.Y. She married, in England, **JOHN WILMOT**, born in 1605 at

---

[390] Hill, *Fundy to Chesapeake*, 319. This line of descent depends on the possibility that Catherine ?Willets, who m. John Townsend III, is a daughter of Thomas Willets and his wife Dinah Townsend.
[391] Hill, *Fundy to Chesapeake*, 227.

Yetminster, co. Dorset, England; died in 1698 in Westchester Co., N.Y. The 22-year difference in their ages, suggests that she may have been his second wife. They probably came to America in about 1649, because their daughter, Mary Wilmot, who married Thomas Oakley, son of MILES OAKLEY, was born at Great Neck, L.I., in that year. John and Bridget (Waters) Wilmot are ancestors of Sarah D. Rundall.

MARGARET WATSON

MARGARET WATSON[392] was born at Bannockburn, Stirlingshire, Scotland, in 1682. She married, in about 1719, in Ireland or Massachusetts, as his second wife, **GAIN ROBINSON**, son of Munster and Catherine (Fitzgerald) Robinson; born in Scotland in about 1682; died at East Bridgewater, Plymouth Co., Mass., 7 July 1763. He came to America with two children by his first wife, and she and Gain had twelve more children in Massachusetts. Their daughter Martha is an ancestor of William H. Thompson.

WILLIAM WEAVER

WILLIAM WEAVER[393] was probably an immigrant in the mid-eighteenth century from one of the states that now comprise the Republic of Germany. He was living in the German-speaking community of Rhinebeck, N.Y., at the time that his daughter, Catherine, met and married JOHN SAXE, who emigrated to Pennsylvania, learned the trade of a miller, and was moving north to look for work at Rhinebeck, N.Y. Many others named Weaver also appeared in Rhinebeck at about that time.

William WEAVER = _____ _____
John SAXE = Catherine WEAVER
Godfrey SAXE = _____
Joseph H. STOCKWELL = Anna Maria SAXE
Benajah Flavel STOCKWELL = Emily Lodiweska (Emma F.) HYDE
George J. HILL = Jessie Fidelia STOCKWELL

_____ (_____) WEAVER

_____ _____ was the wife of WILLIAM WEAVER and mother of Catherine, who married JOHN SAXE. She probably accompanied her husband from Germany and died in Rhinebeck, N.Y. There are many graves of men and women named Weaver in the Reformed Church cemetery in Rhinebeck.

RICHARD WEBB

RICHARD WEBB,[394] born probably in England in about 1623; died at Stamford, Conn., 15 March 1675/6. He was first mentioned in New Haven, Conn., in 1643 as "fined for coming late to train" and he took the oath of allegiance, in company with Robert Bassett, 1 July 1644. His will named his wife Margery, his son Joseph, who took the mill at Stamford and ran it jointly with his mother; his son Joshua, who had the "lands at Newfield, and the tools which were in Huntington [Long Island]." He married, in say 1653, **MARGERY (_____) BASSETT**. They had eight children, born at Stamford.

Richard WEBB = Margery (_____) BASSETT
Samuel WEBB = _____ _____
Francis BROWN = Mercy WEBB
David BROWN = Sarah WEED, prob. dau of Ebenezer Weed
David BROWN [II] = Deborah JESSUP
Shadrack RUNDALL Sr. = Phebe BROWN
Reuben John RUNDALL = Martha TOMPKINS
Silas William RUNDALL = Rachel MANLY
William Henry "Will" THOMPSON = Sarah D. "Sadie" RUNDALL

---

[392] Hill, *Fundy to Chesapeake*, 13.
[393] Hill, *Western Pilgrims*, 218; and Hill, *John Saxe, Loyalist (1732-1808) and his Descendants for Five Generations*.
[394] Hill, *Fundy to Chesapeake*, 183.

MARGERY (_____) (BASSETT) WEBB

MARGERY _____,[395] who married (1) _____ **BASSETT**, married (2), at a time and place unknown, **RICHARD WEBB**. He was probably born in England in 1623 and died at Stamford, Conn., 15 March 1675/6. He came to America in 1643, and was first mentioned in New Haven. He later owned and operated a large mill in Stamford, which he bequeathed to his wife and son (see preceding).

JONAS WEED

JONAS WEED,[396] born in England by 1610, based on date of freemanship; died at Stamford, Conn., between making his will on 26 November 1672 and the inventory of his estate on 5 June 1676, probably closer to the latter date. He came to New England in 1630 and settled at Watertown, Mass., where he became freeman, 18 May 1631. He was a member of the Watertown church prior to 29 March 1636, when he was dismissed from that church to form a new church at Wethersfield. In 1672, he had several parcels of land in Stamford. He married **MARY _____**, who died in 1690. If she was his only wife, they had ten children, of whom the second son, Daniel, is probably an ancestor of Sarah D. Rundall.

Jonas WEED = Mary _____
Daniel WEED = Ruth _____
Ebenezer WEED = Mary BELL
David BROWN = Sarah WEED, prob. dau of Ebenezer Weed
David BROWN (II) = Deborah JESSUP
Shadrack RUNDALL Sr. = Phebe BROWN
Reuben John RUNDALL = Martha TOMPKINS
Silas William RUNDALL = Rachel MANLY
William Henry "Will" THOMPSON = Sarah D. "Sadie" RUNDALL

MARY (_____) WEED

MARY _____, who died in Stamford, Conn., in 1690, married, at a time and place unrecorded, **JONAS WEED**, born in England by 1610 and died between 1672 and 1676. He came to New England in 1630 and settled at Watertown, Mass. He later relocated to Wethersfield and Stamford, where he became a miller and land owner. If she was his only wife, they had ten children (see preceding).

JOANE WHEEL

JOANE WHEEL,[397] born in Gloucestershire, about 1640; died at Cheltenham, Pa., 2 Feb 1701/2, married **RICHARD WALL, Sr.,** and emigrated to Pennsylvania with him and their son, Richard, Jr., in 1682. They came in "the Welcome Fleet" of ships that accompanied William Penn. The house that they built in Cheltenham Township was later used as the residence of their granddaughter, Sarah, and her husband, George Shoemaker, Jr. It is still preserved as a museum, and the name of the town has been changed from Shoemakertown to Elkins Park. She is an ancestor of Dr. William T. Shoemaker.

ELIZABETH WHEELER

ELIZABETH WHEELER,[398] known as "Phoebe," was born at Cranfield, Bedford, England, in about 1604. She was murdered by Indians at Southampton, N.Y., in 1649. She married **THOMAS HALSEY,** son of Robert and Dorothy (Downes) Halsey; baptized at the parsonage in Great Gaddesen, Hertfordshire, England, 2 January 1592; died at Southampton, Long Island, 27 August 1678. Her son Isaac is an ancestor of **Fleet Admiral William F. Halsey, Jr.** She is an ancestor of George Hill, the Iowa Pioneer.

---

[395] Hill, *Fundy to Chesapeake*, 183.
[396] Hill, *Fundy to Chesapeake*, 187. This line is based on the probability that Sarah Weed is the daughter of Ebenezer.
[397] Hill, *Quakers and Puritans*, 8.
[398] Hill, *Western Pilgrims*, 150.

SARAH WHEELER

SARAH WHEELER,[399] whose origin is unknown, married **JAMES BRISCOE**. They were of Milford, Conn., when their daughter Ruth Briscoe was born in 1682. She is an ancestor of George J. Hill.

THOMAS WHEELER

Lieut. **THOMAS WHEELER, Sr.**,[400] was born in England, perhaps near Odell, Bedfordshire; died in 1654, probably in Fairfield, Conn. He was one of the earliest settlers of Concord, Mass., where he arrived in about 1639-40. He removed to Fairfield, Conn. He married, perhaps at co. Bedford, before 5 May 1613, **ANN _____, perhaps HALSEY**; died in 1659. They had five children, born in England.

Lieut. Thomas WHEELER = Ann ____ (perhaps HALSEY)
Sgt. Thomas WHEELER = Sarah MERRIAM
Deacon Joseph WARREN = Ruth WHEELER
Joseph WARREN Jr. = Tabitha PARKER
Capt. Joseph WARREN = Joanna FLETCHER
Jeduthan WARREN = Joanna MOORS
Jesse WARREN = Betsy JACKSON
Herbert Marshall WARREN = Eliza Caroline COPP
Dr. William Toy SHOEMAKER = Mabel WARREN

ANN (_____) WHEELER

ANN _____, perhaps HALSEY, married, in England, **THOMAS WHEELER**, later known as Lieut. Thomas Wheeler. They were perhaps married at Cranefield, co. Bedford, before 5 May 1613, and had five children before they emigrated to America in 1639-40. They settled first at Concord, Mass., and then relocated to Fairfield, Conn., in 1644 (see preceding).

JOHN WHITE

Elder **JOHN WHITE**,[401] son of Robert and Bridget (Allgar) White of Messing, co. Essex, England, was born in about 1597; died at Hartford, Conn., 23 January 1683/4. He came to America on the *Lyon* in 1632, and first resided at Cambridge. He was the ruling elder of the Second Church at Hartford and deputy for Hadley to the Massachusetts Bay General Court in 1664 and 1669. He married, at Messing, 26 December 1622, **MARY LEVIT**, who predeceased him.

Elder John WHITE = Mary LEVIT
Nathaniel WHITE = Elizabeth BREWSTER
Nathaniel TOMPKINS = Elizabeth WHITE
Nathaniel TOMPKINS [II] = Elizabeth CORNELL
Nathaniel TOMPKINS [III] = Mary FORSHAY
Nathaniel TOMPKINS [IV] = Elizabeth "Polly" OAKLEY
Bartholomew TOMPKINS = [unmarried] Martha LAKE
Reuben John RUNDALL = Martha TOMPKINS
Silas William RUNDALL = Rachel MANLY
William Henry "Will" THOMPSON = Sarah D. "Sadie" RUNDALL

JOHN WHITNEY

JOHN WHITNEY,[402] tailor of London and emigrant to Massachusetts, was son of Thomas and Mary (Bray) Whitney. He was baptized at St. Margaret's Church, Westminster, Middlesex, England, 20 July

---

[399] Hill, *Western Pilgrims*, 142.
[400] Hill, *Quakers and Puritans*, 162-3.
[401] Hill, *Fundy to Chesapeake*, 220.
[402] Hill, *Western Pilgrims*, 212-14. Not previously cited: *Great Migration* 7:366-72 ("JOHN WHITNEY").

1592; died in Watertown, Mass, 1 June 1673. John Whitney came from London on the *Elizabeth and Ann*, in April 1635. From June 1635 until he died in June 1673, he lived at Watertown, Mass. Before 1619, John Whitney married (1) **ELINOR** _____, at or near London; probably born between 1597-99 at London; died at Watertown, 11 May 1659. They had ten children. He is an ancestor of **Eli Whitney**, inventor of the cotton gin. He married (2) **Mrs. Judah _____ CLEMENT**, without further issue.

John WHITNEY = Elinor (aka Ellen, Ellin) _____
Benjamin WHITNEY = Jane _____
Jonathan MORSE = Jane WHITNEY
Joseph PARTRIDGE = Eunice MORSE
Lt. Aaron HOLBROOK = Hannah PARTRIDGE
Ebenezer STOCKWELL = Abi HOLBROOK
Joseph H. STOCKWELL = Anna Maria SAXE
Benajah Flavel STOCKWELL = Emily Lodiweska (Emma F.) HYDE
George J. HILL = Jessie Fidelia STOCKWELL

ELINOR (_____) WHITNEY

ELINOR _____, also known as Eleanor or Ellin, was probably born in London, England, between 1597-99; died at Watertown, Mass., 11 May 1659. She married, at or near London, **JOHN WHITNEY**, tailor of London. His father and grandfather were members of the Taylors Company of England. They had ten children, and came to America in 1635, in the Great Migration (see preceding).

ROBERT WHITTON

ROBERT WHITTON[403] died after 1723, when he signed the marriage certificate of his grandson, Samuel Spencer 2nd. The name and time of death of his wife is illegible in the Bible entry for the family, in which their six children were shown.

Robert WHITTON = _____ _____
Samuel SPENCER Sr. = Elizabeth WHITTON
Samuel SPENCER, Jr. = Mary DAWES
Joseph LUKENS = Elizabeth SPENCER
Jonathan SHOEMAKER Esq. = Hannah LUKENS
Charles SHOEMAKER = Rachel COMLY
Julien SHOEMAKER = Hannah Ann HESTER
William Toy SHOEMAKER = Mabel WARREN

_____ (WHITTON) _____

_____ _____ married **ROBERT WHITTON**, an early settler of Pennsylvania. He died after 1723, but her name and date of death is illegible in the family Bible. She had six children (see preceding).

WILLIAM WILCOCKSON

WILLIAM WILCOCKSON[404] **(aka WILCOX)**, a linen weaver, was born in 1601 at St. Albans, Hertfortshire, England; died in 1652, probably at Stratford, Conn. He came to America in 1635 at the age of 34 in the *Planter*, with a certificate from the minister at St. Albans, and was admitted as a freeman of Massachusetts, 7 December 1636. In 1639 he removed to Stratford, Conn., and was Deputy to the general court at Hartford in 1647. He married **MARGARET HARVEY**, daughter of James Harvey of Ilkeson, Derbyshire; born in 1611. They had nine children, the last seven born in America.

---

[403] Hill, *Quakers and Puritans*, 73.

[404] Hill, *Western Pilgrims*, 24. The account of William Wilcockson and his wife Margaret Harvey is taken from *Great Migration* 7:396-401 (WILLIAM WILCOCKSON). He was called Wilcox in *Western Pilgrims*, as the family name has become normalized, but in his lifetime, the documents quoted show that it was always spelled Wilcockson.

William WILCOCKSON = Margaret HARVEY
Sergeant Samuel WILCOCKSON = Hannah RICE
Samuel WILCOX [Jr.] = _____ _____
Ephriam WILCOX = Hannah HILL
Michael JACKSON = Susannah WILCOX
Sergeant Isaiah J. HENDRYX = Esther JACKSON
Josiah (Isaiah) RILEY = Susannah HENDRYX
Simeon RILEY = Katharine "Catherine" GILLETT
Charles W. HILL = Adelia Catharine "Delia" RILEY
George J. HILL = Jessie Fidelia STOCKWELL

ANN WILKINSON

ANN WILKINSON[405] was born about 1646, probably in co. Antrim, Ireland; died at Christiana Hundred, New Castle Co., Pa., in January 1692. She married, at Antrim Quaker Meeting, 11mo. 5, 1702, **WILLIAM GREGG,** son of William Gregg; born in Argyllshire, Scotland, or Antrim, Ireland, in about 1642; died at Christiana Hundred, 1 September 1687. They came to America sometime after 1682, perhaps in the ship *Caledonia*, and settled at Stand Milas in 1684. Their daughter Ann Gregg married William Dixon, son of HENRY DIXON, and is an ancestor of Sarah D. Rundall.

SIMON WILLARD

Major SIMON WILLARD, Esq.,[406] son of Richard and Margery (Humphrey) Willard, was baptized 7 April 1605 at Horsmandon, co. Kent, England; died at Charlestown, Mass., 24 or 25 April 1677. He came to Massachusetts in May 1634 from Marden, co. Kent, with his wife and three children. They first came to Cambridge, Mass., but removed, finally, in 1676, to Charlestown. He was a man with many occupations, and he was uncommonly successful at all of them. He married, at Marden, co. Kent, England, 13 October 1628, **MARY SHARPE,** daughter of Henry and Jane (Ffeylde) Sharpe; christened 10 October 1614, Horsmandon, co. Kent; died at Concord, Mass., before 1653. They had nine children. He married (2), by 1653, **Mary _____**. Simon Willard had eight children with his second wife.

Major Simon WILLARD = Mary SHARPE
Nathaniel HOWARD = Sarah WILLARD
Benjamin PARKER = Sarah HOWARD
Joseph WARREN Jr. = Tabitha PARKER
Capt. Joseph WARREN = Joanna FLETCHER
Jeduthan WARREN = Joanna MOORS
Jesse WARREN = Betsy JACKSON
Herbert Marshall WARREN = Eliza Caroline COPP
William Toy SHOEMAKER = Mabel WARREN

GEERTRUY WILLEMS

GEERTRUY WILLEMS,[407] born in the Netherlands, came to New Amsterdam from Amsterdam. She married, at New Amsterdam, by banns on 26 September 1661, **FRANCOIS DU PUY,** a Huguenot from Calais, France. She is an ancestor of Sarah D. Rundall.

RICHARD WILLET

RICHARD WILLET,[408] whose origin is unknown, died at Jericho, Long Island, N.Y., in 1667. He was at Hempstead, L.I., then New Netherlands, in 1657, although he was probably there much earlier. He

---

[405] Hill, *Fundy to Chesapeake*, 337.
[406] Hill, *Quakers and Puritans*, 174-5. Additional details in *Great Migration* 7:413-24.
[407] Hill, *Fundy to Chesapeake*, 226.
[408] Hill, *Fundy to Chesapeake*, 316. This genealogy depends on the possibility that Catherine ?Willets, who married John Townsend III, is a daughter of Thomas Willets and his wife Dinah Townsend.

then had 28 acres of land, 6 head of cattle and 6 milk cows. Although he was a Quaker, he held public offices, as surveyor of highways in 1659, and as townsman. He is an ancestor of **Richard M. Nixon, 37th President of the United States.** He married, before 1650, **Mary WASHBURN**, daughter of WILLIAM WASHBURN and his wife JANE, of Oyster Bay; born about 1629; died 17, 12 mo. 1713/14. She "lived for fifty years a widow, removing to Jericho where she became a 'Friend,' bringing up her children in that faith, in which she became a minister."

Richard WILLET = Mary WASHBURN
Thomas WILLETS Sr. = Dinah TOWNSEND
John TOWNSEND [III], Jr. = Catherine (?) WILLITS (poss. dau. of Thomas Willets and Dinah Townsend)
Daniel MERCER = Rebecca TOWNSEND
Solomon MERCER = Abigail SHARPLES
William WALTER = Phebe MERCER
William H. MANLY = Sarah D. WALTER
Silas William RUNDALL = Rachel MANLY
William Henry "Will" THOMPSON = Sarah D. "Sadie" RUNDALL

REBECCA WILLIAMS

REBECCA WILLIAMS[409] married, at Friends Meeting House in Philadelphia, 3 mo. 9, 1705, **THOMAS IREDELL**, son of Robert and Ellinor (Jackson) Iredell, born at co. Cumberland, England, in 1676; died in Pennsylvania. They had a son, who is an ancestor of Dr. William T. Shoemaker.

[WILLOUGHBY D'ERESBY]

[*WILLOUGHBY D'ERESBY*[410] was proposed by J. G. Hunt to be an ancestor of GEORGE MORTON (c.v.). His research was based on an imagined connection. See discussion in the Notes for *Western Pilgrims*, summarized above in *WILLIAM SKIPWITH*. See also *CONSTABLE of HALSHAM*.]

JOHN WILMOT

JOHN WILMOT,[411] born 1605, Yetminster, co. Dorset, England; died in 1698, Westchester Co., N.Y. He married, in England, **BRIDGET WATERS**, born 1627, Oakley Parish, co. Cumberland, England; died in 1698 in Westchester Co., N.Y. He was more than 20 years older than his wife, which is a bit unusual, and suggests that she may be a second wife. They had at least one child, a daughter, born at Great Neck, L.I., in 1649, so John and Bridget probably came to America by 1649.

John WILMOT = Bridget WATERS
Miles OAKLEY [II] = Mary WILMOT
Thomas OAKLEY = Abigail FARRINGTON
Elisha OAKLEY = Elizabeth YEOMAN
Nathaniel TOMPKINS [IV] = Elizabeth "Polly" OAKLEY
Bartholomew TOMPKINS = [unmarried] Martha LAKE (possibly daughter of Daniel Lake)
Reuben John RUNDALL = Martha TOMPKINS
Silas William RUNDALL = Rachel MANLY
William Henry "Will" THOMPSON = Sarah D. "Sadie" RUNDALL

ALEXANDER WILSON

ALEXANDER WILSON[412] was born in Londonderry, Ireland, in 1659; died in New Hampshire, 4 March 1752. He married ____, and had a daughter, Janet Wilson, who married MATTHEW TAYLOR.

Alexander WILSON = _____ _____
Matthew TAYLOR Sr. = Janet WILSON

---

[409] Hill, *Quakers and Puritans*, 67.
[410] Hill, *Western Pilgrims*, 704.
[411] Hill, *Fundy to Chesapeake*, 227.
[412] Hill, *Fundy to Chesapeake*, 51.

Samuel ARCHIBALD = Eleanor TAYLOR
Lt. Col. John ARCHIBALD 2nd = Margaret FISHER
William ARCHIBALD = Susannah "Susan" PUTNAM
Joseph Scott THOMPSON = Ruth E. ARCHIBALD
James Everett THOMPSON = Jane GRANT
William Henry "Will" THOMPSON = Sarah D. "Sadie" RUNDALL

_____ (_____) WILSON

_____ _____, whose name is unknown, married **ALEXANDER WILSON**, born at Londonderry, Ireland, in 1659 and died in New Hampshire in 1752. Her daughter Janet Wilson is an ancestor of William H. Thompson (see preceding).

JEAN WILSON

JEAN WILSON,[413] married **ERROLL BOYD**. He was born in about 1752, perhaps in Scotland; died at Halifax, N.S., 24 February 1828. She is an ancestor of William Thompson.

JOHN WOOD

Sergeant JOHN WOOD(S)[414] was probably born in England; died at Marlborough, Mass., 10 July 1678. He was a pinmaker, and sergeant of Marlboro garrison houses in 1675. He married **MARY_____**, who was probably born in England in about 1610; died in Marlborough in 1690. They had six children.

Sergeant John WOOD = Mary _____
Deacon John WOODS = Lydia _____
Abraham EAGER = Lydia WOODS
Jabez WARD = Phebe EAGER
Corporal Jabez WARD = Jemima ALLEN
Private Henry HYDE = Thyrina (Therina) WARD
Luther HYDE = Phoebe GIDDINGS
Harvey HYDE = Fidelia Gadcourt POTTER
Benajah Flavel STOCKWELL = Emily Lodiweska (Emma F.) HYDE
George J. HILL = Jessie Fidelia STOCKWELL

MARY (_____) WOOD

MARY _____, wife of **JOHN WOOD(S)**, was probably born in England in about 1610; died at Marlborough, Mass., in 1690. Her husband was a pinmaker and was sergeant of the local militia company. He was probably born in England and died at Marlborough on 10 July 1678. The eldest of their children became a deacon and is an ancestor of Jessie F. Stockwell (see preceding).

SUSAN WOOD

SUSAN WOOD,[415] daughter of Edmund Wood, of Shelf in Halifax, Yorkshire, and sister of Edmund Wood (Jr.); probably died in Stamford, Conn., after 1646. She married, (1) **Thomas BUTTERFIELD**, who died, leaving her a childless widow in England. His brother, Samuel Butterfield came to America and was said to have been cruelly killed, "roasted," by Indians at Groton, Mass., but more likely was captured and survived. Susan (Wood) Butterfield was "of Ovenden," Yorkshire, when she married, (2) **MATTHEW MITCHELL**, at Halifax, Yorkshire, England, 16 April 1616. She had eight children with him. The entire family came on the *James* of Bristol in 1635, and he became the wealthiest man in Stamford. The date of her death is unknown, but her husband's will, proved 16 June 1646, left the

---

[413] Hill, *Fundy to Chesapeake*, 109.
[414] Hill, *Western Pilgrims*, 327.
[415] Hill, *Fundy to Chesapeake*, 195-7; *Great Migration* 5:125-31 (Matthew Mitchell), and 7:491-6 (Edmund Wood).

residue of his estate to her, "to claim the rest £1700." Their daughter Abigail married the Rev. Abraham Pierson, Sr., and is probably an ancestor of Sarah D. Rundall.

WILLIAM WOODBURY

WILLIAM WOODBURY,[416] son of _____ Woodbury, was born in 1589 in England, probably in South Petherton, co. Somerset; died at Beverly, Mass., 29 January 1677. He probably came to Massachusetts with his brother John in June 1638. He served in the Port Royal Expedition in 1654. He married, at South Petherton, 29 January 1616/17, **ELIZABETH PATCH**, who was baptized at South Petherton, 16 April 1593. Their son Nicholas married, in Salem, by about 1652, ANN PALGRAVE, daughter of Richard and Joan (Harris) Paulsgrave; she was orphaned and came to America with her step-father, the Rev. John Youngs. William and Elizabeth (Patch) Woodbury have two lines of descent to Mabel Warren.

William WOODBURY = Elizabeth PATCH
Nicholas WOODBURY = Ann PALGRAVE   James PATCH = Hannah WOODBURY
Richard OBER = Abigail WOODBURY   Capt. Paul THORNDIKE = Mary PATCH
Hezekiah OBER = Ann (Anna) MORGAN   Capt. John THORNDIKE = Joanna LARKIN
James THORNDIKE = Anna OBER
Simeon MOORS = Joanna THORNDIKE
Jeduthan WARREN = Joanna MOORS
Jesse WARREN = Betsy JACKSON
Herbert Marshall WARREN = Eliza Caroline COPP
William Toy SHOEMAKER = Mabel WARREN

THOMAS WOODFORD

THOMAS WOODFORD,[417] born about 1641, a steward, came to America in 1632 on the *William & Francis*; died in 1666/7. He first resided at Roxbury, Mass., and was a freeman on 4 March 1634/5. He married, by about 1636, **Mary BLOTT**, daughter of ROBERT BLOTT and SUSANNAH SELBEE; baptized at Harrold, co. Bedford, 24 December 1609; died before 27 May 1662. They removed to Hartford, Conn., where he was one of the first settlers. As a steward, or "man servant," he was literate, and had a library, including a "new Bible." He had three daughters. His younger two daughters married sons of Samuel and Ann Allen. His daughter Sarah was an ancestor of **Ethan Allen.**

Thomas WOODFORD = Mary BLOTT
Samuel ALLEN = Hannah WOODFORD
Deacon Samuel ALLEN = Sarah RUST
Samuel ALLEN = Hannah MILLER
Jabez WARD = Jemima ALLEN
Henry HYDE = Thyrina WARD
Luther HYDE = Phoebe GIDDINGS
Harvey HYDE = Fidelia Gadcourt POTTER
Benajah Flavel STOCKWELL = Emily Lodiweska HYDE
George J. HILL = Jessie Fidelia STOCKWELL

RICHARD WOODWARD

RICHARD WOODWARD,[418] born in England in about 1589; died at Watertown, Mass., 16 February 1665. He came to America from Ipswich, England, in 1634 in the *Elizabeth* with his wife and two sons and settled in Watertown. He married, in England, **ROSE____**; born about 1584; died in Watertown, 6 October 1662. They had two children. He married (2), as her second husband, **Ann (____) GATES**, without further issue.

---

[416] Hill, *Quakers and Puritans*, 179.
[417] Hill, *Western Pilgrims*, 334. Anderson, *Great Migration Begins* 3:2057-60 (THOMAS WOODFORD).
[418] Hill, *Western Pilgrims*, 237. Anderson, *Great Migration*, 7:528-31.

Richard WOODWARD = Rose _____
George WOODWARD = Mary _____
John WOODWARD = Rebecca ROBBINS
John WOODWARD = Hannah HYDE
Henry BACON = Hannah WOODWARD
Jabez HYDE = Hannah BACON
Private Henry HYDE = Thyrina (Therina) WARD
Luther HYDE = Phoebe GIDDINGS
Harvey HYDE = Fidelia Gadcourt POTTER
Benajah Flavel STOCKWELL = Emily Lodiweska (Emma F.) HYDE
George J. HILL = Jessie Fidelia STOCKWELL

ROSE (_____) WOODWARD

ROSE _____, born about 1584; died in Watertown, Mass., 6 October 1662; married, in England, **RICHARD WOODWARD**, born in England in about 1589; died at Watertown, Mass., 16 February 1665. They came to America from Ipswich, England, in 1634, and settled in Watertown with their two children (see preceding).

MARY WRIGHT

MARY WRIGHT,[419] daughter of Edmund Wright, Esq., of Suffolk and Norfolk, was buried at Badinham, 4 March 1621/2. She married *WILLIAM DEREHAUGH*, son of John Derehaugh of Badinham, Suffolk and his wife Agnes; born about 10 February 1559; buried 4 September 1610. Mary Wright is a descendant of **John "Lackland," King of England**, and is an ancestor of Mabel Warren.

MARGARET WYATT

MARGARET WYATT,[420] daughter of John and Frances (Chichester) Wyatt, was baptized in Braunton, Devon, 8 March 1594/5; died in Windsor, Conn., 12 September 1675. She is of **Royal Descent**. She married, in Braunton, co. Devon, England, 2 February 1626/7, **Hon. MATTHEW ALLYN**, merchant, son of Richard and Margaret (Wyatt) Allen; baptized at Braunton, 17 April 1605; died at Windsor, Conn., 1 February 1670/1. They had three children. Margaret Wyatt and her husband Matthew Allyn are ancestors of **President Grover Cleveland**, and of Ellen Axson (wife of **Woodrow Wilson**), Elizabeth "Bess" Wallace (wife of **Harry Truman**), and Anne Robbins (wife of **Ronald Reagan**; name changed to Nancy Davis after her mother m. [2] Loyal Davis). They are ancestors of Jessie F. Stockwell.

MARGARET YARWOOD

MARGARET YARWOOD,[421] married, 4 mo. 13, 1678, in England, perhaps as his second wife, **BARTHOLOMEW COPPOCK, Sr.,** born at Saltney, Cheshire, England; died at Marple, Chester Co., Pa., 20 December 1718. She died 7 mo. 1735. He had five children. She is the mother of his son Bartholomew Coppock, Jr., who is an ancestor of Sarah D. Rundall.

ROBERT YEOMANS

ROBERT YEOMANS[422] was the father of Elizabeth Yeomans, who was born at Cortland, Westchester Co., N.Y., 20 June 1732, and died at Yorktown, N.Y., in about 1751, perhaps with the birth of her first child with Elisha Oakley.

---

[419] Hill, *Quakers and Puritans*, 148; Roberts, *Royal Descents of 600 Immigrants*, 397; Richardson, *Royal Ancestry*, "Derehaugh," 2:439-40.

[420] Hill, *Western Pilgrims*, 347. Richardson, *Royal Ancestry*, 1:111-5, traces the line of Margaret Wyatt back to Alice of Normandy, sister of King William the Conqueror, and thus to his ancestor, Charlemagne. Also see Weis, *Ancestral Roots*, 8th ed., 61, line 52; and Roberts, *Royal Descents*, 489-50.

[421] Hill, *Fundy to Chesapeake*, 300.

[422] Hill, *Fundy to Chesapeake*, 228.

Robert YEOMANS = _____
Elisha OAKLEY = Elizabeth YEOMANS
Nathaniel TOMPKINS [IV] = Elizabeth "Polly" OAKLEY
Bartholomew TOMPKINS = [unmarried] Martha LAKE (possibly daughter of Daniel Lake)
Reuben John RUNDALL = Martha TOMPKINS
Silas William RUNDALL = Rachel MANLY
William Henry "Will" THOMPSON = Sarah D. "Sadie" RUNDALL

JOHN ZIMMERMANN

JOHN ZIMMERMANN, Sr.,[423] son of Johann and Anna Ursula (Yäger) Zimmermann, was born at Gussenstadt, Heidenheim district, kingdom of Württemberg (now Baden-Württemberg, Germany), 18 November 1855; died at Philadelphia, Pa., 23 May 1936. His ancestor, Mattis Zimmermann, was born in that district in 1550, and the family had probably lived there for many generations. John was taught by his father to weave rugs in a small workshop in the house that had been in his father's family for three generations. He came to America at age 19 in 1874, initially living with relatives in Elmira, New York. He moved to Philadelphia two years later. With his imaginative inventions of improvements in looms and dyeing, and his leadership in the German community, and with his partners' financing and marketing skills, John Zimmermann and the Wassermann brothers created a series of successful fabric companies. Their companies eventually coalesced under that name of Artloom, which became one of the largest maker of fabrics in American. He became a Mormon, and after he became successful in the carpet business, he became a Bishop of that church. He married (1), in Philadelphia, **EVA KATHARINE KELLENBENZ**, daughter of Johann Michael and Clara (Grozinger) Kellenbenz; born at Kleineislingen (now Eislingen), Dönau, Württemberg, Germany, 28 September 1855; died at Philadelphia, Pa., 12 October 1920. After she died, he married (2), 23 November 1922, in Decater Co., Iowa, **Mrs. Anna (ANDERSON) DANCER**, without additional issue. John and Eva (Kellenbenz) Zimmermann had seven children, six of whom survived. *American Dreams* tells the story of the remarkable successes that they had, and of the successes of their families.

Mattis ZIMMERMANN = _____
Adam ZIMMERMANN = Catharina BOLLINGER
Herr Jakob ZIMMERMANN = Appolonia _____
Bürgurmeister Johann Jakob ZIMMERMANN = Anna WALTER
Johann Michael ZIMMERMANN = Maria BARTH
Georg Christoph ZIMMERMANN = Margareta SATTLER
Sigmund Christoph ZIMMERMANN = Appolonia BÜHNER
Johann Georg ZIMMERMANN = _____ _____
Jakob ZIMMERMANN = _____ _____.
Johannes ZIMMERMANN = Anna Ursula JÄGER
John ZIMMERMANN = Eva Katherine KELLENBENZ
Albert Walter ZIMMERMANN = Barbara SHOEMAKER
George James HILL = Helene ZIMMERMANN

---

[423] Hill, *American Dreams*, 1-31 (The Zimmermann Family); 75-96 (John Zimmermann and Eva Kellenbenz)

Corrections and Additions

I would like to call attention to the following corrections and additions to the four books of this tetralogy:

In *Western Pilgrims*, a footnote on page 7, copied and repeated on pages 83, 88, 90, 92, 96, 103, 107, and 112, should be corrected, to substitute **Jerusha** (whose name I show in bold) for Sarah, as follows:
> "The Introduction to Chapter 7 discusses the issue of the genealogy of the families mentioned in Chapters 7 and 14-21. This genealogy depends on the assumption that ~~Sarah~~ **Jerusha** P., wife of Rufus Herrick [III], is ~~Sarah~~ **Jerusha** Pierce, and that she is the daughter of Willard and Jerusha (Pellet) Pierce."

Sorry to say, but I repeatedly erred in stating in these footnotes that the woman in question is Sarah P. or Sarah Pierce. As mentioned in the text, the name of the woman in question should be JERUSHA P. and JERUSHA PIERCE.

On p.168, the reader is directed to follow the children of William and Alice (Carpenter) (Southworth) Bradford by a notation to "See Morton Family." This was an inadvertent error. The direction should have been to "See Bradford Family." The children of William and Alice (Carpenter) Southworth appear on p.99.

On the list of ancestral families, the name Constable appears. This was an error; the surname Constable does not appear in this book. And the surname Lane appears in error in the name list of *Western Pilgrims*. It refers to John Lane, who was a son-in-law of the immigrant, John Wallis and his wife Mary Phippen, but not a direct ancestor of either George J. Hill or Jessie Stockwell.

Silence Dunklee appears in *Western Pilgrims*, p. 225, as the wife of Caleb Putnam, and it is said that Silence Dunklee was a descendant of the Rev. John Lothrop. However, in *Fundy to Chesapeake*, p. 75, the name of Caleb Putnam's wife is shown to be Silence (Phillips) Dunklee. She married (1) to _____ Dunklee; and (2) to Caleb Putnam. The Dunklee line would connect with the Rev. John Lothrop, but not the line of Phillips. The comments about the Lothrop, Learned, Dunklee families in Chapter 43, p. 225, are therefore no longer relevant.[424]

On p. xxiv, the Ahnentafel for George J. Hill shows 705 Elizabeth WORTHINGTON as the wife of 704 Thomas PIERCE. This is erroneous. She was Thomas Pierce's second wife. His first wife, whose name is unknown, was the mother of 352 Thomas Pierce, Jr.

I mentioned on p. 293 that JANE LAWRENCE, wife of GEORGE GIDDINGS, "was said to be of Royal descent." I can now confirm this: Douglas Richardson, *Royal Ancestry* 3:548-52, shows the Lawrence Family's descent from Alice of Normandy to Jane Lawrence, wife of George Giddings.

On p. 62, I showed that Elizabeth Galley was the wife of OSMOND TRASK, and mother of Elizabeth Trask. In this *Synopsis*, I have added more information about Elizabeth Galley and her parents, JOHN and FLORENCE GALLEY, from Anderson, *Great Migration Begins*.

WILLIAM WILCOX and his wife MARGARET ____ are given brief treatment on pages 24-5. I have now amplified their biographies, based on the account in Anderson, *Great Migration*, 7:396-401

---

[424] I wrote in *Western Pilgrims*, "William French married (2) 6 May 1669, in Billerica, Mass., Mrs. Mary (LOTHROP) STEARNS, widow of John Stearns. She was the daughter of Thomas[2] Lothrop and his wife Sarah[2] (Learned) (Ewer) Lothrop; granddaughter of the Rev. John Lothrop, and his first wife Hannah House . . .William and Mary (Lothrop) (Stearns) French had the following children, born at Billerica, surname French: i. MARY, b. 30 Apr 1670; d. Lexington., Mass., 17 Sep 1729; m. (1) possibly Woburn, Mass., 20 Jun 1687, Robert SHARP; m. (2) in Dedham, 23 Mar 1693, Nathaniel DUNKLEE, son of Elnathan and Silence (Bowers) Duncklee … Issue: 8, incl. 1. **Silence DUNKLEE who m. Caleb Putnam**, at Salem, 7 Dec 1720; they are maternal ancestors of GJH, author of this work." In *Fundy to Chesapeake*, I corrected this statement, as follows: "**Caleb PUTNAM**, born 14 Feb 1693/4, Salem Village (now Danvers), Mass.; married 7 Dec 1720, Salem Village, **Silence PHILLIPS**, b. Salem; bapt.. there, 17 Sep 1693; she m. (2nd) as his 1st wife, to _____[3] **Dunklee**, son of Nathaniel[2] Dunklee (Elnathan[1]) and Mary French, dau of Capt William French and Mary[3] Lothrop (Thomas[2], Rev. John[1] Lothrop)." When she married Caleb Putnam, Silence Dunklee was her married name.

(WILLIAM WILCOCKSON and his wife MARGARET HARVEY); and 6:49-52, regarding their son Samuel, who married Hannah Rice, daughter of RICHARD RICE and his wife ELIZABETH.

In my discussion of the possible origin of JAMES PRESCOTT, who appeared in Hampton, N.H., in 1665, I restate with emphasis that he could be the James Prescott who was declared a fugitive from Parliament in 1659/60. This assumption was accepted by the late Timothy Field Beard, Genealogist General of the Baronial Order of the Magna Charta. I also restate that he could not be the same James Prescott who was baptized in Rearsby, Leicestershire, in 1637/8, because that is surely the same James Prescott who was buried eight months later in the adjacent village of Rothley. However, he nevertheless could be an unrecorded son of Sir William and Margaret (Babington) Prescott, who had at least six other children, and Margaret was still bearing children at the time that a James (2d) would have been born.

I would re-emphasize the comment that I made in *Western Pilgrims* (pp. 161-3): GEORGE MORTON is probably a member of the Morton family of Bawtry, Yorkshire, which is descended from Royalty. I first published this conclusion in *Mayflower Quarterly* 79 (No. 4, December 2013), 324-8; and to this date, no one has challenged it.

In *Fundy to Chesapeake*, p. 218, a typographical error should be corrected:
I wrote that Martha Tompkins was "conceived in October 1705; born at Trenton ... 14 July 1806." The year of her conception was 1805, not 1705.

On p. 332, a correction is made in the birth year of JOH STEVENS, from 1521 to 1621.

In *Quakers and Puritans*, I erred in not mentioning in the Bibliography the two most important reference works that were cited in the text and shown in the footnotes. The text references are on the first page of Part II, the Warren Family (p.121). Therefore, to the Bibliography, these books should be added:
> Betsey Warren Davis, *The Warren, Jackson, and Allied Families* (Philadelphia, J. B. Lippincott, 1903), and Warren Woden Foster, M.D., *Some Descendants of Arthur Warren of Weymouth, Massachusetts Bay Colony* (Washington, D.C.: Judd & Detwiler, 1911).

The Ahnentafel of Mabel Warren should be corrected to show:
> 176. **Daniel PEIRCE**, b. 1 Jan 1639/40, Watertown, Mass.; d. about 1723; m.
> 177. **Elizabeth** _____, b. 1642.

The text of *Quakers and Pilgrims* (pp. 252-3) was not correctly summarized in the Ahnentafel in respect to the wife of Daniel SMITH, Sr. Her name was shown as Elizabeth PORTER. However, as the text shows, PORTER was the name of her step-father, Roger Porter; her birth name was Elizabeth ROGERS. The Ahnentafel of Mabel Warren should be corrected to show:
> 357. **Elizabeth ROGERS**, b. Dedham, co. Essex, 1617; died aft July 1660.
> Her parents were:
> 714. **Thomas ROGERS**, b. abt 1588; d. Watertown, Mass., 12 Nov 1638; m.
> 715. **Grace RAVENS**, b. abt 1591, co. Suffolk; d. Watertown, Mass., 3 Jun 1662; she m.

(1) John Sherman; and (3), as his 2d wife, Roger Porter

APPENDIX

APPENDIX A

Research on Hannah Scott

AncestryProGenealogists
324 S. State Street, Suite 100, Salt Lake City, UT 84111 • Phone 801-596-3230 • Fax 801-596-3380 •
www.progenealogists.com
May 30, 2017

Research Session: Dates: Researcher: Scott 5 (S28345) August 2016 - May 2017 Johanne Gervais
Repository: Nova Scotia Archives, Halifax, Nova Scotia

Research Objective: **The objective of this research session is to locate information on Hannah Scott, the wife of James Thompson and mother of Joseph Scott Thompson.** Research is to take place at the Nova Scotia Archives in Halifax, Nova Scotia, reviewing microfilm records for two churches in Halifax County for the years 1785 to 1868 that contain records for Musquodoboit: 1). Christ Church Anglican, which includes baptisms from 1793–1984, marriages from 1793–1981, and burials from 1817–1992 and 2). Saint Paul's Anglican Church, which includes baptisms from 1749–1950, marriages from 1749–1954, and burials from 1749–1954.

Nova Scotia Archives, Halifax, Nova Scotia, Canada, Saint Paul's Anglican Church, Halifax County, "Marriage Licenses 1757–1863"; Nova Scotia Archives Microfilm 11549, accessed May 2017. Hannah Scott, James Thompson marriage / Nothing was found

Nova Scotia Archives, Halifax, Nova Scotia, Canada, Saint Paul's Anglican Church, Halifax County, "Baptisms 1753–1790"; Nova Scotia Archives Microfilm 11552, accessed May 2017. Baptism of Joseph Scott Thompson / Nothing was found (Includes records from St. John's Church in Lunenburg recorded at Saint Paul's Halifax 1749–1905 and records from Windsor recorded at Saint Paul's Halifax 1774–1795.)

Nova Scotia Archives, Halifax, Nova Scotia, Canada, Saint Paul's Anglican Church, Halifax County, "Marriages 1752–1792, Burials 1753–1789, Baptisms 1791–1854"; Nova Scotia Archives Microfilm 11553, accessed May 2017. Hannah Scott, James Thompson marriage; Joseph Scott Thompson baptism; Hannah Scott burial / Nothing was found

Nova Scotia Archives, Halifax, Nova Scotia, Canada, Saint Paul's Anglican Church, Halifax County, "Marriages, Baptisms, Burials 1749–1792, 1752– 1756, 1785–1792"; Nova Scotia Archives Microfilm 11551, accessed May 2017. Hannah Scott, James Thompson marriage; Joseph Scott Thompson baptism; Hannah Scott burial / Nothing was found

Nova Scotia Archives, Halifax, Nova Scotia, Canada, Saint Paul's Anglican Church, Halifax County, "Marriage Licenses 1783–1785"; Nova Scotia Archives Microfilm 11536 accessed May 2017. Hannah Scott, James Thompson marriage / Nothing was found

Nova Scotia Archives, Halifax, Nova Scotia, Canada, Saint Paul's Anglican Church, Halifax County, "Marriage Licenses 1785–1790"; Nova Scotia Archives Microfilm 11537 accessed May 2017. Hannah Scott, James Thompson marriage / Nothing was found

Nova Scotia Archives, Halifax, Nova Scotia, Canada, Christ Church Anglican, Dartmouth, Halifax County, "Marriages 1793–1795"; Nova Scotia Archives Microfilm 11308 accessed May 2017. Hannah Scott, James Thompson marriage / Nothing was found

Nova Scotia Archives, Halifax, Nova Scotia, Canada, Christ Church Anglican, Dartmouth, Halifax

----

May 30, 2017

George J. Hill
3 Silver Spring Road
West Orange, NJ 07052
Dear George:
I am pleased to present to you the findings of our continued research into your Scott family. Your goal in this session was to locate marriage or burial information on Hannah Scott, the daughter of Joseph Scott

and Sarah Cutting, and baptismal information on Joseph Scott Thompson. Previous research sessions have not been able to find documentation to prove that this Hannah was the wife of James Thompson and mother of Joseph Scott Thompson who was born 8 June 1800 in Musquodoboit, Nova Scotia, and married Ruth Archibald around 1824 in Nova Scotia. At the recommendation of our associate, Johanne Gervais, additional research has taken place at the Nova Scotia Archives in Halifax, Nova Scotia, having reviewed microfilm records from two churches in Halifax County that included records for Musquodoboit: 1). Christ Church Anglican with baptisms from 1793–1984, marriages from 1793–1981, and burials from 1817–1992 and 2). Saint Paul's Anglican Church with baptisms from 1749–1950, marriages from 1749–1954, and burials from 1749-1954. This session concentrated on Musquodoboit church records, since Joseph Scott Thompson was presumably born on 8 June 1800 in Musquodoboit. Unfortunately, no additional information was learned for this family. The following session summary appears below for your review.

After a lengthy discussion with the archivist at the Nova Scotia Archives regarding the research previously completed on the Scott family, the archivist recommended to first search the microfilm of marriage licenses at Saint Paul's Anglican Church. She mentioned that the archivists and compilers have not indexed or documented these marriage licenses in any register at the Archives. Three sets of microfilm for Saint Paul's Anglican Church contained marriage licenses for the years 1757–1863, 1783–1785, and 1785–1790. Research found no marriage licenses for Hannah Scott, James Thompson, Joseph Scott Thompson, or any of Hannah Scott's siblings. Research continued with three more boxes of microfilm for Saint Paul's Anglican Church, which included baptisms from 1753–1790; marriages from 1752–1792, burials from 1753–1789, baptisms from 1791–1854; and marriages, baptisms, and burials for the years 1749–1792, 1752–1756, 1785–1792. Research found no records for the marriage or burial of Hannah Scott or the baptism of Joseph Scott Thompson.

The Christ Church Anglican records were on eight reels of microfilm but only two microfilms included relevant years—baptisms from 1 March 1793–19 June 1842 and marriages from 1793–1795. Neither the baptism of Joseph Scott Thompson nor the marriage of Hannah Scott was found. This session found no information related to Hanna Scott, James Thompson, or Joseph Scott Thompson.

At this point, research turned to the inventory of what was known / discovered through previous sessions (see the attached compilation of Scott Family Research Completed) in order to see what research may have missed. We know that Hannah Scott was born in Horton in 1768 and the Onslow Township book recorded her birth. Her siblings were also born in Onslow and Horton. Hannah's parents were Joseph Scott and Sarah Cutting, both born in Massachusetts. Joseph Scott travelled from Horton to Onslow frequently and was the Sheriff of Colchester County for many years. Hannah's parents lived in Nova Scotia from about 1765 to at least 1804. Online family genealogies state Joseph Scott Thompson's birth as 8 June 1800 at Musquodoboit, Halifax County, Nova Scotia with no source records. He married Ruth Archibald around 1824, had children in Nova Scotia, and died on 7 March 1866 at Somerville, Massachusetts. Joseph Scott Thompson's birth date provides an approximate period and location of where and when Hannah Scott and James Thompson might have been married.

Previous research sessions covered the Horton Township book in Kings County and three churches in the Horton area—the Methodist Church, St. John's Anglican Church, and the Roman Catholic Church. Research in Colchester County. All record books for Hants County have been searched, which included Douglas, Falmouth, Newport, and Windsor Townships. Birth, marriages, and deaths for the districts of Fort Lawrence, Franklin Manor, Maccan, and Southampton in Cumberland County have been searched as well as the Parrsboro Township Record book. Church records in Halifax County, which also included Musquodoboit were examined. Books and compilations on Nova Scotia marriage bonds; marriages; historical records of Colchester County; New England Planters; death, burial, and probate records; Colchester County and Musquodoboit pioneers; estate papers; and newspaper vital statistics have also been examined.

Although a previous research session reviewed Horton Township records for Kings County, where Hannah was born, the township records for nearby Aylesford and Cornwallis, also located in Kings County, were not examined. In addition, an analysis of the list of township books for Cumberland County

located at the Nova Scotia Archives also revealed another township record not yet searched, Westchester Township. This township may be relevant, since Joseph Scott had land in Parrsboro Township, which was only a short distance from Westchester. It is possible that Hannah moved to Aylesford, Cornwallis, or Westchester Township when she married. Alternatively, Hannah might have moved to a township in any of the counties neighboring King's County, where she was born. Township books in Nova Scotia are very detailed and according to local genealogists, they provide the most complete information regarding births, marriages, and deaths. Based on the preceding assumption and since research found no further clues, a future research session would:
• Complete the research of Kings County by reviewing the township books for Aylesford and Cornwallis.
• Complete the research of Cumberland County by reviewing the Westchester Township book.
• Review township books in the remaining two counties that are adjacent to King's County, those of Annapolis County and Lunenburg County.
• Review the Sackville Township records in Westmorland County. This county, adjacent and to the west of Cumberland County, was established as a Nova Scotia township in 1772 and reestablished as a New Brunswick parish in 1786. It is possible the marriage record for Hannah Scott and her children are located in New Brunswick, not Nova Scotia.

The following calendar of sources has now been investigated thus far in the effort:

Colchester County
Township Records for Onslow
Church Records (no records earlier than 1850)
Truro Township Records and Index 1770-1837
Londonderry Township Records 1780-1835
Westchester Township Book, 1782-1970
Economy Township
Registry of Probate Colchester County 1770-1969
Colchester County Index of Estates 1802-1948
The Book of Records for Births, Deaths & Marriages for the Township of Onslow, NS Beginning in 1761
Onslow Township Cemeteries and Index #49 – McCallum Settlement to #58 – Belmont (Hillside Cemetery)
Kings County, Horton Township
Township Book 1751-1895
Methodist Church records
St. John's Anglican Church records
Roman Catholic Church records
Hants County
Douglas Township, Hants County, Series "P" Vols 1-5 BMD 1725-1873
Falmouth Township, Hants County, BMD 1747-1825
Newport Township, Hants County, BMD 1752-1845
Windsor Township, Hants County, BMD 1761-1819
Cumberland County
Fort Lawrence District, Cumberland County, Births 1766-1889, Marriages 1777-1891, Deaths 1780-1891
Franklin Manor District, Cumberland County, Births 1766-1889, Marriages 1777-1891, Deaths 1780-1891
Maccan District, Cumberland County, Births 1766-1889, Marriages 1777-1891, Deaths 1780-1891
Southampton District, Cumberland County, Births 1766-1889, Marriages 1777-1891, Deaths 1780-1891
Parrsboro Township Record Book
Musquodoboit, Halifax County
Holy Trinity Church
Truro St. John's Anglican Church

Musquodoboit United Church baptism
Musquodoboit Harbour St. Stephen's Anglican Church
Musquodoboit Harbour St. James United
Halifax County
Saint Paul's Anglican Church, Halifax County, "Marriage Licenses 1757-1863"
Saint Paul's Anglican Church, Halifax County, "Baptisms 1753-1790",
Saint Paul's Anglican Church, Halifax County, "Marriages 1752-1792, Burials 1753-1789, Baptisms 1791-1854"
Saint Paul's Anglican Church, Halifax County, "Marriages, Baptisms, Burials 1749-1792, 1752 1756, 1785-1792",
Saint Paul's Anglican Church, Halifax County, "Marriage Licenses 1783-1785"
Saint Paul's Anglican Church, Halifax County, "Marriage Licenses 1785-1790"
Christ Church Anglican, Dartmouth, Halifax County, "Baptisms 1 March 1793-19 June 1842"
Christ Church Anglican, Dartmouth, Halifax County, "Marriages 1793-1795"
Books/Compilations
Marriage Bonds 1763-1872 Nova Scotia Provincial Secretary and Lieutenant-Governor
Marriage Bonds Index, Jean M. Holder and Marion D. Oldershaw
Marriages in Nova Scotia (excluding Halifax City) 1752-1841
Marriages of **Colchester County** Nova Scotia: 1763-1864, William T. Hill
Historical and Genealogical Record of the First Settlers of Colchester County (N.S.) Down to the Present Time, Thomas Miller
Deaths, Burials, and Probate of Nova Scotians, 1749-1799, Volume 2 (L-Z), Allan Everett Marble
Deaths, Burials, and Probate of Nova Scotians, 1800-1850, From Primary Sources Volume 4 (P Z), Allan Everett Marble
Index to Historical and Genealogical Records of the First Settlers of Colchester County, Allan Everett Marble
Planters and Grantees of Cobequid, Nova Scotia, 1761-1780 Volume 2 L-Y, Carol Campbell and James F. Smith
My Pioneer Ancestors, M.G. Burris
People of the Musquodoboit Valley A Community Genealogy Second Edition, Bryon K. Jennings
Musquodoboit Pioneers A Record of Seventy Families, Their Homesteads and Genealogies
1780 - 1980 Volumes I & II, Jennie Reid
Census Returns, 1811, 1817 and 1818, (Census Returns, Assessment and Poll Tax Records 1767 1838
Original Estate Papers Halifax County 1750-1841
Religious Marriages in Halifax, 1768-1841, from primary sources, Terrence M. Punch
Nova Scotia Vital Statistics From Newspapers 1762-1812, Terrence M. Punch
Nova Scotia Vital Statistics From Newspapers 1813 -1822, Terrence M. Punch
The Settling of Colchester County by New England Puritans and Ulster Scotsman, Arthur Eaton
Israel Longworth's History of Colchester County, Sandra Creighton
The Settlement of Colchester County, Harry E Nelson
Notes on The Scott Family of Musquodoboit, Volume 218, #17A & 18

As before, as you review the report, please be certain to examine the research journal which lists all of the sources we used in the session. Some of these are not directly discussed in the report, because they did not provide substantive information, but it was important to have reviewed them. Copies of key documents accompany the report. The private Ancestry tree that was shared with you previously, and we can continue to build upon it in future sessions.
Sincerely, Jeffery Lensman, MBA Research Manager

APPENDIX B

LINEAGE AND HERITAGE SOCIEITES WITH DESCENT PROVED
FROM ANCESTORS IN THESE FOUR BOOKS

Listed in Order of Founding, from Heritage Society Community of America
Qualifying ancestor or Gateway ancestor shown in parentheses
* = Held office as state officer or board member
** = Held office as national officer or board member

Ancient and Honorable Artillery Company of Massachusetts (Robert Long)
Saint Andrew's Society of the State of New York (Errol Boyd)
Society of the Friendly Sons of Saint Patrick of Philadelphia (John Archibald)
Society of the Cincinnati (Richard Howell)
Saint Nicholas Society of the City of New York (Edward Howell)
Aztec Club of 1847 (Franklin Pierce)
General Society Sons of the Revolution (Isaac Hill, Jr.) *
Sons of Union Veterans of the Civil War (Edward B. Thompson)
Huguenot Society of America (Jonathan Gillette)
National Society of the Sons of the American Revolution (Isaac Hill, Jr.)   * **
Naval Order of the United States (CAPT George J. Hill – by right of service)
National Society of The Colonial Dames of America (Helene Z. Hill, descent from Toby Leech)
General Society of Colonial Wars (Isaac Hill, Jr.) * **
General Society of the War of 1812 (Joseph Gillett) * **
Colonial Society of Pennsylvania (John Sharples)
Order of Indian Wars of the United States (Matthew Fuller)
Order of the Founders and Patriots of America (Luke Hill, Sr.; and Isaac Hill, Jr.) * **
General Society of Mayflower Descendants (Edward Fuller) * **
Baronial Order of Magna Charta (James Prescott; later disproved, but eligible from Edward Howell) **
Welcome Society of Pennsylvania (John Sharples; and Helene Hill, from Richard Wall)
National Society Americans of Royal Descent (Gateway: Thomas Trowbridge)
National Society Sons and Daughters of the Pilgrims (Henry Herrick) * **
United Empire Loyalists' Association of Canada (William Irish)
Military Order of the World Wars (George Hill, by right of service; Helene by descent from her father)
Society of the Descendants of the Colonial Clergy (Obadiah Holmes)
Military Order of the Crusades (Gateway: Thomas Trowbridge) **
Jamestowne Society (James Feake, as investor) *
Order of Three Crusades 1096-1192 (Gateway: Thomas Trowbridge)
Order of the Crown of Charlemagne in the United States of America (Gateway: Thomas Trowbridge for
    both George and Helene Hill)
National Society of the Sons of American Colonists (Honorary Member)
Dutch Colonial Society (John Morton)
Flagon and Trencher (Robert Long)
Hereditary Order Descendants Loyalists & Patriots American Revolution (Isaac Hill and John Saxe) **
Order of Descendants of Colonial Physicians and Chirurgiens (Matthew Fuller) **
Son of a Witch (Rebecca [Towne] Nurse)
National Guild of Saint Margaret of Scotland (James Prescott, disproved; eligible: Edward Howell)
National Society Descendants of Early Quakers (John Sharples) **
Descendants of the Founders of New Jersey (Obadiah Holmes) **
Hereditary Order of the First Families of Massachusetts (John Johnson)
Associated Daughters of Early American Witches (Sarah Hill, from Rebecca [Towne] Nurse)

National Order of the Blue and Gray (Edward Thompson – blue) **
Order of the First Families of Rhode Island and Providence Plantations (Obadiah Holmes)
Fuller Society (Edward Fuller)
Sons and Daughters of the Colonial and Antebellum Bench and Bar (Obadiah Holmes)
Winthrop Society (John Johnson) **
Order of the First Families of Maryland (John Manley)
Order of the First Families of Maine (John Alcock)
Hereditary Order of the Families of Presidents & First Ladies (Rutherford Hayes & Varina Davis)
Order of the Merovingian Dynasty (Thomas Trowbridge) **
Guild of Colonial Artisans and Tradesmen 1607-1783 (Shadrack Rundle)
Order of First Families of Connecticut 1633-1662 (Thomas Trowbridge)
Order of the First Families of New Hampshire 1622-1680 (James Prescott) **
Order of First Families of Vermont 1609-1791 (Freeborn Potter)
National Society of Saints and Sinners (Gateway: Thomas Trowbridge)
Descendants of Sheriffs & Constables of Colonial & Antebellum America (Obadiah Holmes) **
Order of Descendants of the Justiciars (Gateway: Thomas Trowbridge) **
Society of Descendants of Lady Godiva (Gateway: Thomas Trowbridge) **
Order of the Norman Conquest (Gateway: Edward Howell for George Hill; Helene's Gateway: John
    Thorndike; both Gateway ancestors are descendants of William of Warenne)
Descendants of Cape Cod and the Islands (Matthew Fuller)
Order of the Monarchs of Rheims (Gateway: Edward Howell)

Also:

Order of the Gavel, as the Governor General of the Founders of New Jersey; in addition, Governor
    General of the First Families of New Hampshire
Order of New England, as a member of the First Families of all six New England states
Hereditary Society Community of the United States of America, as an Honorary Member (2017)

BIBLIOGRAPHY

Abbott, Susan Woodruff, and Jacquelyn L. Ricker. *Families of Early Milford, Connecticut*. Baltimore: Genealogical Publishing Co., 1979 (on CD-ROM, 2000).

Adams, James Trulow. *The Epic of America*. Boston: Little, Brown & Co., 1931.

Anderson, Bart. *The Sharples-Sharpless Family*. 3 vols. West Chester, Penn.: Bart Anderson, 1971.

Anderson, Robert Charles. *The Great Migration Begins* and *The Great Migration*. Online database. AmericanAncestors.org. New England Historic Genealogical Society, 2009-2012.

[Barbour, Lucius Barnes, *Barbour Collection*] *Connecticut Town Birth Records, pre-1870* (*Barbour Collection*). White, Lorraine Cook, ed. Genealogical Publishing Co., 1994-2002.

Connecticut Nutmegger

Davis, Betsey Warren. *The Warren, Jackson, and Allied Families*. Philadelphia: J. B. Lippincott, 1903.

Doherty, Frank J. *The Settlers of Beekman Patent*. 10 vols. Pleasant Valley, N.Y.: Frank J. Doherty, 1990-2003.

Fisher, David Hackett. *Albion's Seed: Four British Folkways in America*. New York: Oxford University Press, 1989.

Hill, George J. *John Saxe, Loyalist (1732–1808) and His Descendants for Five Generations*. Westminster, Md.: Heritage Books, 2010.

_____. *Hill: The Ferry Keeper's Family; Luke Hill and Mary Hout, Who Were Married in Windsor, Connecticut, in 1651, and Fourteen Generations of Their Known and Possible Descendants*. Westminster, Md.: Heritage Books, 2011.

_____. *Western Pilgrims: The Hill, Stockwell and Allied Families; Ancestors and Descendants of George J. Hill and Jessie Fidelia Stockwell, Who Were Married in Wright County, Iowa, in 1882*. Berwyn Heights, Md.: Heritage Books, 2014.

_____. *Quakers and Pilgrims: The Shoemaker, Warren and Allied Families; Ancestors and Descendants of William Toy Shoemaker and Mabel Warren, Who Were Married in Philadelphia in 1895*. Berwyn Heights, Md.: Heritage Books, 2015.

_____. *Fundy to Chesapeake: The Thompson, Rundall and Allied Families; Ancestors and Descendants of William Henry Thompson and Sarah D. Rundall, Who Were Married in Linn County, Iowa, in 1889*. Berwyn Heights, Md.: Heritage Books, 2016.

_____. *American Dreams: Ancestors and Descendants of John Zimmerman and Eva Katherine Kellenbenz, Who Were Married in Philadelphia in 1885*. Berwyn Heights, Md.: Heritage Books, 2017.

Jacobus, Donald Lines. *History and Genealogy of the Families of Old Fairfield*. 1929; reprint, 3 vols. into 2, Baltimore, Md.: Genealogical Publishing Co., n.d.

Miller, Arthur. *The Crucible (A Play in Four Acts).* Introduction by Christopher Miller Bigsby. Clayton, Del.: Prestwick House, Inc., 1982; 1st presented in 1953.

Pope, Charles Henry. *Pioneers of Massachusetts.* 1901; reprint by Heritage Books, Bowie, Md., 1991.

Richardson, Douglas and Kimball G. Everingham, eds. *Royal Ancestry: A Study in Colonial and Medieval Families.* 5 Vols. Salt Lake City, Utah: Douglas Richardson, 2013.

Roberts, Gary Boyd. *The Royal Descent of 600 Immigrants to the American Colonies or the United States.* Baltimore: Genealogical Publishing Co., 2004.

_____. *Ancestors of American Presidents.* First Authoritative Edition. Santa Clarita, Calif.: Carl Boyer, 3rd; with New England Historic Genealogical Society, Boston, Mass., 1995.

Savage, James. *Genealogical Dictionary of the First Settlers of New England.* Boston: Little, Brown and Co., 1906.

Shiller, Robert J. "The Transformation of the 'American Dream'" *New York Times* (6 August 2017), Business section, p.3. Shiller discusses the evolution of the term "American Dreams." He says that it was popularized in 1931 by James Truslow Adams in *The Epic of America.*

Torrey, Clarence Almon. *New England Marriages Prior to 1700.* Baltimore: Genealogical Publishing Co., 1997.

ABBREVIATIONS

aka or a.k.a. = also known as

dau. = daughter

NEHGS = New England Historic Genealogical Society

poss. = possibly

prob. = probably

Index

This Index is in two parts. The name of each immigrant person is shown in unitalicized capital letters, followed by initials which show the name of the book and the page number in this Synopsis, viz.: ADAMS, HENRY (WP) 3, meaning that HENRY ADAMS is in *Western Pilgrims*, and he is summarized on p.3 of this Synopsis. Italics indicate that the person did not emigrate from Europe, viz.: *CHARLEMAGNE*. If the name is in brackets in Part I, the individual or family is not an ancestor or cognate descendant of any of the four families in this tetralogy, and is discussed briefly, viz.: [MATHER]. In Part II, brackets are used differently (see below). There are 415 names listed alphabetically in Part I: 278 men and 90 women are names of immigrants or first known ancestors in America; 31 are European ancestors; and 16 are mentioned as disproved or not-related by blood. In Part II, 113 women are listed.

COMEE, DAVID (QP)	29	GEORGE, JOHN (QP)	47
COMLY, HENRY (QP)	29	GIBBS, ISRAEL (WP)	47
CONANT, ROGER (QP)	29	GIBBS, MERIBAH	48
[CONSTABLE HALSHAM (WP)]	30	GIDDINGS, GEORGE (WP)	48
COOK, SUSANNA (WP)	30	GILLETT, JONATHAN (WP)	48
COOKE, ELIZABETH (QP)	30	GODFREY, RICHARD (WP)	48
[COOLIDGE, JOHN] (QP)	30	*GOODSPEED, ___ (FC)*	49
COPP, ELIZA CAROLINE (QP)	30	GOULD, PRISCILLA (FC)	49
COPPOCK, BART. (FC)	31	GRANT, CHRISTOPHER (QP)	49
CORNELL, ELIZABETH (FC)	31	GRANT, WILLIAM (FC)	50
CROASDALE, THOMAS (QP)	31	GREELEY, ANDREW (WP)	50
CROKER, THOMAS (WP)	31	GREENWOOD, THOMAS (QP)	50
CROSS, ROBERT (WP)	32	GREGG, WILLIAM (FC)	50
CUTLER, JAMES (FC)	32	HALE, ROBERT (QP)	51
CUTTING, RICHARD (FC)	32	[HALLOCK, JOHN] (FC)	51
DARBY, JOHN (QP)	33	HALSEY, THOMAS (WP)	51
DAVIS, AARON (WP)	33	[HARCOURT, RICHARD] (FC)	52
DAWES, ABRAHAM (QP)	34	HARDY, SAMUEL (FC)	52
DE PUY, FRANCOIS (FC)	34	HARVEY, MARGARET (WP)	52
DENISON, WILLIAM (WP)	34	HATHORNTHWAITE, AG. (QP)	52
DEREHAUGH, WILIAM (QP)	35	*HAWTEN, EDWARD (WP)*	52
DICKINSON, ALICE (QP)	35	HAYES, MARY (QP)	53
DIPPOLT, JOHN GEORGE (QP)	35	[HAYWARD] (WP)	53
DIXEY, WILLIAM (QP)	35	*HEATH, MARY (WP)*	53
DIXON, HENRY (FC)	36	HEATON, ROBERT (QP)	53
DOLBERE, MARY (WP)	36	*HEDGE, JAMES (QP)*	54
DORMER, GEOFFREY (WP)	36	HENDERSON, PATRICK (FC)	54
DOVER, ANNE (WP)	37	HENDRICHS, SARAH (QP)	54
DUNCAN, SAMUEL (FC)	37	HENDRYX, ISAIAH (WP)	54
[DUNKLEE, EL. (WP, FC)]	37	HERRICK, HENRY (WP)	55
EAGER, WILLIAM (WP)	37	HESTER, JACOB (QP)	55
EDMONDS, WILLIAM (FC)	38	HILL, ABRAHAM (WP)	55
EVANS, ANN (FC)	38	HILL, LUKE (WP)	56
EVANS, ROBERT (QP)	38	HINE, THOMAS (WP)	56
EYRE, JOHN (WP)	39	HOBBY, JOHN (FC)	56
FARRINGTON, THOMAS (FC)	39	HODGES, JOHN (WP)	57
FEAKE, JUDITH (FC)	39	HOLBROOK, THOMAS (WP)	57
FENNER, SARAH (WP)	40	HOLLINGSWORTH, VAL. (FC)	58
FISHER, ANTHONY (WP)	40	HOLMES, OBADIAH (WP)	58
FISHER, EDWARD (WP)	40	HONOR, ALICE (WP)	58
FISHER, JOHN (FC)	41	HORTON, SARAH (QP)	58
FISKE, NATHAN (WP)	41	HOUGH, ABIGAIL (WP)	59
FLEMING, MARGARET (WP)	41	HOUT, MARY (WP)	59
FLETCHER, ROBERT (WP, QP)	42	*HOW, JOHN (QP)*	59
FOLGER, JOHN (FC)	42	HOWARD, NATHANIEL (QP)	59
FORD, THOMAS (WP)	43	HOWELL, EDWARD (WP)	59
FORSHAY/LeFAUCHEUR (FC)	43	HOYT, SIMON (FC)	60
FOWLE, JOANE (WP)	44	HUNT, AARON (WP)	60
FREDD, JOHN (FC)	44	HUSTED, ROBERT (FC)	60
FRENCH, WILLIAM (WP)	44	HYDE, JONATHAN (WP)	61
FROST, WILLIAM (WP)	45	HYDE, KATHERINE (WP)	61
FULLER, EDWARD (WP)	45	IREDELL, THOMAS (QP)	61
FURBURST, REBECCA (FC)	45	IRISH, JOHN (WP)	62
GALE, RICHARD (WP)	45	JACKSON, EDWARD (QP)	62
GALLEY, JOHN (WP)	46	JACKSON, EPHRAIM (FC)	63
GAMLIN, ROBERT (WP)	46	JACKSON, ISAAC (FC)	63

JACKSON, JOSEPH (WP)	63		MOORE, FRANCIS (WP)	81
JASPER, ELIZABETH (WP)	63		MOORS, JOSEPH (QP)	81
JEFTS, HENRY (QP)	64		MORGAN, ROBERT (QP)	82
JESSUP, JOHN (FC)	64		MORSE, SAMUEL (WP)	82
JEWELL, THOMAS (WP)	64		MORTON, GEORGE (WP)	82
JOHNSON, JOHN (WP)	65		MOULTON, THOMAS (FC)	83
JOHNSON, KATHERINE (WP)	65		MOYSE, JOSEPH (WP)	83
JONES, THOMAS (QP)	65		MUNROE, WILLIAM (QP)	84
JORDAN, STEPHEN (WP)	66		NEWBERRY, THOMAS (WP)	84
JORDAN, THOMAS (WP)	66		NEWLIN, NICHOLAS (FC)	84
KELLENBENZ, EVA (AD)	66		NEWMAN, LYDIA (WP)	85
KIDDER, JAMES (WP)	66		NORMAN, ESTHER (WP)	85
KINGMAN, HENRY (WP)	67		NORMAN, RICHARD (QP)	85
KINSMAN, ROBERT (WP)	67		NURSE, FRANCIS (FC)	85
KNAPP, NICHOLAS (FC)	68		OAKLEY, MILES (FC)	86
KNOWLES, HENRY (WP)	68		OBER, RICHARD (QP)	86
KNOWLES, JOSEPH (QP)	69		OGDEN, JOHN (FC)	86
LAKE, HENRY (FC)	69		OP den GRAEFF, MARY (QP)	87
LAMBERT, WILLIAM (WP)	69		OVIATT, THOMAS (WP)	87
LARKIN, EDWARD (QP)	69		PALGRAVE, ANN (QP)	88
LASKIN, HUGH (WP)	70		[PALMER, JERUSHA (WP)]	88
LAWRENCE, THOMAS (WP)	70		PALMER, WILLIAM (FC)	88
LAY, ROBERT (WP)	71		PANTON, MARY (FC)	89
[LEARNED, WILLIAM] (WP)	71		PARKER, JACOB (QP)	89
LEECH, TOBY (QP)	71		PARTRIDGE, JOHN (WP)	89
LEVIT, MARY (FC)	71		PATCH, ELIZABETH (QP)	89
LIPPITT, JOHN (WP)	72		[PEABODY, SUSANNAH] (WP)	90
LLOYD, LLOYD (QP)	72		PEET, SARAH (FC)	90
LONG, ROBERT (WP)	72		PEIRCE, JOHN (QP)	90
[LONGFORD, WILLIAM] (WP)	73		*PELLETT, THOMAS* (WP)	90
LORING, WELTHEAN (WP)	73		PENNELL, ROBERT (FC)	91
[LOTHROP, JOHN] (FC, WP)	73		PENNINGTON, HENRY (FC)	92
LUKENS, JAN (QP)	73		PENNY, CICELY (WP)	92
LUM, SAMUEL (FC)	74		PENROSE, BART. (QP)	92
LYON, THOMAS (FC)	74		PHELPS, WILLIAM (WP)	92
MAKENNE, ALEXANDER (FC)	74		PHILLIPS, JAMES (FC)	93
MALLORY, PETER (WP)	75		PHILLIPS, WALTER (FC)	93
MANLEY, JOHN (FC)	75		PHIPPEN, DAVID (WP)	93
MANSFIELD, ROBERT (QP)	75		PIERCE, THOMAS (WP)	94
MARCHE, EULALIA (WP)	76		PIERSON, ABRAHAM (FC)	94
MARSHALL, ELIZABETH (WP)	76		*PLOMER, GYLES* (WP)	95
MASTERS, JOHN (WP)	76		PORTER, ELIZABETH (WP)	95
[MATHER (WP, QP)]	77		POTTER, ROBERT (WP)	95
MCVAUGH, EDMOND (QP)	77		POTTS, DAVID (QP)	96
MEAD, WILLIAM (FC)	77		POWYS, JANE (WP)	96
MERCER, THOMAS (FC)	78		PRATT, PHINEAS (FC)	96
MERRIAM, JOSEPH (QP)	78		PRESCOTT, JAMES (FC)	96
MICHELL, JOHN (WP)	79		PRESTON, WILLIAM (WP)	97
MILLER, JOHN (FC)	79		PRIEST, DEGORY (FC)	97
MILLER, MARY (FC)	79		PRINCE, JOHN (WP)	98
MILLER, WILLIAM (WP)	79		PRINCE, REBECCA (FC)	98
MILLS, GEORGE (FC)	80		*PROWSE, AGNES* (QP)	98
MITCHELL, MATTHEW (FC)	80		PUTNAM, JOHN (FC)	99
MITCHELL, THOMAS (FC)	80		RAVENS, GRACE (QP)	99
MONTGOMERY, ELIZ.	117		RAY, DANIEL (FC)	99
MOOR, JANE (FC)	81		RAYMENT, RICHARD (WP)	100

RICE, RICHARD	100		TOWNSEND, RICHARD (FC)	117
RICHARDS, THOMAS (WP)	101		TRASK, OSMOND (WP)	118
RICHARDSON, EZEKIEL (QP)	101		TROWBRIDGE, TH. (WP, QP)	118
RILEY, JOHN (WP)	101		TURNER, JOHN (WP)	118
RINDGE, DANIEL (WP)	102		TYLER, JOAN (QP)	119
ROBBINS, RICHARD (WP)	102		TYSON, MARY (QP)	119
ROBERTS, SARAH (QP)	103		UNDERWOOD, WM. (WP, QP)	119
ROBINSON, GAIN (FC)	103		UTTER, NICHOLAS (WP)	120
ROGERS, THOMAS (QP)	103		VICKERY, GEORGE (WP)	120
RUNDLE, WILLIAM (FC)	104		*VYE, HARRY* (WP)	120
[RUSSELL, JOHN] (QP)	104		WAKELEE, JAMES (WP)	121
RUST, ISRAEL (WP)	104		WALES, MARY (QP, FC)	121
SANFORD, EZEKIEL (WP)	105		WALES, NATHANIEL (FC)	121
SANGHURST, ELIZABETH (FC)	105		WALL, RICHARD (QP)	122
SAXE, JOHN (WP)	105		WALTER, GODWIN (FC)	122
SCOTT, BENJAMIN (WP)	105		WALTON, WILLIAM (QP)	122
SCOTT, SARAH (WP)	106		WARD, WILLIAM (WP, QP)	123
SEELEY, SARAH (WP)	106		WARREN, ARTHUR (QP)	123
SELBEE, SUSANNAH (WP)	106		WASHBURN, WILLIAM (FC)	124
SHARP, MARY (QP)	106		WATERS, BRIDGET (FC)	124
SHARPLES, JOHN (FC)	106		WATSON, MARGARET (WP)	125
[SHEFFIELD, EDMOND] (WP)	107		WEAVER, WILLIAM (WP)	125
[SHERMAN, JOHN] (QP)	107		WEBB, RICHARD (FC)	125
SHOEMAKER, GEORGE (QP)	107		WEED, JONAS (FC)	126
SINGLETARY, RICHARD (WP)	107		WHEEL, JOANE (QP)	126
[*SKIPWITH, WILLIAM*] (WP)	108		WHEELER, ELIZABETH (WP)	126
SMITH, ____ (QP)	108		WHEELER, SARAH (WP)	127
SMITH, JOHN (WP)	108		WHEELER, THOMAS (QP)	127
SMITH, JOHN (FC)	109		WHITE, JOHN (FC)	127
SMITH, NEHEMIAH (WP)	109		WHITNEY, JOHN (WP)	127
SPALDING, EDWARD (WP)	109		WHITTON, ROBERT (QP)	128
SPENCER, JOHN (QP)	110		WILCOCKSON, WILLIAM (WP)	128
SQUIRE, EDITH (WP)	110		WILKINSON, ANN (FC)	129
STARKEY, CATHERINE (FC)	110		WILLARD, SIMON (QP)	129
STEPHENSON, MARG. (FC)	111		WILLEMS, GEERTRUY (FC)	129
STEVENS, JOHN (FC)	111		WILLET, RICHARD (FC)	129
STEVENSON, ANN (WP)	111		WILLIAMS, REBECCA (QP)	130
STOCKWELL, WILLIAM (WP)	111		[*WILLOUGHBY D'ERESBY*] (WP)	130
STRATTON, ELIZABETH (QP)	112		WILMOT, JOHN (FC)	130
SWAINE, RICHARD (FC)	112		WILSON, ALEXANDER (FC)	130
TABER, PHILIP (WP)	112		WILSON, JEAN (FC)	131
TANNER, NICHOLAS (FC)	113		WOOD, JOHN (WP)	131
TAYLOR, HANNAH (FC)	113		WOOD, SUSAN (FC)	131
TAYLOR, MATTHEW (FC)	113		WOODBURY, WILLIAM (QP)	132
TAYLOR, ROBERT (FC)	114		WOODFORD, THOMAS (WP)	132
TAYLOR, ROBERT (WP)	114		WOODWARD, RICHARD (WP)	132
TAYLOR, SARAH (WP)	114		*WRIGHT, MARY* (QP)	133
THATCHER, RICHARD (FC)	115		WYATT, MARGARET (WP)	133
THOMPSON, ARCHIBALD (FC)	115		YARWOOD, MARGARET (FC)	133
THOMPSON, MARGARET (FC)	115		YEOMANS, ROBERT (FC)	133
THORNDIKE, JOHN (QP)	115		ZIMMERMANN, JOHN (AD)	134
THORNE, JOHN (QP)	116			
TILLINGHAST, PARDON (WP)	116			
TOMPKINS, JOHN (FC)	116			
TOWNE, WILLIAM (FC)	117			
TOWNSEND, JOHN (FC)	117			

Part II

In Part II, 113 women are listed; 96, whose family name before marriage is unknown; and 17 whose name is completely unknown. The following women are known only by their first name and married name, which is shown in brackets, viz: [ALBEE]. For example, in the records, Hannah (_____) Albee is known only by her married name as Hannah Albee. She is shown therefore shown below as _____ [ALBEE], HANNAH. Not even the given name is known for some women; e.g., the wife of Edward Fuller is shown below as _____ [FULLER], _____. These women are known as *femmes coverts*. Some of the completely unknown wives have been omitted from the list below.

_____ [ALBEE], HANNAH (WP)	3	
_____ [ALCOCK], ELIZABETH (WP)	4	
_____ [ALLEN], ANN (WP)	4	
_____ [BACHELOR], JANE (FC)	9	
_____ [BACON], MARGARET (WP)	9	
_____ [BAKER], ELIZABETH (FC)	10	
_____ [BAKER], ELIZABETH (QP)	10	
_____ [BELKNAP], MARY (WP)	11	
_____ [BELL], REBECCA (FC)	12	
_____ [BOURNE], ELIZABETH (WP)	14	
_____ [BREWSTER], LUCY (FC)	16	
_____ [BROWN], ABIGAIL (WP)	17	
_____ [BROWN], DOROTHY (FC)	18	
_____ [BROWN], MARTHA	17	
_____ [BUDD], KATEREN (FC)	19	
_____ [BULLARD], MAGDALEN (WP)	19	
_____ [BULLER], _____ (FC)	20	
_____ [BURLINGAME], MARY (WP)	20	
_____ [BUTTERFIELD], ANN (QP)	21	
_____ [CANFIELD], PHEBE (WP)	22	
_____ [CLARKE], SARAH (WP)	26	
_____ [CLIFFORD], _____ (WP)	27	
_____ [COLE], [H]ARRALD (WP)	27	
_____ [COLVIN], DOROTHY (WP)	29	
_____ [COMEE], ELIZABETH (QP)	29	
_____ [CUTLER], ANN (FC)	32	
_____ [CUTTING], SARAH (FC)	33	
_____ [DARBY], ALICE (QP)	33	
_____ [DAVIS], MARY (WP)	34	
_____ [DAWES], EDITH (QP)	34	
_____ [DIXEY], ANN (QP)	36	
_____ [DIXON], ROSE (FC)	36	
_____ [DUNCAN], MARY (FC)	37	
_____ [EDMANDS], MARY (FC)	38	
_____ [EVANS], ELLEN (QP)	39	
_____ [FISHER], MARY (WP)	40	
_____ [FISHER], JUDITH (WP)	41	
_____ [FISHER], SARAH (FC)	41	
_____ [FISKE], SUSANNAH (WP)	41	
_____ [FLETCHER], _____ (WP)	42	
_____ [LeFAUCHEUR], JUDITH (WP)	43	
_____ [FRENCH], ELIZABETH (WP)	44	
_____ [FULLER], _____ (WP)	45	
_____ [GALE], MARY (WP)	46	

_____ [GALLEY], FLORENCE (WP)	46	
_____ [GEORGE], ELIZABETH (QP)	47	
_____ [GIBBS], _____ (WP)	47	
_____ [GRANT], MARY (QP)	49	
_____ [HALE], JOANNA (QP)	51	
_____ [HEATON], ALICE (QP)	54	
_____ [HENDERSON], KATH (FC)	54	
_____ [HOBBY], _____ (FC)	57	
_____ [HOYT], SUSANNAH (FC)	60	
_____ [HUSTED], ELIZABETH (FC)	61	
_____ [IRISH], ELIZABETH (QP)	62	
_____ [JACKSON], FRANCES (QP)	62	
_____ [JESSUP], JOANNA (FC)	64	
_____ [KINGMAN], JOAN (WP)	67	
_____ [KINSMAN], _____ (WP)	68	
_____ [KNAPP], ELINOR (WP)	68	
_____ [KNOWLES] _____ (WP)	68	
_____ [LAKE], ALICE (FC)	69	
_____ [LARKIN], JOANNA (QP)	70	
_____ [LASKIN], ALICE (WP)	70	
_____ [LIPPITT], _____ (WP)	72	
_____ [LUM], ANN (FC)	74	
_____ [MAKENNE], MARY (FC)	75	
_____ [MANLEY], _____ (FC)	75	
_____ [MANSFIELD], ELIZABETH (QP)	76	
_____ [MASTERS], JANE (WP)	77	
_____ [MEAD], PHILLIP (QP)	78	
_____ [MERCER], MARY (FC)	78	
_____ [MERRIAM], SARAH (QP)	78	
_____ [MILLER], PATIENCE (WP)	80	
_____ [MOORE], KATHERINE (WP)	81	
_____ [MORTON], LETTICE (WP)	83	
_____ [MOULTON], JANE (WP)	83	
_____ [MOYSE], HANNAH (WP)	84	
_____ [NEWLIN], ELIZABETH (FC)	85	
_____ [NORMAN], FLORENCE (QP)	85	
_____ [OVIATT], FRANCES (WP)	88	
_____ [PARKER], SARAH (QP)	89	
_____ [PEIRCE], ELIZABETH (QP)	90	
_____ *[PELLET]*, SARAH (WP)	91	
_____ [PENNELL], HANNAH (FC)	92	
_____ [PENNINGTON], R (FC)	92	
_____ [PHILLIPS], _____ (FC)	93	
_____ [PHIPPEN], SARAH (WP)	94	

149

From Find A Grave, by Kevin O'Sullivan, 4/8/2008

Major General HUMPHREY ATHERTON (1608-1661)
Gravestone in Dorchester North Burying Ground, Dorchester, Mass.

Ancestor of Mabel Warren and perhaps also William H. Thompson

Other Books by the Author

Leprosy in Five Young Men
Outpatient Surgery (3 editions)
Clinical Oncology, with John Horton
Edison's Environment (2 editions)
Intimate Relationships: Church and State in the U.S. and Liberia (2 editions)
Proceed to Peshawar

©JanPressPhotomedia

ABOUT THE AUTHOR

GEORGE J. HILL, M.D., M.A., D.Litt., is Professor of Surgery Emeritus at the New Jersey Medical School, Rutgers University. He has been a Fellow in Molecular Biology at Princeton University and he was an Adjunct Professor of History at Kean University, Union, New Jersey. A native of Iowa, Dr. Hill received his B.A. degree with honors from Yale University and the M.D. from Harvard. After retiring from the practice of surgery, he earned an M.A. in history at Rutgers-Newark and the D.Litt. in history from Drew University. Dr. Hill has written more than a dozen books on a wide range of topics, including prize-winning books on surgery, oncology, and leprosy. His master's thesis became a book on the environmental impact of Thomas Edison, and his doctoral thesis on church and state in the U.S. and Liberia was also published as a book. He received the 2012 David A. Cowen Award from the Medical History Society of New Jersey. Dr. Hill was a non-commissioned officer in the U.S. Marine Corps Reserve during the Korean War, and he was on active duty with the U.S. Public Health Service during the Cuban Missile Crisis. As a U.S. Navy Medical Officer, he served in Vietnam and he was recalled for duty as a surgeon during the First Gulf War. In 2013 the Naval Institute Press published his book, *Proceed to Peshawar*, about a secret and long forgotten mission taken by his father-in-law as a Naval Intelligence Officer in World War II. He received the U.S. Meritorious Service Medal when he retired as a Captain in 1992. Dr. Hill is also an alpinist and an explorer, having hiked and climbed on all seven continents.

As a student of genealogy, Dr. Hill has proved his descent from many early Americans. He is a member of more than sixty lineage societies. His ancestors include James Feake, Sr., a goldsmith of London in 1615; Edward Fuller, who came on the *Mayflower* in 1620; Luke Hill and Mary Hout, who were married in Windsor, Connecticut, in 1651; Jonathan Gillett, who died there in 1677; Henry Herrick, who became a freeman of Salem, Mass., in 1630; Rebecca (Towne) Nurse, who was hanged there in 1692; Edward Howell, a Lord of the Manor in England who came to New England in 1638 and was a founder of the Hamptons on Long Island; Thomas Trowbridge, who was in New Haven, Conn., in 1638, and who had Royal ancestors; Robert Long, a member of the Ancient and Honorable Artillery Company in 1639; William Irish, descendant of early settlers of Rhode Island and a Loyalist in the American Revolution; James Prescott, of Hampton, New Hampshire, in 1665; William Rundle, a freeholder of Greenwich, Conn., in 1667; John Sharples, who came to Pennsylvania in 1682 with William Penn; John Manley, of Cecil County, Maryland, in 1712; and John Archibald, who died in Derry, New Hampshire, in 1651, and whose descendants were pioneer settlers of Truro, Nova Scotia. Dr. Hill was elected to Honorary Membership by the Heritage Society Community of the United States of America in 2017.

153

www.ingramcontent.com/pod-product-compliance
Lightning Source LLC
Chambersburg PA
CBHW080614270326
41928CB00016B/3048